Praise for *Happiness*

"This is the most authoritative and informative book about happiness ever written. That's not surprising, given that its authors are the world's leading happiness researcher and his psychologist son, whose vocation is coaching people toward happier lives."

> David G. Myers, Hope College, author, The Pursuit of Happiness:
> Who is Happy, and Why

"A great gift from the leading professional scientist of happiness in the world and his son, the 'Indiana Jones' of positive psychology."

> Martin E. P. Seligman, Fox Leadership Professor of Psychology, University
> of Pennsylvania and author, Authentic Happiness

"This book is a must read! If you want science-based advice on what can make you truly happy, Dr. Diener, with his son Robert-Biswas Diener, bring to life over thirty years of cutting-edge research on how to achieve real psychological wealth. The Dieners are the real deal. No one has studied happiness more than Ed Diener, and few people have conducted field research in more exciting places than Robert. You'll quickly see why Ed Diener is called Dr. Happy and why Robert is called the 'Indiana Jones' of Positive Psychology."

> David J. Pollay, B.A. Yale, M.A.P.P. University of Pennsylvania, President of
> The Momentum Project, *syndicated columnist, and author*,
> The Law of the Garbage Truck™

"The collaboration between the foremost authority on happiness research and the 'Indiana Jones' of psychology makes for a great mix of interesting examples and solid research. I have never seen a book that does such a good job offering useful practical advice while basing this advice on completely sound empirical research."

> Richard E. Lucas, Professor of Psychology, Michigan State University

"This is a happiness book by the world authority, the pre-eminent scholar in the field along with an in-the-trenches coach who teaches and adapts this material every day for practical use with coaching clients. Robert is also an international researcher and coaching scholar in his own right. This is to say that these are scholars who do the research and not just journalists or pop psychologists reporting it second hand. These folks know happiness from the inside out."

Michael B. Frisch, Psychologist and Neuroscientist, Baylor University;
Positive Psychologist/Coach and Clinical Psychologist

"In the huge happiness industry that has grown up over the past few years, this book is the very best overview of research and self-help manual available. It is written by the most productive, respected psychologist in the field of happiness studies and his son. It is the most readable, comprehensive overview and self-help manual available on happiness. If an ordinary citizen wanted to know about the contemporary science of happiness, it would be the place to begin.

Alex C. Michalos, Ph.D., F.R.S.C., Chancellor Director,
Institute for Social Research and Evaluation

"Finally the definitive book on happiness from the world's leading expert, Ed Diener, and his son, Robert Biswas-Diener, known as the 'Indiana Jones' of Positive Psychology. The authors bring over thirty years of research and practice into this engaging book that reveals the secrets of psychological wealth — your true net worth — which includes your attitudes toward life, social support, spiritual development, material resources, and health. This is a landmark book that should be read not only by laypersons but also scholars, educators, business leaders, and decision-makers interested in global well-being and human happiness."

Jim Clifton, Chairman & CEO, The Gallup Organization

Happiness

Unlocking the Mysteries of
Psychological Wealth

Ed Diener and
Robert Biswas-Diener

Blackwell
Publishing

© 2008 by Ed Diener and Robert Biswas-Diener

BLACKWELL PUBLISHING

350 Main Street, Malden, MA 02148-5020, USA
9600 Garsington Road, Oxford OX4 2DQ, UK
550 Swanston Street, Carlton, Victoria 3053, Australia

The right of Ed Diener and Robert Biswas-Diener to be identified as the authors of this work has been asserted in accordance with the UK Copyright, Designs, and Patents Act 1988.

Designations used by companies to distinguish their products are often claimed as trademarks. All brand names and product names used in this book are trade names, service marks, trademarks, or registered trademarks of their respective owners. The publisher is not associated with any product or vendor mentioned in this book.

This publication is designed to provide accurate and authoritative information in regard to the subject matter covered. It is sold on the understanding that the publisher is not engaged in rendering professional services. If professional advice or other expert assistance is required, the services of a competent professional should be sought.

First published 2008 by Blackwell Publishing Ltd

4   2011

Library of Congress Cataloging-in-Publication Data

Diener, Ed.
    Happiness : unlocking the mysteries of psychological wealth / Ed Diener and Robert Biswas-Diener.
        p. cm.
    Includes bibliographical references and index.
    ISBN 978-1-4051-4661-6 (hardcover : alk. paper)   1. Happiness.
I. Biswas-Diener, Robert.   II. Title.

    BF575.H27D54 2008
    158–dc22

                                                    2008013328

A catalogue record for this title is available from the British Library.

Set in 10/12.5pt Meridien
by Graphicraft Limited Hong Kong
Printed and bound in United States of America
by Sheridan Books, Inc.

The publisher's policy is to use permanent paper from mills that operate a sustainable forestry policy, and which has been manufactured from pulp processed using acid-free and elementary chlorine-free practices. Furthermore, the publisher ensures that the text paper and cover board used have met acceptable environmental accreditation standards.

For further information on Blackwell Publishing, visit our website at
www.blackwellpublishing.com

To our wives, Carol and Keya, who have been so helpful to us in our writing of the book, and to the Gallup Organization, for their encouragement and support.

Contents

Contents

Foreword

With so many books about happiness on the market, why should you read this particular one? David Myers, psychologist and author of many books, including *The Pursuit of Happiness*, calls Ed Diener the "Jedi Master of Happiness Studies." He is referring to the fact that – over the course of a thirty-year career in psychology – Ed has pioneered the field of happiness studies, publishing more than two hundred scholarly papers and chapters on the topic. And Robert, labeled the Indiana Jones of Positive Psychology by one of the field's leaders, has pursued the secrets of psychological wealth in places such as India, Greenland, Kenya and in remote areas around the globe. Intrigued? Let me tell you a bit more about the authors, who happen to be my husband, Ed, and our son, Robert.

The road to being a world authority on happiness began for Ed on a farm in California. Ed grew up in the years after World War II, the youngest of six children. As his older siblings grew up and moved away, and his parents were busy with farming, Ed was often left to entertain himself. Of course, like many an unsupervised boy, he got into trouble. His curiosity led him to make a flame thrower, to throw bullets into an open fire, and to drive a car at age ten. By the time Ed was twelve, he drew up plans for a genetically modified monkey-dog (smart like a monkey but loyal like a dog!). Ed was intrigued by numbers and science. He filled his afternoons reading biographies of scientific luminaries such as Isaac Newton and the astronomer, Tycho Brahe, and attempted to recreate some of their classic studies at home. He discovered how to calculate the amount of water displacement of a brick and other objects by immersing them in the bathtub to determine their volume.

When he arrived at college, Ed focused his curiosity on human behavior. Why do people laugh and cry, why do people seek social situations, why do people do things that are bad for their health, and most importantly, what is happiness and how is it achieved? Ed suggested this last question as the topic of his research in college. Specifically, he proposed to study the happiness of farm workers. However, his professor would not approve the study, informing Ed that "it is impossible to study happiness . . . it can never be measured." Besides, the professor opined, "I already know the answer. Farm workers cannot be happy." Discouraged, Ed wrote a paper on conformity instead.

After pursuing other research studies, Ed landed a faculty position at the highly ranked University of Illinois. When Ed earned tenure, we took a sabbatical to the Virgin Islands. There the idea of making a serious study of happiness returned. Ed spent much of his time reading the works of Aristotle, St. Thomas Aquinas, Maslow, and other great thinkers. He mapped out an ambitious plan for the serious study of happiness which he termed "subjective well-being" to lend it an air of scientific legitimacy to a skeptical academic world. During this same year, we took our three children out of school for trips to Haiti and South America. We motored up remote tributaries of the Amazon and were virtually alone in the deep jungle, surrounded by river porpoises, wooly monkeys, macaws, and piranha. After hours of travel we arrived at a settlement of Yagua people. The Yagua, who lived in stick houses and wore almost no clothing, were as fascinated by us as we were with them. But no one was more intrigued by the interactions than Robert. The tribal children crowded around him to look at his Mickey Mouse watch, and they let him shoot their blow darts at tree trunks. A village elder tried to give Robert curare poison for use with his blow gun, which we sensibly declined. However, the impact of this trip on Robert was immense. The realization that there were people who lived so differently from our neighbors in the American Midwest was a revelation that had a great influence on his adult career.

Following that sabbatical, Ed published his first article on subjective well-being. Over the years, he has studied how to effectively define and measure happiness, the relation between income and happiness, how cultures differ in happiness, how memory affects happiness, the benefits of happiness, and mental processes that affect people's happiness. He has turned a scientific eye to the role that people's values, relationships, resources, genetics, and economics play in the happiness equation. He has measured the happiness of people from the Forbes list of richest Americans, of identical twins, of cloistered nuns, and of sex workers. He has collected and analyzed data on happiness from hundreds of thousands of people from representative samples of more than a hundred countries. Because he has done more research on human happiness than any other individual in the world, Ed is frequently quoted and relied upon by other happiness scholars and popular writers. He has dialogued with the Dalai Lama on the subject of happiness and talked with world leaders about measuring societal happiness.

And most recently, his idea of using a gross national happiness index, in conjunction with the commonly used gross domestic product, to measure the wealth of cities, states, and countries is gaining momentum and interest throughout the world. This is a man who in the evening says, "I am tired so I think I will go analyze some data." The study of happiness has energized him for the past thirty years.

Not only is Ed a psychologist, but so am I, our twin daughters, Marissa and Mary Beth, and our son, Robert. An unusual atmosphere of psychological inquiry and experimentation filled our household from the time there was the patter of little feet. On the weekend and evenings, we sometimes carried out psychology projects with our children. For example, Robert did his first science project on the relation of mood and weather. As the children grew into teenagers, dinner table discussions frequently centered around topics such as "how people differ and how they are the same" and "how emotion affects memory." In this atmosphere of intellectual curiosity, Ed and Robert forged a partnership that combined scientific inquiry with real world application.

Building on his childhood experiences and his curiosity about foreign cultures that began in the Amazon, Robert pursued research on happiness in atypical places such as Greenland, the African savannah, and the slums of Calcutta. To give you a taste of just how adventurous his field research has been, Robert had a small grant to conduct research among the Maasai in Kenya. In order to garner the trust of the Maasai and to obtain accurate data, Robert allowed himself to be branded by the Maasai, not once but three times, to prove his worthiness to work with them. He also billed the granting agency for a goat which he bought as a sacrifice for a good hunt. Certainly not your typical laboratory research!

Robert has continued to travel and study happiness throughout the world. He visited the gold souks of Dubai, the markets of Istanbul, the gardens of the Vatican, the mountain villages of Morocco, the Inuit of Greenland, seaside towns in Nicaragua, cultural festivals in Taiwan, markets in Cambodia, the Australian outback, and countless other places. Everywhere he went he was more captivated by conversations with local inhabitants than he was by the famous tourist sites. Like his father, Robert is intensely interested in the quality of life of everyday people such as postal employees, bus drivers, and hairdressers around the globe.

The father-son collaboration is a natural fit. Robert extended Ed's work from the research laboratory to the field. Robert contacted remote and hard-to-access groups such as tribal Kenyans, the Greenland Inuits, and the Amish, and conducted subjective well-being research in these communities. Although Robert has published nearly two dozen professional articles on happiness, he is also interested in how this research can be applied to help people live better lives. He opened a coaching practice as a way to put innovations in the science of happiness into practice, and works with dozens of clients across the English-speaking world. He co-authored a book on using positive psychology in practice and regularly consults with organizations interested in applications of positive psychology.

So what does all this life history of the Diener clan have to do with this book? Why should you listen to Ed's and Robert's views on the topic of happiness? After all, it seems that everyone has a theory of happiness and "knows" what is important for happiness. I believe that the answer lies in the fact that not all opinions are created equal. Most of us would prefer to get investment tips from the BBC's financial analyst and car maintenance advice from an experienced mechanic, and not the other way around. We seek expert advice on everything from health care to hair coloring. Ed and Robert are the experts – in the modern scientific sense of the word – on the topic of happiness. They spend many, if not most, of their waking hours considering the fine points of emotional well-being, and have conducted a rigorous investigation of this topic for decades by collecting data from tens of thousands of people from all walks of life and every corner of the globe. They have examined the happiness of billionaires and homeless people and have looked at potential influences of happiness ranging from old age to the spring break trips of college students.

Happiness is Ed's and Robert's job and their passion. In this book they combine their scientific knowledge with personal wisdom and diverse experiences. There are many myths, half-truths, fact and fiction in the popular media on happiness. Here is the opportunity to let the Jedi Master and Indiana Jones of Happiness unlock the mysteries of psychological wealth for you and to find out the true secrets of happiness.

Carol Diener, PhD, JD

Acknowledgments

We are grateful to the many people who have made this book better, through their advice and encouragement. We have discussed the ideas in this work for endless hours with our spouses, Carol Diener and Keya Biswas-Diener. We thank them also for reading countless drafts and giving us insightful feedback. Chris Cardone at Blackwell Publishing has been of great help to us, especially because of her continuing encouragement. A number of assistants were responsible for searching for relevant studies, and for readying the book for publication, and we express our gratitude for the hundreds of hours they spent: Rebecca Sigmon Hernandez, Deborah Dexter, Alice Moon, and Lindsey Markel.

A group of scholars went beyond the call of duty in reading a draft of the entire document, and their comments served to strengthen many aspects of this book: Michael Frisch, Richard Lucas, Alex Michalos, David Myers, and Chris Peterson. We are also thankful to the reviewers who read individual chapters and gave us helpful feedback: Shigehiro Oishi, Sarah Pressman, John Helliwell, Rutt Veenhoven, Harry Reis, Gerald Clore, Raymond Paloutzian, Robert Emmons, George Vaillant, Chu Kim-Prieto, Timothy Wilson, Barry Schwartz, Andrew Clark, Ulrich Schimmack, Thomas Wright, Timothy Judge, Jim Clifton, Amy Wreszniewski, Jeanne Tsai, Christopher Hsee, William Pavot, Sheldon Cohen, Christie Scollon, and Nansook Park.

Part I
Understanding True Wealth

1

Psychological Wealth:
The Balanced Portfolio

Recently, the world held its breath for the final *Harry Potter* installment. The boy wizard is an international phenomenon, and the author, J. K. Rowling, a surprise literary sensation. As captivating as the stories of magic wands and Muggles are, Rowling's personal story is equally compelling. A single mother writing on cocktail napkins in Edinburgh pubs to save money on heat at home, Rowling spun a hobby into a multibillion-dollar franchise. Currently, Rowling is among the richest women in the world, and reportedly is worth more than the Queen of England. As such, she has entered into the public discourse about the fabulously wealthy.

Most of us are fascinated by financial stardom, and television shows, magazines, and exposés offer tantalizing peeks into the lives of the superrich. For example, we ask, who is the richest person in the world? Is it the computer billionaire Bill Gates? Maybe it is the oil-rich sultan of Brunei, or the business-savvy sheik of Dubai? Why not consider the highly influential Oprah Winfrey? Perhaps a dictator who has squirreled away billions in a Swiss bank? You would be wrong if you thought of any of these folks. Although they are extremely wealthy when it comes to money, these well-heeled people with private jets and homes around the world may not be at the top when it comes to true riches, psychological wealth.

In this book, we will describe the new concept of psychological wealth, which extends beyond material riches and beyond popular concepts like emotional intelligence and social capital. Psychological wealth is your true total net worth, and includes your attitudes toward life, social support, spiritual development, material resources, health, and the activities in which you engage. In this book, we show how psychological wealth depends on happiness and life satisfaction,

3

and the factors that lead to them. We will explain why monetary wealth is only one component of true wealth, and why other aspects are usually more important. In our final chapter, you can measure your own psychological wealth and see if you qualify for our Richest 400 list.

We have devoted our professional lives as psychologists to the careful study of happiness. We have worked from the ground up to re-examine long-held conclusions about well-being, and ask new questions about the subject. We have investigated the emotional lives of the very wealthy, and of the destitute. We have looked at the role that relationships, religion, culture, and positive attitudes play in happiness. We have collected data from tens of thousands of people in dozens of nations, including postal workers in India, tribal people in Kenya, Inuits above the Arctic Circle, and Hispanic students in California. The results of our studies of happiness have shown us that there are many important, and often counterintuitive, aspects of this emotional Holy Grail. After decades of research, we have findings that will re-confirm some of your beliefs about happiness, and turn others on their head. Our book is intended to help laypeople and psychologists alike to rethink their beliefs about happiness, the core of psychological wealth.

If you are like most people, one of the first things you will want to ask us is to define happiness. We refer to "happiness" as "subjective well-being" in scientific parlance, because it is about how people evaluate their lives and what is important to them. An individual's subjective well-being is often related to some degree to their objective circumstances, but it also depends on how people think and feel about these conditions. Subjective well-being encompasses people's life satisfaction and their evaluation of important domains of life such as work, health, and relationships. It also includes their emotions such as joy and engagement, and the relatively rare experience of unpleasant emotions such as anger, sadness, and fear. In other words, happiness is the name we put on thinking and feeling positively about one's life.

If you are anything like us, when you tried to think of the richest person in the world, you did not consider your parish priest, your neighbor, or your aunt, even though these people might be very wealthy in friends, spirituality, and energy. Most folks think of wealth in monetary terms, although few people would disagree with the idea that psychological wealth – experiencing happiness and satisfaction due to positive attitudes, intimate relationships, spirituality, and engagement with meaningful goals – represents a much deeper form of riches. Despite this fact, money and its pursuit occupy most of people's attention. We allot time to other concerns, such as health and friendships. We go to the gym, to church, or on dates – perhaps even regularly – to cultivate health, spirituality, and positive relationships. But think how much time is spent on the acquisition and management of money: creating budgets, paying taxes, going to the bank, writing checks, saving for a vacation, celebrating a pay raise, reading about the salaries of famous people, arguing with a spouse over finances, paying bills, and using credit cards. And of course there is earning money, which takes more time than any other waking activity.

Despite how useful money is, many people have a love-hate relationship with it. Consider for a moment the ambivalence we have had throughout human history about the wealthy among us. They are both admired and envied. They are the focus of endless attention, as exemplified by the immense popularity of lists of the richest people. At the same time, people with piles of money are also often the source of derision and hostility. When we think of rich people, works of great philanthropy might come to mind, but we might think just as easily of instances of injustice and downright stealing by wealthy people through history. Ill-treatment of workers, callous attitudes toward the poor, and crass materialism are associated in our minds with wealth, just as much as the great public works that rich folks have sometimes donated to society.

In the eighth century BC there was a legendary king of Phrygia named Midas, and we all know his name. According to myth, Midas won the favor of the god Dionysus. Midas was offered a wish and chose the power to turn everything he touched into gold. He was delighted by his new talent and tried it out on the world around him, transforming stones to precious metal. When he returned home to his castle, Midas ordered a feast laid out to celebrate his good fortune. Unfortunately, the wine and food turned to gold and Midas went hungry. He soon realized that his new power had a hidden cost, and this point was driven home when he touched his daughter, and she changed into a golden statue. Heartbroken, King Midas prayed to Dionysus to remove the power, and his wish was granted. The story of Midas captures our ambivalence about money and wealth, and it provides an important cautionary tale about avarice. The pursuit of material riches is not worthwhile if it means giving up relationships, suffering ill health, or being spiritually bankrupt. Psychological wealth is much broader than monetary wealth because when we have it, we truly do "have it all." If we give up too many other aspects of true wealth to obtain money, our materialism decreases our net worth.

A Psychological Wealth Primer

Psychological wealth is the experience of well-being and a high quality of life. It is more than simple fleeting joy, and more than an absence of depression and anxiety. Psychological wealth is the experience that our life is excellent – that we are living in a rewarding, engaged, meaningful, and enjoyable way. Psychological wealth includes life satisfaction, the feeling that life is full of meaning, a sense of engagement in interesting activities, the pursuit of important goals, the experience of positive emotional feelings, and a sense of spirituality that connects people to things larger than themselves. Taken together, these fundamental psychological experiences constitute true wealth. After all, if you have them, you have all one would want from life, whereas when you are rich with money, you have only one desirable resource from the list. In addition to the internal aspects of psychological wealth, there are universals such as health and positive social relationships that are so intricately interwoven with the experience of well-being that they too are part of psychological wealth. What then are the ingredients of psychological wealth? Here are some essential components of true wealth:

- Life satisfaction and happiness
- Spirituality and meaning in life
- Positive attitudes and emotions
- Loving social relationships
- Engaging activities and work
- Values and life goals to achieve them
- Physical and mental health
- Material sufficiency to meet our needs

Ultimately, the quality of your life will suffer if you do not develop each aspect of true wealth. However, when you have all the elements, you truly are rich! You need not be a monetary millionaire to be wealthy. After all, if you experience your life as wonderful, what more would you want? Even if you don't have billions of dollars, if you love your life, you have everything you need and want. If you have psychological wealth, it will be of little concern if you have only a moderate amount of money.

We all know the traditional markers of a financially wealthy person. We know that such a person is likely to have luxury goods and status symbols: a large house, with a modern kitchen that includes granite counters and stainless-steel appliances; a regular vacation spot; a new car loaded with amenities; and perhaps some eye-catching jewelry or original artwork. Probably a Mercedes and a swimming pool. What are the indicators of psychological wealth? How might we recognize someone who is truly wealthy? You can't tell too much from looks – a psychologically wealthy person could be short or tall, old or young, a bus driver, a housewife, or a small-business owner. It is likely that they are not living in destitution. They probably have a close circle of family and friends. But after these few traits, you must look deeper to recognize them. The psychologically wealthy are characterized by the ability to see what is good in the world, but nevertheless to be grounded in reality. They are involved in activities that they believe are meaningful and important, and they have found activities in which they can use their strengths.

Take, for example, superdad Dick Hoyt, who lived every parent's nightmare when problems with delivery left his son, Rick, severely physically handicapped. Doctors initially recommended that Rick be institutionalized, but Dick raised money and worked with a team of engineers to design a computer that allowed his son to communicate by typing with head movements. When Rick was in high school, the father-son duo participated in a five-mile run – with an out-of-shape Dick pushing his son in a wheelchair – to benefit a local student who had become paralyzed. The experience of completing the race was transformative for both of them. For Rick, competing in a race, even though he was being pushed, made him feel as if he weren't handicapped. For Dick, the opportunity to help his son find meaning was invaluable. Dick had a new reason to take care of his health, and his fitness quickly improved.

Together, the Hoyt pair went on to compete in more than eighty marathons, triathlons, and Iron Man competitions. They redefined what "ability" means, and found a deep sense of purpose in their athletic feats. Dick and Rick appear to be psychologically wealthy: they have a great relationship, enjoy sports and find personal meaning through competition, and have Olympic-class positive attitudes. Most of all, psychologically wealthy people like Dick and Rick Hoyt possess happiness and life satisfaction. The positive emotions they experience are not simply joy and other fleeting pleasant feelings, but also an abundance of feelings such as love, commitment, and gratitude that connect them to others. These are the type of people who are grounded in values we admire, and who are remarkably free of pettiness and negativity. They are not in a frenetic search for new spouses, billions of dollars, and new thrills because they already are so deeply embedded in meaningful relationships and activities.

In this book, we will examine each of the different facets of psychological wealth in detail. Each of the elements is needed for consummate wealth, and an exclusive emphasis on one can detract from the others. If we pursue only happiness, for example, to the exclusion of spirituality and meaning, we may become hedonists who do not find true well-being. And as we have said, if we pursue money to the extent that we ignore the other facets of psychological wealth, we will have failed. In the end, understanding psychological wealth is about having a "balanced portfolio." This book provides an overview of the elements of psychological wealth that research reveals are good investments.

Part I: Understanding True Wealth

Although on its surface psychological wealth sounds like age-old wisdom – a morality story that cautions us that there is more to happiness than just money – there is more to this concept than meets the eye. Of course, most folks intuitively know and agree with the idea that spirituality, health, and relationships are vital to the quality of our lives. Philosophers, religious scholars, and grandparents have been teaching this same lesson since the dawn of civilization. What is radical about the idea of psychological wealth is its basis in new and often counterintuitive research. The modern science of subjective well-being has turned many commonsense notions about happiness on their heads. For instance, we now know that there is an optimum level of happiness. That is, it appears that in certain domains of life it is possible to have too much happiness, a point beyond which people might perform less well rather than better.

In chapter 2, we turn to this body of research and present two of the most exciting and important principles underlying psychological wealth. The first principle is that happiness is a process, not a place. For ages, people have assumed that happiness is an emotional end goal, a pleasant state that comes from obtaining favorable life circumstances such as health, a good marriage, and a large paycheck. The logic is that if a person can line up enough desirable circumstances, then happiness will necessarily follow. As commonsensical as this notion is, science shows that psychological wealth cannot be produced by circumstances alone. Although money, national origin, and marital status are correlated with subjective well-being, the relationship is sometimes small relative to other causes of happiness. Rather, happiness is an ongoing process that requires a way of experiencing life and the world that includes positive attitudes, meaning, and spirituality. Being truly rich is as much about the attitudes within us as the circumstances surrounding us.

The second major principle necessary in rethinking happiness and understanding psychological wealth is that it is beneficial to effective functioning. Historically, happiness has suffered from a bad reputation. Many people think of happiness as shallow, selfish, naïve, and complacent. Critics of the emotion claim that happiness cannot last, and cynics charge that joy is a fundamentally unrealistic feeling. The pursuit of happiness is seen as a waste of time. There is now a body of evidence from scientific studies that indicates precisely the opposite, that positive feelings are functional and beneficial. Research on the benefits of positive emotions show that they help people connect with friends, think more creatively, and become interested in new activities. Happiness, then, is itself a resource you can tap to achieve the things you want in life. In chapter 2, we explain why happiness is beneficial to effective functioning. Happiness is a cornerstone of psychological wealth in part because it is emotional currency that can be spent on other desirable goals, such as friendships and success at work. It is when we are feeling positive and energized that we often make the largest gains: we think of new ideas, take up new hobbies, tend to our relationships, maintain our health, and find meaning in life.

Part II: Happy People Function Better

In Part II, we focus on three aspects of psychological wealth – health, relationships, and meaningful work – that are directly related to happiness. It is here that we see that psychological wealth is closely related to happiness because it cannot be attained without positive emotions. The links between happiness and health, relationships, and work are the foundation of a portfolio of psychological wealth. Success in these life domains tends to boost happiness, and positive emotions, in turn, tend to lead to success in these life domains. In this section, we make the case that happiness is the fundamental building block of psychological wealth, but that it is important not just because it feels good, but because it is so beneficial in so many areas of life. Rethinking happiness requires us to understand that it is not just a pleasant goal, but necessary to achieving success in many domains of life.

Part III: Causes of Happiness and Genuine Wealth

For as long as folks have been trying to figure out the best route to happiness, the lion's share of people's attention has centered on life circumstances. It makes sense that people would attempt to increase their happiness by improving their lot in life. Common sense tells us that getting a new job, making more money, being healthier, or finding just the right spouse will lead to feelings of well-being. But does it? Research on subjective well-being reveals that most life circumstances, such as whether you are a man or a woman, or young or old, have only a small effect on happiness. There are a few areas, however, that are significantly linked to emotional well-being. We now have a solid understanding of how income buys some happiness and whether being religious adds to or takes away from emotional bliss. In Part III, we discuss the life circumstances that have been shown to be influential to psychological wealth, including income, spirituality, and culture.

Later in Part III, we discuss the psychological factors that influence happiness and, in turn, psychological wealth. People have long used phrases like "Life is what you make it," "See the silver lining in every cloud," and "Look at the world through rose-colored glasses." These phrases hint that part of our quality of life and happiness is due to our personal approach to, and interpretation of, the world. Some folks seem to be perennially up-beat, while the smallest problems drag other people into anger or depression. A variety of everyday mental processes exert a powerful influence on your well-being, including adaptation, emotional forecasting, and positive attitudes. Taken together, these mental processes are an essential part of psychological wealth.

Part IV: Putting It All Together

In the last section, we offer advice for integrating the various aspects of psychological wealth in the service of living a truly rich life. Importantly, we caution you against seeking unbridled happiness. Many people pursue intense, permanent feelings of happiness, believing this most-desired of emotions is truly a cup that can never overflow. New evidence suggests that there may be an optimal level of happiness, and people who are "too happy" actually appear to perform less well at work and school and may even be less healthy than folks who are optimally happy. This new line of research shows us that psychological wealth, like all wealth, is best when it is balanced and used wisely. Thus, we hope our book serves as a counterpoint to the self-help works that counsel feeling intensely happy as the be-all of existence.

In the end, the good life is really all about having psychological wealth. When we pursue a secure material existence, develop ourselves spiritually, and use our strengths in pursuit of valued goals, we are building our psychological wealth balance sheet. As physical beings, we are part of the material world and need to build our tangible resources to experience security and comfort. But we are also spiritual, needing a sense of meaning and purpose that is larger than ourselves, and that connects us to humanity and nature. Finally, we are psychological beings who interpret the world around us, and this means that our happiness depends in part on the mental habits we develop. True wealth requires material, spiritual, social, and psychological resources.

In the final chapter, we present measures of psychological wealth so that you can determine the net worth on your psychological wealth balance sheet. How rich are you? In the appendix, we describe how the Diener family is using science to understand happiness. With the virtues of the scientific method – controlled studies, large representative samples, and sophisticated statistical analyses – we are in a position to integrate and refine the historic wisdom about leading a good life drawn from philosophy, religion, and personal experience. But we hope that we are also more than science nerds. Ed Diener has been labeled the "Jedi Master of Happiness" not only because he has trained so many of the experts in the field, but also because, like Yoda, he did not conform to popular fads. And Robert has been called the "Indiana

Jones of psychology" because of his adventures in exotic places around the globe while collecting happiness data. We hope you enjoy seeing how our personalities and life histories have led to the conclusions we present in this book.

We believe that you will enjoy reading this book, and know that you will come away rethinking your views on happiness!

2

Two Principles of Psychological Wealth

There are two key components to understanding psychological wealth in general, and happiness in particular. Both are vitally important and frequently discussed, but often misunderstood. The first is that happiness is more than achieving desirable life circumstances, such as health, wealth, success at work, and a happy family. Although it is certainly logical to think that when all the pieces of life's puzzle fall neatly into place, you will feel happy, there is more to happiness than meets the eye. Happiness, as we will show you, is much more of a process than an emotional destination. People, probably through no fault of their own, frequently overlook the process side of happiness in their pursuit of the good life. You likely can think of examples of folks who focus on potential happiness down the road – a summer vacation or remodeled kitchen – but who also forget to stop and smell the roses along the way. We make the case that while goals that produce happiness are important, understanding that happiness itself is a process is even more important.

The second principle crucial to understanding psychological wealth is seeing happiness for its functions rather than for its pleasantries. Undoubtedly, happiness – by almost anyone's definition – feels good, and most folks like to savor the experience. But happiness doesn't just feel good; it is good for you in a number of surprising ways, helping people to function effectively in many areas of life. Understanding how happiness can be used beneficially is important to cultivating true psychological wealth.

Happiness is a Process, Not a Place

North America's tallest peak, Mount McKinley, is a challenging and dangerous mountain to climb. It sits in the rugged, remote interior of Alaska, and McKinley's summit has been a prized goal for mountaineers for the last century. A friend of ours, the University of Illinois psychologist Art Kramer, has been on the upper slopes of the mountain several times as part of his research on how oxygen – and the lack thereof – affects people's thinking. As humans become deprived of oxygen, whether because of circulatory problems or thin air, their thinking slows, they become confused, and good decisions are difficult. The rarefied air at twenty thousand feet offers a perfect laboratory for Art's research. But because research ethics do not allow scientists to place their research participants in mortal danger, Art cannot go the usual route of recruiting university students to study. Instead, he climbs and conducts research with the United States Navy, whose elite soldiers scale the mountain as part of their training.

On a recent climbing expedition, Kramer was ascending a steep snow bank when he came upon a team of less experienced Canadian mountaineers who were uncertain in which direction they ought to head. Art took the team to the ridge leading to the summit, and then did something remarkable. Instead of hiking the final few hundred meters himself, he turned his back on the summit and descended to camp. Because climbing to the top of Mount McKinley could cast doubt on the scientific integrity of the expedition – creating the impression that Professor Kramer was using government research funds to finance his private ambition – he turned around before reaching the summit. The hardest part of the climb was behind him; all that lay between him and the summit was a straightforward walk up a gentle slope. He could easily have ascended to the top, but chose instead to turn back. In an age where summit fever has led to highly publicized accounts of tragedy, Art's attitude toward the peak is refreshing.

When we suggested to Art that *not* reaching the summit might haunt him for the rest of his life, he laughed. Rather than worrying about "the one that got away," Art views climbing Mount McKinley as far more about the activity than the end goal. He once said to us, "Climbing has never been about the summit for me. It's always been about the process of climbing." His sentiment is easy enough to say, but let's be honest: the summit of a mountain can be an important goal. But if we side-step this traditional goal, what does that leave us?

If climbing is not about getting to the top of the mountain, then what is to keep a person huffing and puffing uphill? The answer, according to Art, is that there are many enjoyable, rewarding moments along the way. The entire process of climbing can be an emotional payoff, from training at home, to the feeling of "flow" while climbing, to gorgeous views, to victory beers with friends after the climb. Art can easily point to many of his favorite aspects of spending time at high altitudes: "Climbing is about being out in the wilderness and enjoying the beauty. It's also about the challenge of route finding." When we spoke about his Mount McKinley expedition, he added, with a childlike twinkle in his eye, "And climbing is definitely about making snow caves; I've enjoyed that." Success, for Art, is more about how enjoyable the journey is than whether or not he achieves the summit.

While you may not be a climber, you can likely recognize the metaphorical implications of this story. In so many ways, and for so many people, the pursuit of goals is like a climb up the side of a mountain. There are better routes and worse routes; there are hazards and setbacks; effort is required; and there is the hope of ultimate success. Perhaps most important, the summit is only one small part of the climb. Just as climbers eagerly anticipate their expedition, enjoy the relief of an occasional rest, and savor the memory of their trips, happiness is often less about achieving goals than it is about enjoyment along the way, and fond recollections afterward. In this way, Art Kramer's story beautifully illustrates one of the main points of this book: happiness is not just a destination. That's right: despite the fact that many people seek out lasting fulfillment – and it is natural and understandable to do so – happiness is not an emotional finish line in the race of life. We should repeat that: happiness should *not* be looked at just as a destination we try to reach, but as a beneficial way we learn to travel. A key to psychological wealth is to understand the importance of the journey itself to happiness.

What does it mean to say that happiness is a process, not a place? There are several important lessons in the dictum. The Art Kramer story illustrates one meaning – that happiness often comes from doing rather than having. If we enjoy the activities needed in working for our goals, many hours and years of pleasure are provided, whereas reaching summits provides only the occasional short-term high. Another important meaning of the "process, not a place" maxim is that no matter what good life circumstances we obtain, things can still go wrong. Furthermore, even in good circumstances we need to find new challenges and goals, or things will grow boring. We adapt to good things and need to move on to new goals to continue to enjoy life to the fullest.

Caveat Emptor: Bad Stuff Happens . . . Even to Princesses

Take a moment and recall the classic story of Cinderella. Remember how she was cruelly mistreated by her stepsisters and their wicked mother? Do you recall how they made her slave away at the daily household chores? Remember how the dress she labored so hard over was torn to shreds in a fit of jealousy, and her hopes of going to the royal ball lay in tatters? Of course, you probably best remember the happy ending of the fairy tale: Cinderella's magical godmother arrives in the nick of time, whisks her away to the dance, and engineers a quick infatuation, with the result that the beloved protagonist marries the charming prince. But is that the end of the story, or just the beginning?

It is interesting to consider what happened to Cinderella next, after she was betrothed and took up residence in Charming Castle. For people who believe that happiness is a matter of favorable circumstances, the story of Cinderella turns out to be a slam dunk. With a Hollywood-handsome husband, a royal title, all the riches she could want, and soldiers to guard her from the paparazzi, how could our belle of the ball not be happy? But for folks who are inclined to think of happiness as a process, the matter of Cinderella's emotional fate is far from clear. Did Cinderella's husband treat her well, or was he a philanderer in later life? Did she find some meaningful pastime to keep her occupied on the palace grounds? Were her children spoiled brats? Did she harbor resentment about her upbringing, or try to get revenge on her stepsisters? Did she grow bored with royal balls and court intrigue, or did she organize a dance program for the poor kids in her kingdom? Happiness, as we have said, is a process, not a destination. Just as Cinderella's life did not end with her royal wedding, your emotional bliss is not complete once you have obtained some important goal. Life goes on, and even those great circumstances you achieve will not ensure you lasting happiness. For one thing, bad things can happen even to beautiful young princesses. But even if Cinderella's life encountered few bumps on the fairyland road, she might have grown bored with the wonderful circumstances surrounding her, and needed new aims and activities to add zest to her life.

In the end, Cinderella's quality of life was probably dictated less by her favorable circumstances and more by how she construed them. Hardships are an inevitable part of life, and having psychological wealth does not mean there are never any risks or losses. Of course there are. Happiness is not the complete absence of tough times, because that would be unrealistic. But, as we shall see later in this chapter and later in this book, negative emotions have a place in psychological wealth, and subjective interpretation plays an important role in happiness.

Needing the Rigors of the Game

We sometimes ask our students whether they would accept the following pact with a genie. After floating out of his lamp, he offers to give you *everything* you desire, and as soon as the wish comes into your head, without the typical three-wish limit. The smirking genie says that anything you want will instantly come to you. You can't wish for happiness, and you can't wish that you will need to work for things to obtain them: no trickery of this type is allowed. Just solid old-school wishing for gold, castles, travel, beauty, friends, sports talent, intelligence, musical talent, good-looking dates, fast cars, and the like is permitted. Of course, most students wave their hands wildly, signaling that of course they would accept this great offer. Undoubtedly they are thinking of school loans, good grades, summers in Paris, and body fat. But – typically – as the class discussion proceeds, doubts begin to creep in. Maybe this all-wishes-granted deal, having everything and working for nothing, would become boring. Maybe you would adapt to all your blessings and they would no longer produce happiness. The discussion proceeds a bit further, and a few students begin to think the infinite-wishes deal might be hell on earth. Things would become boring, they reason, and life would lose its zest.

Students' qualms about receiving everything without effort express our intuitive understanding that working for things we desire can be part of the pleasure of obtaining them. Just as climbing the mountain may be the major part of the fun, and simply being boosted to the top by a genie would be much less rewarding, much in life might be more meaningful and rewarding because of the efforts needed to obtain it.

Not only will the eventual reward be more exciting, but the activities needed to gain the reward can themselves be very rewarding. The former justice of the United States Supreme Court Benjamin Cardozo expressed this well: "In the end the great truth will have been learned: that the quest is greater than what is sought, the effort finer than the prize (or, rather, that the effort *is* the prize), the victory cheap and hollow were it not for the rigor of the game." The renowned justice went beyond saying that the goal-seeking activities enhance the final reward; he claimed that these activities are in fact the prize itself!

The Lessons of Part III

Part III is particularly relevant to happiness as a process. Chapter 9 of that section is about adaptation, and shows that we adapt to some degree to the good conditions we encounter in life. At first they produce a thrill; then we grow used to them. This is why we need continuing new goals to remain happy, and why rewarding activities are so important to happiness. We can continue to enjoy mountain climbing even if the thrill of summiting wears off. In fact, just as the euphoria of summiting may decline, the enjoyment of climbing can grow as one's skills improve.

Chapter 10 is about happiness forecasting and is also relevant to happiness as a process. To lead a happy life, we need to make good decisions, and this involves the recognition that problems invariably arise, even in good circumstances. Our Prince Charming might not be a philanderer, but he won't be perfect either – he forgets birthdays and is a workaholic. He grows a paunch and develops bad breath. Making good choices in life depends on recognizing not just rewards, but the likely problems in choices as well. Happiness depends in part on our ongoing choices, not just on a set of lucky circumstances.

Finally, Chapter 11 describes our AIM (attention, interpretation, memory) model, which is central to the idea that happiness is a process rather than a place. The idea behind the AIM model is that how people interpret the world has as much, or more, to do with their happiness than what is actually going on in their world. The processes of attending to some events and not others, of interpreting ambiguous events in positive rather than negative ways, and of tending to recall the good times instead of the bad times from the past are about the internal processes of being happy. Without these processes it is hard to stay happy for long. This is why some people are happy and some are not when living in very similar circumstances. Happiness as a process means that our daily interpretation of things determines our feelings of well-being, and learning to interpret most events in a positive light is a valuable skill.

Happiness as a process, not a place, is a core principle of beneficial happiness that captures many ideas about the effective way of living a happy life. Always remember that happiness is a way of traveling as much as it is a final destination. Of course, some routes and destinations are better than others, and Paris can be quite fun once you get there. A trip to Hawaii is usually more rewarding than one to Newark. So enjoy both the trip and the destination.

Happiness is Beneficial

Modern psychological science has added a fascinating and counter-intuitive new dimension to the age-old discussion of happiness: happiness is beneficial. Rather than viewing happiness as a pleasant or peaceful state of mind, research tells us that happiness is helpful and functional. It is a resource to be used rather than only to be enjoyed.

Some people believe that happiness is about as beneficial as injecting heroin, and that feelings of joy are about as helpful as making a wish when you blow out candles on your birthday cake. The playwright and Nobel laureate George Bernard Shaw once said, "A lifetime of happiness! No man alive could bear it; it would be hell on earth." The great medical missionary and Nobel laureate Albert Schweitzer similarly undermined the importance of happiness when he quipped, "Happiness is nothing more than good health and a bad memory." Among the most vocal critics of all time was the French writer Gustave Flaubert, who was famously opposed to the pursuit of happiness. When Flaubert wasn't busy penning his steamy novel *Madame Bovary*, he was usually criticizing middle-class society and the quest for happiness. Flaubert opined, "To be stupid, selfish, and have good health are three requirements for happiness, though if stupidity is lacking, all is lost." To the curmudgeonly Flaubert, happiness was a case of investing energy and resources in the wrong places. At its best, according to Flaubert, happiness is a pleasant feeling; at its worst, happiness is a dangerous golden calf that suckers whole societies into complacency, destructive hedonism, and softheadedness.

Flaubert was dead wrong in his assertion that happiness is stupid and selfish. Happiness, as it turns out, not only feels good, but is often good for you and for society. In Part II, we will discuss research showing that happiness is associated with a wide variety of tangible benefits, ranging from improved health, to better marriages, to increased chances of attaining personal goals. For most people, happiness is that emotional pot of gold at the end of the emotional rainbow. Happiness is most commonly thought of as a destination, a state we work toward and hope to achieve in some lasting way. However, studies show that happiness is not only a worthy aspiration, but that it is actually a resource as well; it is emotional capital we can spend in the pursuit of other attractive outcomes. Research shows that happy people live longer, succumb to fewer illnesses, stay married longer, commit fewer crimes, produce more creative ideas, work harder and better on the job, make more money, and help others more. Who wouldn't want to be happier if it increased one's chances of being physically fit, financially secure, helpful, and surrounded by friends? If you think about the times in your own life when you have been upbeat, you probably recognize that these were periods of creativity, energy, hope, and social connection. In the end, happiness is far more than hedonism or complacency; it is helpful and healthy.

The first hints of the new way of looking at happiness surfaced in the early 1970s, when the researcher Alice Isen and her colleagues investigated the potential outcomes of good moods. In one classic study, she secretly planted coins in the change slot of a telephone booth. When unsuspecting callers "found" the money, they were subsequently more likely than those who had not found change to help a bystander (a research accomplice) carry books or pick up dropped papers. Similarly, in a study where Isen and her colleagues gave physicians a gift bag of candies and chocolates, the boost of positivity led the doctors to be better diagnosticians, able to integrate information, arrive at a diagnosis earlier, and show more flexible thinking. If you want to improve your chances of a correct diagnosis on your next clinic visit, bring a small gift!

Human anatomy and human psychology have something in common: both serve specific functions. Our hands, with their dexterous fingers and opposable thumbs, are perfect for grasping. Our sweat glands are essential to our ability to cool ourselves. It makes sense, given the so-called mind-body connection (which holds that emotions and other psychological processes are rooted in our biology), that our emotions are not just products of random chance that serve no purpose, but that they too are functional.

Our feelings help us interpret the quality of our lives and the world around us, and motivate us to behave accordingly. It is easy to understand the benefits of negative emotions like guilt and fear. Fear functions to keep us safe by motivating us to avoid perceived dangers, and guilt functions to guide our behavior through moral decision making, and thereby helps preserve harmony in families and communities. Imagine how dysfunctional the world would be if people did not grieve for their deceased loved ones, feel pangs of guilt when they cheated on tests, or become angry when they were treated unjustly. This is one reason we do not advocate a happy-only approach to life, but insist that bad moods are not only inevitable, but can be useful. Although negative emotions are unpleasant to experience, they often serve a purpose.

Broaden and Build

The function of positive emotions seems less obvious. What good is being cheerful? How might feeling joyful help us? It turns out that feeling good is a special gift that helps us thrive and function. According to Barbara Fredrickson, a psychologist at the University of North Carolina, positive emotions serve a definite purpose: they "broaden and build" our *personal* resources. Just as our paychecks can be spent on material items like hybrid cars and *Harry Potter* books, our positive moods lead us to seek out and cultivate relationships, think more creatively, and show curiosity and interest in new activities. In one study, for instance, participants who felt happy expressed interest in engaging in more activities than did those who were in a negative mood. In another study, people put in a good mood expressed more interest in both active and passive social and nonsocial activities. They also expressed more energy for doing the activities. You probably recognize this phenomenon from your own life: when you are feeling sad you don't feel like doing much, but when you are feeling joyful many activities sound great.

Few people realize that many of our personal resources, whether it is our closest friendships, success at work, or a new skill, are accumulated when we are in positive moods. Positive emotions energize us to develop our physical, intellectual, and social resources. To investigate this possibility, Fredrickson conducted a study in which she assessed people's moods and then examined their creative coping strategies in the moment and at a follow-up session five weeks later. Sure enough, the folks who were in a good mood during the initial research session were more likely to exhibit creative problem solving and better coping strategies.

One aspect of building resources you may not have considered is the process of play. When we are feeling joyful, our playful spirit emerges. Play is more than just idle leisure time; it is an opportunity to practice new skills and bond with others. For children, play is unscripted, and offers the opportunity to try new ways of doing things, or practice newly acquired abilities. For parents, the sight of their sons and daughters mimicking the skills of adulthood is common. Kids pretend to change diapers, make bottles, grocery shop, cook and clean, pack for a trip, buy goods with credit cards and money, build homes, drive cars, put on makeup, and style their hair. These are practice runs for later in life, when they will be applying these skills in earnest.

For adults, play is no less functional. Although adults generally do not engage in make-believe play, they participate in board games, sports, and leisure activities such as hiking and painting. In each instance, adult recreation subtly builds our resources. Many board games, for example, require social coalition building, challenge us to make creative connections, hone our strategic abilities, help to build our working vocabularies, and give our minds some exercise. Similarly, athletic activities offer an opportunity for us to maintain our physical fitness, as well as form bonds of loyalty. Games of chance and ability are the testing grounds for the ideas, words, friendships, and skills that we will call upon later when the stakes are higher. But, as useful as play is, we mostly want to do it when we are in a good mood. We usually experience positive emotions when things are going well, and these are the times when we can afford to build our resources for the future. Play may have seemed like just relaxation to you before now, and a few people even consider it to be a waste of time, but many forms of leisure are in fact quite helpful in living a more successful life.

Another broadening and building benefit of positive emotion is the way in which we seek out and connect with others. When we feel affection toward other people, whether it is platonic or romantic, we tend to want to spend time socially with them. Happiness and love lead us to listen with concern, help when called upon, and exert the effort to maintain existing relationships. We are far more likely to go dancing with our friends or attend a party if we are feeling upbeat and energetic. We are even more likely to brave new experiences, such as attending a new church, giving a new sport a try, or choosing a new coffee shop or restaurant when we are in a good mood.

Cheerfulness and optimism serve to widen our social circle. How does this process work? Consider the case of human infants. Babies smile, even before their eyesight is developed enough to clearly see adult faces, suggesting this is an innate behavior. Adults, in turn, react to smiling babies with predictable ooh-ing and ah-ing, and shower the infant with attention. Thus, the smile, as an outward manifestation of happiness, serves from the beginning to connect us to others. Further proof for this comes from research that found that people who suffer from facial paralysis, and who cannot smile, have difficulty in social relationships. Thus, we are prewired to make connections with others – relationships that are necessary for our personal and physical well-being – and happiness is the grease that allows this evolutionary machinery to work.

In the end, our personal and social capital – our knowledge, insight, friends, families, skills, and creativity – are more valuable even than our material resources. Luckily, we are evolutionarily adapted to develop these important assets when we are feeling good. Happiness and related positive emotions function to encourage us to broaden and build a wide range of resources that, ultimately, lead to personal fulfillment and societal well-being.

Regulating Negative Emotions

We explained that negative emotions such as sadness and guilt are functional, and that we ought to experience them some small portion of the time. What we have not said, and what many readers will be able to attest to, is that negative feelings have a downside in that they can feed on themselves. Although embarrassment and anger are not necessarily pleasant to experience, they can be habit forming. For some people, anger is exciting, and they can learn to feed off the negative emotional dramas in their lives. For other people, self-pity can act as a blanket, one that individuals can swaddle themselves in for a kind of perverse security. The danger of negative feelings isn't in experiencing them – we all do – but in getting too comfortable with them, so that they rival our positive emotions in frequency and intensity. Fortunately, positive emotions can serve to regulate and dampen these unpleasant feelings if they become too strong or common. In this way, emotions are like a teeter-totter, in which the heavier weight of good feelings controls the seesaw action.

Consider the case of a couple in the middle of a fight, an inevitable experience familiar to most of us. Marital arguments, unfortunately, have a way of dragging on longer than they should. Who hasn't followed their spouse into the next room, even after the debate is supposedly over? Anger can keep the fight going long after the issue itself is resolved. Fortunately, happiness can serve as an emotional firewall, protecting us from doing further harm to our relationships. Frequently, for instance, either the husband or the wife will abruptly make a joke, or something will occur that will suddenly seem funny to both parties. Intensely negative arguments sometimes deteriorate into quizzical laughter, in which the spouses wonder at the absurdity of what, only moments earlier, seemed worth fighting over. This is our natural positivity defense kicking in, and it is the way in which the referee of happiness calls the end to the game of negativity.

Positive emotions serve to bring us back to our baseline by undoing our negative feelings. Just as sweating helps cool us down to our normal temperature after exercise, happiness can restore us after a negative emotional event. In fact, happiness, like sweating, has a direct effect on our physiological arousal. Fredrickson conducted a study in which she showed short scary movies to the participants. As expected, the films were arousing, and were accompanied by reactions of fear. After screening the horror films, Fredrickson showed clips from funny, neutral, or depressing movies. Participants who saw the amusing clips returned to their baseline cardiovascular levels within twenty seconds, compared with the forty to sixty seconds their counterparts who were exposed to the neutral and negative movies required.

Fredrickson found similar results in a study in which participants were affected by real-world conditions. In a sample of college students whose moods were tested both before and after the terror attacks of September 11, 2001, positive emotions were associated with less depression, more resilience, and more personal growth among the happier students. This suggests that positive individuals have an advantage over others, in that they can bounce back more easily from the occasional negative situations they will certainly encounter.

Challenges Look Easier When You Are Happy

Another clear benefit of good moods is the effect they have on our motivation. Research shows that positive emotions make goals seem easier to achieve, and therefore happiness adds an extra boost of enthusiasm and perseverance to our personal pursuits. Professors Dennis Proffitt and Gerald Clore from the University of Virginia found that people in a good mood see the world as an easier place than those in a negative mood, who see it as scarier and more difficult. In an early study, they asked research participants to estimate the steepness of a hill in front of them. The researchers instructed participants to wear a heavy backpack. Under the increased physical load, people guessed that the hill was far steeper than the backpack-free participants had estimated.

In the next round of research, Proffitt and Clore took a new group of participants to the same hill, and played classical music composed by either the upbeat, bouncy Mozart or the despondent Mahler. This time, when the participants made their slope estimates, those who had been subjected to the emotionally heavy Mahler pieces estimated the steepness of the hill at 31 degrees. Compare this with the estimate of 19 degrees made by those who were treated to the light, flute-filled Mozart compositions.

The researchers next manipulated moods more directly. They took the research participants to the top of the hill and had them estimate the slope from above. Some of the participants had to stand on the top of a stable wooden box when making their guesses, while others stood atop a wobbly skateboard. As you might imagine, those folks who were on the less stable footing of the skateboard reported more fear, and thought the angle of the hill was steeper than did those on the solid box. Same hill, different perceptions. In yet another study, conducted at the University of Virginia, students were asked how far it would be to walk to Monticello, the famed home of Thomas Jefferson. The students guessed that it was closer if they were with a friend than they did if they were alone. Thus, negative emotions can make the world look frightening, whereas positive moods make the hills of life appear smaller and distances look shorter.

Coming Chapters on Happiness and Psychological Wealth

It is because happiness is associated with action and forward thinking that we are not only able to survive, but to thrive, develop, and progress. When people are in a good mood, they are more likely to be sociable, creative, playful, and energetic – all of which can help them further build their resources. Happiness, then, helps create psychological wealth.

The following chapters of this book outline the evidence showing that the benefits of happiness are obvious in concrete ways in areas such as health and longevity, work and income, and social relationships. Indeed, for social relationships, positive emotions may be the primary elixir. Even for something as seemingly ephemeral as spirituality, positive emotions are helpful.

As important as happiness is for effective functioning in diverse realms of life, there are limits. One need not be intensely happy to function well, and a smidgeon of negative emotions at the right times is helpful. Thus, in chapter 12, we describe how the best level of happiness for doing well varies in different domains. We also discuss how seeking continual bliss is not only doomed to failure, but can be destructive. Thus, being happy most of the time is good, but euphoria is necessarily a rare occurrence. In the rest of this book, we will describe the scientific evidence for our two principles, and give concrete examples of how they are manifested in life.

Part II
Happy People Function Better

3

Health and Happiness

Take a moment and picture your next physical exam. You wait for fifteen minutes reading old copies of *People* to catch up on celebrity gossip, and then you are called to the examination room. As usual, your doctor peers into your ears and nose, checks your blood pressure, listens to your heart, hits your knees with a rubber hammer, and administers the digital rectal exam to check your prostate, if you happen to have one. All the while he or she peppers you with questions about your exercise, diet, and smoking habits. Then the doctor does something completely unexpected and asks about how happy, optimistic, and satisfied you are. What is going on here? This is a medical office, not a psychotherapist's couch! Nonetheless, an emerging body of research suggests that probing your happiness is one of the most important things your doctor can do to predict your health and longevity, and to offer you advice on how to live healthier and longer. Yet few physical exams actually include this easy assessment. This is not a criticism of doctors; of course, the vast majority of them do a remarkable job of treating their patients. Instead, ignoring your feelings is simply a component of how we tend to think of health in general. In health-conscious modern societies, most folks pay attention to diet and exercise, but overlook emotion's vital role in overall health. Books about your "real age," for example, help you calculate your longevity based on a variety of health indicators, but rarely do they include how happy you are. We are out to set the record straight!

Ample evidence now indicates that happiness is very important to your health, and we believe that your doctor must ask about your happiness if he or she really wants to keep you physically and mentally healthy. Along with Lipitor for your high cholesterol, beta blockers for your high blood pressure, a nicotine patch to cure your smoking habit, and diet and exercise to correct your obesity, your physician could assign you gratitude exercises and savoring training to reduce your unhappy moods and create more positive emotions in you. Among the proof that happiness is beneficial to health is the fact that people who are happy become sick less often than unhappy people. Just imagine a life with fewer doctor's office visits, shorter hospital stays, and more health and vitality! In scientific studies of happy people, those who are satisfied with their lives and have an optimistic outlook tend to report fewer symptoms of illness, and actually get sick less often when measured objectively. In this chapter, we will present compelling evidence that happiness influences health in a variety of ways. We hope to convince not only you, but your doctor as well. Our aim is therefore no less than to improve medical practice around the world.

A Hotel in Pennsylvania, Room 305

We begin our tour of the scientific evidence in Room 305 of a hotel near Pittsburgh, which we will call the Vacation Inn. The Vacation Inn is a typical university campus hotel with long hallways and simple but pleasant rooms. We recently stayed in this hotel for a couple of nights. It was a comfortable stay, but certainly not the Ritz-Carlton at Waikiki Beach. Unlike the Ritz-Carlton, however, the Vacation Inn was once the location for a fascinating study on health and illness. Under the leadership of the Carnegie Mellon professor Sheldon Cohen, a team of scientists sequestered research participants in the hotel. Our stay in Room 305 was an attempt to get a feel of what it would be like to stay isolated there as part of a scientific experiment on health and happiness. Professor Cohen and his colleagues recruited men and women who were willing to be isolated on a floor of the hotel for a week while the scientists ran them through a series of medical tests intended to explore the link between moods and health. The research team paid participants hundreds of dollars apiece to live quarantined in the hotel so that their environment could be carefully controlled. Before arriving at the research site, participants completed surveys at home that asked about their moods, as well as their general positivity and negativity, and were screened for antibodies that indicated whether they suffered from certain illnesses or had been exposed to them in the past.

On their first day at the Vacation Inn, the participants were infected with a cold virus, with a threatening-sounding name like "rhinovirus 39," or a strain of the flu. (Although the experiment was carefully controlled and monitored, we have changed the name of the hotel so that nobody will worry about exposure to stray germs there.) Then they lounged around watching television, reading, or talking on the phone, while the illness slowly crept through their bodies and took hold of them. Over the days that followed, the participants were not allowed to leave their floor of the hotel, did not have close physical contact with anyone (including other participants), and ate only the food that was served to them. They could have no visitors. The participants whiled away the hours and days waiting for the virus to run its course, but they had plenty of medical poking and prodding to break the tedium.

Each day during the study, participants reported to a medical desk where their noses were flushed with a saline solution spray, and researchers carefully analyzed what was washed out. Next, their mucus was weighed. One subject wrote in her diary that "they put a lot of stuff in your nose, but fortunately, they also take a lot of stuff out." When the experimenters were not around, the participants put their dirty tissues in baggies so that the researchers could weigh them. Urine, blood, and saliva samples, as well as daily inspections of ears and throats, completed the medical probing. Finally, the participants answered symptom checklists to complain about the severity of their illness.

Dr. Cohen's research team was not only able to control a participant's diet, activity, and social contact, but also plotted the course of the illness as it slowly worked its way through their bodies. In the end – you guessed it – Cohen and his colleagues found that the people who were happier prior to the experiment reported fewer runny noses, as well as less congestion and sneezing. They also showed fewer objective medical signs of illness, such as excess mucus. Thus, not only did the happier people *think* they were healthier, the objective medical tests also demonstrated that they *were* healthier.

But it makes sense to wonder whether this is an instance of negative moods detracting from health or of positive moods actually contributing to protect health. Cohen found that the people higher in positive emotions were less likely to catch colds; those who did experienced fewer and less severe symptoms. Professor Cohen's studies provide clear evidence of a link between mood and health in which happier people seem to benefit from a natural, emotional inoculation against sickness. The stunning finding is that not only do happy people complain less when they get sick, but they are less likely to succumb to infections in the first place because they tend to have stronger immune systems!

It is difficult to emphasize enough how important Professor Cohen's findings are. Before this particular research, the evidence that happy people are healthier and less likely to succumb to infectious diseases frequently amounted to stories like, "Well, my cousin Megan was happy and she never got sick," or "This fellow I read about watched humorous movies and got over cancer." The problem with this type of anecdotal evidence is that there is always a counterstory. A person can always respond by saying, "But my Uncle George was an incessant complainer, and he never got sick," or "Aunt Matilda was a worrywart and she lived to be 103." Examples and counterexamples such as these can always be found because happiness is only one of many factors important to health, and other influences can override the impact of emotions in specific instances. Thus, the stories of people we know do not provide strong evidence either for or against a link between health and happiness. What is so important about studies such as those conducted at the Vacation Inn is that they demonstrate an objective link between happiness, immune system strength, and the probability of getting an infection. Uncle George and Aunt Matilda, move aside; Professor Cohen is about to take your place.

Three Types of Health

Health has become a modern obsession. There are everincreasing numbers of gyms, diet fads, and television talk shows catering to a new generation of health-conscious customers. Even fast food restaurants are turning their attention to delivering healthier meals. Just about everybody wants health, and many people are willing to invest a fair amount of time, money, sweat, and self-control in the pursuit of it. But what, exactly, is health? Is it bouncing back quickly from a bout of the flu? Or is it something possessed only by those athletic individuals who successfully complete the Boston marathon? Most people have a rough notion of health that includes strength, endurance, flexibility, and resistance to illness. Researchers define and measure health in several concrete ways: the likelihood a person will contract specific illnesses, how long a person lives after contracting a life-threatening illness, and how long a person's lifespan is. We discuss how happiness is related to each of these three types of health – called morbidity, survival, and longevity – and show that positive moods improve all of them.

Morbidity

Simply put, morbidity is whether or not an individual develops or contracts a specific illness, such as pneumonia or breast cancer. We all know that genetics and environmental factors influence who contracts such illnesses, but what role might our moods play in contracting a serious illness? In one long-term study conducted over three decades, research participants were found to have lower rates of many health problems if they were high in positive emotions. These included lower death rates from cardiovascular disease, suicide, accidents, homicides, mental disorders, drug dependency, and liver disease related to alcoholism. The beneficial effects of positive moods persisted even when the researchers took gender, age, and education into consideration. In fact, the only health problem happiness did not predict was whether the subjects were obese. Of course, many of the illnesses examined in the study, such as alcohol and drug dependency, were related in obvious ways to lifestyle and behavior, but there were also surprising instances of illnesses being influenced by happiness. For example, depressed individuals were more likely to have heart attacks and recurrences of heart attacks than happy people. Thus, it appears that happiness can help fend off infectious diseases, guard against lifestyle-related illnesses, and protect against heart disease as well. Unhappiness and depression, by contrast, can actually harm health.

Survival

It is a fact that, ultimately, we all die. None of us will survive indefinitely. When researchers talk about survival, however, they mean something a little more modest. "Survival," or what happens to people once they have already developed a serious illness, is a second definition of health. Health researchers are interested in how people fare once they have developed serious and life-threatening illnesses.

Why do some people succumb quickly while others live on and on? Where emotions are concerned, it is interesting to consider whether people living with the burden of diabetes, HIV, or cancer might do better if they are happy. If you have been paying attention to the take-home message of this chapter, you would probably guess that happiness helps people survive longer. Unfortunately – and surprisingly – just the opposite is true. Reviews of studies linking health and emotions show that survival rates for those people who have serious diseases might be an exception to the health benefits of happiness. Although happiness appears to be generally helpful in promoting health, survival is the one area where happiness is sometimes actually detrimental.

Why might this be the case? If happiness is good for you, and is an emotional tonic that promotes health, how can it, in this instance, be bad for you? There are several possible reasons. First, it is possible that highly positive people may fail to report symptoms of illness, a dangerous tendency that can lead to inadequate treatment. A blotch on the skin or small lump might go ignored or overlooked when it should be examined by a medical professional. Happy people tend to be optimistic, and this might lead them to take their symptoms too lightly, seek treatment too slowly, or follow their physician's orders in a half-hearted way. It is also possible that highly positive people who are seriously ill are more likely to choose to live out the remainder of their lives without the pain and invasiveness of some treatment regimens that might result in their living longer.

Regardless of the reason, being very happy in the face of a serious illness can be detrimental to your health. This reinforces the major theme of this book: happiness, as psychological wealth, is good and good for you, but – just as financial wealth can lead to some undesirable outcomes – being in a giddy mood regardless of circumstances is not necessarily a good thing. One of the most important lessons about happiness is that there is an optimal level, beyond which additional positivity is detrimental. Despite the popular idea that we might be able to wish our way out of cancer with humor and positive thoughts, the scientific evidence for this is tenuous. Our advice is that get-happy techniques probably don't hurt and might even help, as long as they don't interfere with available medical treatments. Happiness is a good thing, but we can't let it cloud our judgment when it comes to our health – a conscientious approach to symptoms and diseases should be combined with an optimistic, positive attitude.

Longevity

If you are anything at all like most people, you probably want to live a long time. In fact, you probably want those golden years to be good ones, in which your mind and body are fit enough to allow you a good quality of life. Longevity, measured by the age at death, is the final method of quantifying health. Age at death, regardless of quality of life, offers an objective number for researchers to use as an outcome in their statistics. From a research standpoint, death is a good variable. There is rarely confusion about when a person is dead, and death is a health outcome about which most of us care a great deal. Although a long life does not always mean a good life, by and large, people prefer to live longer than shorter. Given this, we should ask whether chronically happy people actually live longer than their depressed counterparts. The short answer to this question is yes.

In a fascinating and now-classic study, researchers examined an unusual group to pinpoint the happiness-longevity relationship: Catholic nuns. Like the participants in Sheldon Cohen's hotel studies, religious sisters residing together in a convent live in very similar conditions, and this consistency offers something akin to a controlled laboratory. Among nuns, for instance, there are few differences in illicit drug use, alcohol consumption, diet, sexual risk taking, and other circumstances that could confound other studies that compare happy and unhappy people. In what is now referred to as "the nun study," the University of Kentucky researcher Deborah Danner and her colleagues trained their sights on 180 nuns of the School Sisters of Notre Dame to better understand problems associated with aging, such as Alzheimer's disease. The nuns who participated in Danner's study originally entered convents as young adults in Milwaukee and Baltimore between 1931 and 1943. When they entered, they wrote an autobiography describing their lives and their reasons for joining a religious order. Years later, it was these autobiographies that captured the attention of the researchers.

Danner and her colleagues were interested in the nuns' emotions, and how these might influence their overall health. The research team sifted through the personal stories for indications of positivity and negativity. In particular, they were interested in the presence of language that might reflect positive and negative emotions. They kept an eye out for positive words like "happy," "interested," "love," "hope," and "gratitude." For example, one nun wrote: "I was born in 1909, the eldest of seven children . . . My candidate year was spent in the Motherhouse, teaching chemistry. With God's grace, I intend to do my best for our Order, for the spread of religion, and for my personal sanctification." This autobiography is very practical, very nuts and bolts. Although we have no doubt that the author of these words was a woman of good character, her writing contained little positive emotional content. Contrast her autobiography with that of a sister with high positive emotions, who wrote: "God started my life off well by bestowing upon me a grace of inestimable value . . . The past year which I have spent as a candidate studying at Notre Dame College has been a very happy one. Now I look forward with eager joy to receiving the Holy habit of Our Lady and to a life of union with Love Divine." See the difference? With words like "bestowed upon me grace," "a very happy one," and "I look forward with eager joy," it is easy to picture how upbeat and vital this nun must have been.

Using tallies of the emotional content of the autobiographies as their measure of happiness, the Danner research team divided the study group into happiness quartiles, ranging from the happiest 25 percent to the least happy 25 percent, and examined how long the nuns in each of the four groups lived. At the time of the study, of course, some of the nuns were still alive, while many had passed away. In table 3.1, we show the longevity of the happiest and least happy groups at the time of the study.

The risk of mortality – being dead at the time of the study – was two and a half times higher among the least happy compared to the happiest nuns. Indeed, nuns who used a number of different positive emotion words in their autobiographies – happy, interested, love, hope, grateful, eager, contented, amusement – lived, on average, over ten years longer than those who used few such words. It is enough to

Table 3.1 Nun study: longevity

Number of positive emotion sentences in autobiography	*Percent of nuns still alive*	
	Age 85	*Age 93*
Least Happy	54%	18%
Happiest	79%	52%

Source: Danner, Snowden, and Friesen (2001)

make you take a look at how you speak and write! What is especially compelling about this study, apart from the dramatic health findings, is that the researchers were able to find a group of people who were similar in terms of their social activities, reproductive histories, medical care, occupations, socioeconomic status, and diet. In this case, happiness could be separated from these potentially confounding factors, and in the end, amounted to an influence larger than many of those factors about which your doctor inquires.

Most folks like hearing about the nun study because it includes interesting results and a fascinating sample. Just the same, some people raise the issue that the results of a single study with an unusual group might not translate to the rest of us. Fortunately, the women in the nun study are not isolated examples of a link between positive emotions and health. Using the nun study as her model, the health researcher Sarah Pressman analyzed the autobiographies of 96 famous psychologists. She found that, just as in the nun study, psychologists writing happier life stories were likely to live longer. If the psychologists used more humor or positive feeling words such as "vigor" and "energy" in their autobiographies, they lived about six years longer. In contrast, when they used words such as "nervous" and "tense" in their life stories, they lived about five years less. Interestingly, Pressman also found that when the famous psychologists described their relationships with family members, friends, and colleagues, this also predicted greater longevity. Take heed – when you pen your own autobiography, make sure to write a happy one!

Still not convinced that happiness generally leads to longer life? Perhaps you think that famous psychologists are as unusual a group as nuns. Fortunately, there is even more evidence. In yet another study of longevity, researchers examined the emotions of Mexican-Americans, and followed up two years later to determine who was still alive. They found that people reporting high positivity and an abundance of emotions such as joy and love were half as likely to die during the follow-up period as those who suffered from high amounts of fear, anger, and anxiety! What's more, happiness was associated with a lower risk of dying during the period of the study even after researchers applied fancy statistical controls to account for pre-existing medical conditions and smoking addiction. In other words, comparing people who were initially of similar health led to the conclusion that happiness increased longevity. Happy people of different cultural and ethnic origins seem to experience greater longevity than their unhappy peers. None of the research to date is definitive, but don't bet your life against it by being unhappy for long!

The Pathways from Happiness to Health

We have read many research findings that point to the same conclusion – happiness is usually beneficial to your health and longevity. There ought to be concrete reasons why this is so. We found at least eight ways in which happiness leads to less illness.

Moaners and Groaners

Many doctors believe that chronically unhappy people (those folks psychologists describe as "high in neuroticism") just howl louder about symptoms, aches, and pains. Indeed, they do. We all know critical folks who never seem to be able to see the good in anything. These are the types of people who are constantly on the lookout for something to go wrong or something to complain about. People classified as high in neuroticism, or low in positive emotions, notice small physical symptoms more than other folks, and they complain more about their aches given the same levels of pain or illness. However, studies in which negative moods are experimentally induced in people show that angry, sad, and fearful moods can actually reduce pain tolerance. Thus, unhappy people might actually feel pain more acutely than upbeat people. Your curmudgeonly Aunt Matilda might invoke some eye-rolling and displeasure among the relatives when she complains about the pain in her hip, but she might truly feel more pain.

Good and Bad Habits

Nobody is perfect. We all have small vices, whether it is a love of rich desserts, or occasionally skipping a workout due to sheer laziness. But it is the unhappy folks, on average, who have more bad habits. People who often feel down are far more likely to smoke, take drugs, and drink in excess. Unhappiness may lead people to these bad habits in an attempt to "repair" their negative moods. For example, smokers tend to smoke more when they are distressed, and people who are trying to quit smoking are more likely to relapse when they experience a stressful life event such as tough work at the office or a fight with their spouse.

Many health behaviors are related to happiness, hope, and optimism on the one hand, and to unhappiness and depression on the other. For example, happy people are more likely to exercise, eat well, and take vitamins. By contrast, unhappy people are more likely to die from suicide, homicide, and accidents. When rehabilitation therapy is needed, unhappy people are less likely to stay involved. Because of smoking and alcoholism, unhappy people are also more likely to die from lung cancer and liver disease. Thus, your neighbor Billie Bob might not just complain more about his health; some of his behaviors might have led to health problems in the first place.

Immune Power

As demonstrated by Sheldon Cohen's studies, the immune systems of happy people tend to be more effective than those of depressed people, and therefore they are better able to fight infections. In happy people, the immune system is stronger because of higher levels of infection fighters, such as natural killer cells. In contrast, depressed and distressed people tend to have lower immune reactions. With a weaker immune system, unhappy people are more likely to succumb to the infectious viruses and bacteria to which they are exposed.

Cardiovascular Problems

What is the number-one cause of death in most industrialized nations? Is it cancer? Accidents? It turns out that cardiovascular problems, such as stroke and heart disease, are the leading causes of death in the United States and other industrialized countries. Interestingly, emotions – especially anger and depression – are directly related to these maladies. Depressed people are several times more likely than nondepressed folks to have heart attacks and hypertension. Individuals who work under stress or who have troubled marriages are also more likely to suffer from a heart attack and arterial thickening. In one fascinating study, however, a good marriage helped buffer against the ill effects of a bad work environment in terms of such cardiovascular problems. In another study, researchers found that people in happier nations have fewer problems with high blood pressure. On the positive side, people receiving counseling aimed at reducing hostility and impatience for their "Type A" personalities are less likely to have a second heart attack.

There are several different physiological pathways leading from unhappiness to cardiovascular illness, and one of the most important involves chronic stress. Robert Sapolsky spent years studying the physiological aspects of stress in an unlikely place: the African bush. Sapolsky's research subjects were not college undergrads, but zebras, baboons, and other wild animals, which Sapolsky regularly darted with a tranquilizer gun and drew blood samples from. In his intriguing book *Why Zebras Don't Get Ulcers*, Sapolsky describes the typical zebra day as tedium punctuated by very anxious moments. One moment the zebra is hanging out with his buddies, eating grass, and gossiping about the wildebeest, and the next moment a ferocious lion is breaking up the party. The zebra reacts, physiologically speaking, like the rest of us might. His heart rate quickens, his system is flooded with adrenaline and cortisol, and he runs away. But, according to Sapolsky, an interesting thing happens once the zebra has reached safety: all of his physiological stress responses diminish and the zebra returns back to his normal business-as-usual attitude. Unfortunately, humans – because of their unique ability to predict the future and remember the past – are not always so resilient.

People who experience stressful situations, especially intense ones, often have a difficult time adapting back to normal: that is, they continue to experience physiological distress even after the stressful or traumatic event has happened. The chronic nature of their stress slowly takes a serious toll on their health. Perhaps because of our large brains, we can readily carry with us the traumas of the past. We can also foresee more of the dangers of the future, and therefore we have a greater capacity for chronic stress. Or perhaps it is not how terribly smart we are, but just how complicated our lives have become that makes us susceptible to chronic stress.

Stress elevates heart rate, which in turn puts people at greater risk of stroke and heart disease. In addition, extreme emotional events can serve to directly trigger heart attacks. Yet another way that happiness and unhappiness can influence heart disease is by lowering or raising a blood component called fibrinogen. We need fibrinogen because it is essential in blood clotting when we are injured. However, high fibrinogen levels predict heart disease, and happy people tend to have low levels. In one experiment, unhappy people produced twelve times as much fibrinogen as happy people in reaction to a stressor. High levels of fibrinogen in turn predicted greater rates of heart disease and stroke. Thus, there are many physiological reactions that provide a bridge from our happiness to our hearts. In the modern world, it seems that many people feel "stressed" much of the time. We might write this off as middle-class kvetching if it weren't for the serious health effects it causes.

Recovering from Injuries

Anyone who has bumped a knee, twisted an ankle, broken an arm, or cut a finger knows that the body will heal itself, but that it will take a while. New experimental evidence tells us that organisms recover more slowly from injuries if they are under stress. To examine our ability to physically recover when damage is done to our bodies, scientists create very small wounds – perhaps on your arm or the roof of your mouth – with a sterile puncture device. Not fun, but like having your fingertip pricked when doctors need a small blood sample. The researchers then can track how long the wound takes to heal, and relate that time to circumstances in the subjects' lives. Folks who are in the midst of a stressful event, such as taking care of a chronically sick child or a disabled spouse, have slower wound recovery. Students studying for midterm examinations, for instance, show slower recovery rates than do those who are preparing for a vacation. In highly controlled animal laboratory studies, mice exposed to stress also heal more slowly. Furthermore, if the mice are given a shot to block stress hormones, the mice heal as quickly as the unstressed mice, demonstrating that the bodily stress reactions are indeed the culprit in slow recovery. Thus, although we are all exposed to accidents and illnesses that damage our bodies innumerable times during our lifetimes, happy people tend to heal more quickly from these wounds of slings, arrows, and bicycle accidents.

Growing Old Through Stress

We all know the folk wisdom that says that hard or stressful lives make people age prematurely. Perhaps you even know somebody who has gone completely gray in the midst of a divorce or other difficult event. Most of us look at gray hairs and wrinkles as an indicator of quality of life, as well as a sign of aging. Does that dark-haired 60-year-old beauty dye her hair, or has she led a stress-free life? New research evidence indicates that the rate of bodily aging may indeed be related to stress, and that this occurs at the level of the genetic control of cell replication and replacement.

People's bodies age more quickly if they are exposed to more chronic stress, possibly because they have less capacity to replace worn-out cells. In a recent study on English twins, scientists found that female fraternal twins who had a more stressful life compared to their sisters, as exemplified by the type of job they had, were seven years older in terms of their telomeres, the caps of DNA that protect the ends of our chromosomes. As we age, old cells die and are replaced by new ones. When cells divide to produce new cells, we lose a portion of our telomeres, and the length of our telomeres shortens as we age. When we lose our telomeres, we lose the ability to replicate new cells with fidelity, and our old cells age and eventually die. Telomeres allow our chromosomes to divide and replicate without losing genetic information. Shorter telomeres are associated with death at a younger age, with a greater risk of heart diseases, and with serious infections. We want the longest telomeres we can get, and begin to age mercilessly once we lose them. Thus, the finding that stress correlates with shorter telomeres is of critical importance.

The scientists also found that it makes a difference whom the twins marry. The researchers identified pairs of twins where one had married an upper-class man and the other twin sister had married a lower-status man. In this case, the privileged twin was nine years younger than her twin in terms of telomere age! Besides the obvious lesson for our children to "marry up," the study strongly suggests that stressful and more arduous lives do make us age more quickly. Science has not yet found a way to protect our telomeres, and so we all lose them slowly as our cells replicate. But we don't want to lose our telomeres more quickly than necessary due to stress and unhappiness.

The twin study suggests that stress leads to aging telomeres, and it is known that once telomeres get too small, cell senescence sets in. Other studies support the findings of the twin study with more direct evidence about stress. For example, it was found that among women with chronically ill children, the longer the child had been sick, the shorter the mothers' telomeres. The most stressed mothers had telomeres that were shorter by from nine to seventeen years when compared to the least stressed mothers! Obesity and smoking may also shorten our telomeres, and these conditions are often related to lower happiness as well.

Although our understanding of telomere aging is uncertain and very incomplete, the results of these studies are impressive because they relate feelings of stress and objective conditions of stress to a genetic marker of aging. Stress appears to empower our universal enemy – aging.

Unhappy Hormones

Hormones are vital for health and proper functioning. There are a variety of hormones released in the body that help natural processes ranging from fertility, to sleep, to repairing damaged cells. Cortisol, for example, is a hormone that is released when we are under stress. Its role is to break down damaged tissue so that it can be replaced by new, healthy tissue. It is usually released when there is some type of trauma or stress. However, too much or too little of certain hormones can lead to disease. For instance, large amounts of circulating cortisol in the bloodstream – which could be the result of chronic stress – predict obesity, hypertension, and Type 2 diabetes. Chronic happiness is, fortunately, associated with lower levels of cortisol, as well as better regulation of cortisol through the day. Thus, hormones are yet another route by which our emotions can influence our health.

Family and Friends

The final route from happiness to health is through social relationships. Diverse types of social support, from having loving parents to a strong marriage, are related to better health. In one study, for example, the best predictor of angina (the pains due to insufficient blood to the heart) in men was a question about how loving their wife was. Isolated individuals are more likely to smoke, be obese, and have high blood pressure. On the other hand, those with strong social ties are likely to survive longer after a heart attack. Because happiness and good social relationships are related (see chapter 3), the absence of loneliness is yet another reason that happy people tend to be healthier.

A very important finding comes from Stephanie Brown and her colleagues at the University of Michigan: *giving* support to others is more important to longevity than *receiving* support. She found that elderly individuals who gave little emotional or practical support to others were more than twice as likely to die during the five years she followed them compared to people who gave to others. Even accounting for initial health and other factors, people who gave to a spouse, to friends, and to neighbors were blessed with greater longevity.

We have described eight pathways leading from happiness to health and unhappiness to illness. Future research will refine our knowledge of these causes and explore how they interact. In the meantime, be happy.

Optimal Happiness

We learned earlier that happy people can fail to be vigilant enough in the face of life-threatening illness, but that generally happiness and optimism are good for health. A few studies indicate that highly aroused positive emotions may put us at risk. What about those occasional bouts of unhappiness? Do they also put us at risk? Don't be concerned if you experience sporadic anger, sadness, or worry. Happiness is not the total absence of negative emotions. Brief feelings of sadness and guilt, while unpleasant to experience, can serve important purposes and help us function effectively. How, then, on an individual basis, can we hope to gauge whether we are happy enough to benefit from the health effects of happiness?

One way is by considering "affect balance," the sum total of our unpleasant moods subtracted from our pleasant emotions. Instead of ridding ourselves of all unpleasant emotions, our aim is to experience considerably more pleasant than unpleasant moods and emotions. Researchers examined affect balance in the lives of cardiovascular patients who had previously been hospitalized. They found that affect balance tending toward the negative – that is, with relatively frequent or intense negativity compared to the amount of positivity – was the best predictor of whether the patient relapsed and was readmitted to the hospital. Experiencing negative emotions was not nearly as important as whether a person experienced more negative emotions than positive ones. Using the affect balance approach to happiness, we need to make sure that we commonly experience good feelings, and only infrequently experience negative ones.

A New Healthy Life Checklist

If you want to have a healthy lifestyle and increase your odds of living longer, doctors typically recommend a series of health-promoting behaviors. Many doctors give you a health checklist for the start of your physical exam. Magazine articles and internet sites give formulas for predicting one's length of life from these items. So, to judge your health practices, and how long you can expect to live, please place an X next to the items below that are true:

_____ 1 I don't smoke.
_____ 2 I never drink alcohol, or drink only moderately.
_____ 3 I am a normal weight (not too thin or obese).
_____ 4 I never talk on a cell phone while driving.
_____ 5 I use sunscreen whenever I am outdoors.
_____ 6 I eat fruits, vegetables, and a bit of dark chocolate every day.
_____ 7 I take a baby aspirin many days.
_____ 8 I exercise four or more times a week.
_____ 9 I regularly brush and floss my teeth.
_____ 10 I always wear seat belts.
_____ 11 I frequently feel happy and contented.
_____ 12 I engage in many activities that bring me joy.
_____ 13 I am satisfied with my life.
_____ 14 I feel sad only occasionally.
_____ 15 I feel angry only occasionally.
_____ 16 I feel stressed only occasionally.
_____ 17 I often feel grateful and generally trusting.
_____ 18 I have friends and family members on whom I can depend.
_____ 19 I am an optimistic person.
_____ 20 I am happy with my social relationships.

The first ten items are likely to increase your health and longevity. The next ten items are not only likely to help your health and longevity, but they also will make those extra years a lot more fun! Indeed, whereas a few of the first ten healthy lifestyle items sound like hard work, the last ten healthy lifestyle items make life more enjoyable.

Conclusions

Health is a part of psychological wealth because it provides the energy and ability to do the things needed to live a rewarding life. Of course, there are people with serious chronic illnesses and disabilities who lead full lives. However, these individuals are heroic, and normally ill health is an impediment to complete functioning. A major point of this chapter is that although health can influence feelings of well-being, the reverse is also true.

When Ed was a teenager, he was hospitalized for a small surgical operation, and the nurse gave him the usual embarrassing "barn door" hospital gown to wear. He refused it, insisting that he would wear the crisply pressed shirts he had brought. No, the nurse countered, the hospital rules required that the gown be worn, and not crisply pressed shirts. Ed was unswayed. "Sorry," he replied, "no gowns." Exasperated with this difficult adolescent, the nurse stomped out of the room, unable to tolerate patients who did not comply with her commands. Was Ed just difficult? Probably. But there is another lesson here as well: Ed realized that he would feel more comfortable and happier about himself if he wore the shirts. He felt the shirts would help him to overcome the bleak surroundings of the old hospital. Little did he know that the snappy shirts might have helped him recover more quickly!

The evidence for the effects of happiness on health and longevity is not watertight, and the future will undoubtedly see some minor revisions to our understanding of the health-happiness connection, but the proof is strong enough that you should act on it. The evidence that happy people are more likely to be physically healthier and live longer is becoming compelling; it is so strong that working on one's happiness is a worthwhile health strategy. Doctors once thought that unhappy people just moan and complain more about their health, and they do, but we now know that unhappiness can truly cause worse physical health, whereas happiness can cause objectively better health. Of course, happiness will not prevent all diseases, any more than quitting smoking, wearing seatbelts, or using sunscreen will. But in combination with these other factors, it can help. Not only is a happy person likely to live longer, but he or she is likely to be healthier and more fulfilled during those extra years. No doubt an entrepreneur will soon offer to test the length of your telomeres, and we might try this ourselves. But why not just keep them as long as possible in the first place, by being happy most of the time? We should all think of happiness, hope, and optimism as important health-protective factors. Suggest to your doctor that he or she add these items to the health checklist. And tell your doctor to read this book!

4

Happiness and Social Relationships: You Can't Do Without Them

Imagine a perfect Saturday morning. You don't have to go in to work, you wake up feeling fresh and rested, and you look forward to a leisurely breakfast. However, when you flip on the kitchen lights, something on the table immediately catches your eye. It is a large stone tablet, engraved with strange runes! It reads:

Ωε αρε τηε Δεμονιανσ φρομ τηε Γαλαξψ Ανδρομεδα ανδ αρε χονδυχτινγ α στυδψ οφ ψουρ ωορλδ. Ιν ορδερ το δετερμινε μορε αβουτ ψουρ σπεχιεσ, ωε ηαϖε λεφτ ψου αλονε ιν τηε ωορλδ, ανδ ηα ϖε ρεμοϖεδ αλλ οτηερ πεοπλε. Ψου ωιλλ λιϖε ουτ τηε ρεστ οφ ψουρ λιφε αλονε ον ψουρ πλανετ. Ωε ηαϖε ποωερσ φαρ βεψονδ τηοσε οφ ψουρ σπεχιεσ, ανδ ψου ωιλλ φινδ τηατ ωε ηαϖε αχχομμο δατεδ ψουρ πηψσιχαλ νεεδσ τηερε ωιλλ αλωαψσ βε ηεατινγ ανδ αιρ χονδιτιονινγ, φοοδ, γασολιν ε ανδ φυνχτιοναλ ϖεηιχλεσ ωηερεϖερ ψου γο ιν τηε ωορλδ.

At first you can't make heads or tails of the writing, and think the tablet must be some kind of prop or practical joke. Your family is still asleep, so you get a cup of coffee and a bowl of cereal. As you sit down to eat, you realize there is a pattern to the writing and, before long, you have deciphered the script, which reads:

We are the Demonians from the Galaxy Andromeda and are conducting a study of your world. To determine more about your species, we have left you alone in the world, and have removed all other people. You will live out the rest of your life alone on your planet. We have powers far beyond those of your species, and you will find that we have accommodated your physical needs – there will always be heating and air conditioning, food, gasoline, and functional vehicles wherever you go in the world. Your safety from animals and other dangers is assured. We will not protect you from suicide, however, so that as long as you choose to continue your life without killing yourself, it will signify to us that we have your informed consent for being a subject in this experiment. The entire planet is now yours and belongs to you alone. Our interest is in observing your behavior and, in particular, how you function without others of your species. You should feel free to enjoy your world in whatever way you desire, but you will do so alone. Thanks for participating in our study, and best of luck to you.

Ha, ha, you think, this must be an elaborate practical joke concocted by your kids or your friends. But the more you consider it, the more you wonder exactly where your kids and friends are. The house is conspicuously quiet and there is no traffic out front. Feeling a slow surge of panic, you make some calls. No one answers at any of the numbers you dial. You decide to go for a drive. The streets are empty, the stores are deserted, and you don't see a single pedestrian. You begin what will become a weeklong search of nearby towns, desperate to locate another person.

By the end of the week, panic has given way to a kind of acceptance. You set your mind to thinking about all the exciting possibilities of being in charge of the world. You are free to do whatever you wish. At first, a world without other people seems pretty good. There is no traffic, no lines at movie theaters or grocery stores, no expensive tickets to go skiing, and no one to stop you from exploring Bill Gates's house. Delicious food appears when you enter restaurants. The possibilities are endless.

You spend days exploring museums, private mansions, and sky-scraper penthouses. You visit the homes of famous people and look through their diaries and drawers. You drink their extravagantly expensive wines and wear their jewelry. You drive across the country in the car of your choosing, going as fast as you please. You take a whole month to walk through all the most famous art galleries in the country. You take the pictures you like best home with you. You sleep in the White House and put your feet up on the desk in the Oval Office. You give a speech at the United Nations and drop a watermelon off the top of the Empire State Building. You explore the secret underground bunkers at military installations and take a tour through Area 51 to see if there are really any alien bodies kept there (perhaps a Demonian?). You go camping in all the national parks without having to fight crowds, and you wander the back lots of the major movie studios.

Because the Demonians have made provisions to keep you from all harm, you are free to engage in the thrill-seeking, risky activities about which you have always dreamed. You bungee jump off the Brooklyn Bridge, and scuba dive off the coast of Florida. You wander through the jungles of Central America completely unafraid of the snakes, spiders, and wild cats. You drive a motorcycle through the halls of your old high school and speed a race car down Main Street. You do a hysterical imitation of the Rockettes at Radio City Music Hall, in full costume. Perhaps best of all, there are no annoying cell phones ringing in public places!

One year later, you are lonely beyond belief, and bored out of your mind. You own the world and have lived a dream life, with no restrictions, but you have had no one with whom to share it. There is no one to tell about what you read in the government files, or with whom to visit the ruins outside Mexico City. There is no one with whom to enjoy a drink, a sunset, or sex. There is no current news on the television or radio, no new movies are being made, and no new books are being written. There is not even anyone to compete with, or anyone to challenge you. Each day you wake up dreading the isolation. You talk to God and to the Demonians, but neither of them answers you. You try to domesticate some animals, but they all avoid you. The new challenges you set for yourself, such as learning to play the piano, seem hollow and worthless. Your lifelong dream of learning French is useless. There is nobody left in the world who cares what happens to you, and no one left to care about. The loneliness is crushing, like permanent solitary confinement. You drink a lot of alcohol and try stronger drugs you find in people's homes.

Why is it that such a scenario – one with so much adventure, wealth, creativity, and freedom – could ultimately end up so horribly? Why would a world without other people be a hell on Earth? If it's true that other folks can be annoying – you know, writing irritating letters to the editor and cutting us off in traffic – wouldn't it make sense that the world would be a rosier place without them? Even allowing for people who irritate us, we all understand that, deep down, life is only meaningful if we have people who care about us, people we can show affection to, and folks with whom to share experiences. Perhaps even people who annoy us actually add to the interest life has. Upon reflection, common sense tells us that social relationships are vital to fulfillment. But, as seemingly obvious as this position is, does research support this?

Science, Happiness, and Relationships

Relationships are themselves a crucial part of psychological wealth without which you cannot be truly rich. Simply put, we need others to flourish. Indeed, the results of research on social relationships and happiness are clear on this point: healthy social contact is essential for happiness. Family relationships and close friendships are important to happiness. Many studies show that happy people are also more blessed with good families, friends, and supportive relationships than are people with low life satisfaction.

In fact, the links between happiness and social contact are so strong that many psychologists think that humans are genetically wired to need one another. Humans have a long period of development – from infancy through puberty – during which we depend strongly upon others. Even as adults we function much better when we are embedded in social networks that offer cooperation, support, and enjoyment. The social psychologist Ellen Berscheid writes that the most important factor in the survival of *Homo sapiens* is our social nature, our ability to love one another and work together. Being social is as essential to our survival as our other amazing assets, such as our powerful brains and nimble fingers with opposable thumbs.

The research findings affirm the relation between happiness and being social. But as with all correlational studies, it makes sense to wonder which way the causal arrow points. Does being happy win people more friends? Or does having more friends lead to increased happiness? It turns out that happiness leads to better social relationships. For example, people who have high life satisfaction before marriage are more likely than others to get married, to stay married, and to be happy with their marriages. However, relationships also seem to make people happy.

People's life satisfaction spikes when they get married. On the other hand, research shows that when a spouse dies, widows exhibit a steep decline in life satisfaction, and only slowly recover. In fact, the death of a spouse can be such a serious hit to happiness that it takes, on average, about five to seven years for life satisfaction to return close to the level it was when the spouse was still alive. When people are separated from those they love for a prolonged period of time, they often show signs of "withdrawal," including sadness and homesickness.

You don't need to look any further than the proliferation of cell phones to understand that people like one another a lot. These days, folks can hardly seem to go to the movie theater, grocery store, or the park without checking in with their friends and family. In fact, humans have the ability to connect with one another as never before. Even in the absence of a clear business purpose, people love talking to one another using cell phones, text messaging, Instant Messenger, chat rooms, email, VOIP phones, and Skype, and through social connection websites such as MySpace and Facebook. When you eavesdrop on those cell phone conversations, you realize that the parties often don't really have a concrete need to be talking. You frequently hear questions like "What are you doing right now?" "Where are you?" and "Where are we going to meet?" Basically, people are "connecting."

We don't just need relationships: we need close ones. What are "close relationships"? Of course, just being in frequent contact is one type of intense relationship, but not necessarily one that will produce happiness. The close relationships that produce the most happiness are those characterized by mutual understanding, caring, and validation of the other person as worthwhile. People feel secure in these types of relationships, and are often able to share intimate aspects of themselves with the other. Importantly, they can count on the other person for help if they need it. Although acquaintances and casual friends can be fun, it is the supportive close relationships that are essential to happiness.

Research indicates that social contact influences happiness and health. We know that – on average – people are happier when they are with others compared to the times when they are alone. In one study, for example, we collected mood data from people using the experience sampling method (ESM). Throughout the day, we signaled the research participants with random alarms, after which they would complete a short mood survey and indicate the type of situation they were in: Were they alone, or with other people? Initially, we suspected that introverts would be happier when they were alone and that extroverts would be happier when they were in a social setting. In table 4.1, we show the average intensity of positive feelings of the research participants, which could range from zero (no positive feelings at all) to six (extremely intense positive feelings). The numbers indicate how positive on average introverts and extroverts felt when alone versus with others.

Table 4.1 Introverts, extroverts

	Introverts	Extroverts
Social situations	2.4	2.9
Alone situations	1.5	2.1

As you can see, people generally felt mild positive moods. Even more interesting, and flying in the face of our prediction, both extroverts and introverts had more positive emotions when they were with other people. That's right: even introverts who have the reputation for being social wallflowers enjoyed themselves more when they were in social settings. Although it's true that extroverts spent a bit more time with other people, both groups showed more pleasant moods when they were engaged in social contact. Indeed, the introverts get as much boost from being with people as did extroverts. The Nobel laureate Daniel Kahneman found results parallel to ours. Studying a thousand women, he found that the least happy time of the day was alone (commuting to work), and the happiest times were with others (with family and friends, and having sex). It's certainly not true that we would like to surround ourselves with other people all the time, but when we do, we tend to feel good.

What about the opposite causal direction, the possibility that being happy wins a person more friends? Research findings show that being happy makes a person more sociable, more pleasant, and more rewarding to be around. In one study, psychologists used mood inducers, such as short film clips, to put research participants into a good mood, a neutral mood, or a sad mood. People who were in a good mood expressed greater interest in social activities, helping others, and participating in strenuous activities compared to those in the other two groups. What's more, the happy subjects expected social situations to feel more rewarding, and felt that they had more energy to spend on the encounters. In another study, researchers found that when college men were induced into a positive mood, they made more intimate self-disclosures to a woman with whom they were interacting. Being in a good mood makes people more extroverted.

Other research has supported the notion that happiness leads to social benefits. For instance, psychologists conducted a study in which they examined the yearbook photos of 21-year-old women who attended Mills College during the late 1950s. The researchers were interested in how having a positive attitude might affect the young women later in life. To this end, they assessed the degree to which the women's yearbook photos displayed a "Duchenne smile," a true smile in which the smiling mouth is accompanied by wrinkle lines radiating out from the corners of the eyes. Interestingly, the women with the authentic smiles were more likely to be married in middle age, and more likely to have better marriages, than their classmates with no smiles or artificial smiles. Positivity, even the small amount captured by the flash of a camera, appears to pay off socially and directly improve psychological wealth.

Most of us are drawn to happy individuals much more than we are attracted to unhappy people. You probably have experience with this in your own life. The happy people you know are likely to be fun, optimistic, enthusiastic, and enjoyable to be around. Their positive attitude might even lift your spirits a bit. On the other hand, depressed people tend to be lethargic or apathetic, and can seem to drain your energy. Many unhappy people complain a lot. In laboratory studies, researchers have arranged for people to chat with strangers. The research participants are assigned to meet a stranger and have a short conversation. Their partner is assigned at random, and sometimes it is a person who scores highly on measures of happiness, and sometimes someone who does not. After the conversation is over, the researchers ask both people to rate their partner. As you might expect, people consistently rate the happy folks as more likable, and are more likely to want to have a follow-up conversation with him or her. In short, happy people tend to be more likable and popular.

Why Relationships Matter

We have made the case – and we hope a compelling one – that relationships matter to happiness and are a key part of psychological wealth. But why should they matter? Why are they so crucial to our daily existence? Given the prevalence of violence, divorce, and other social ills in the world, doesn't it sometimes seem like other people are more trouble than they are worth? Isn't it other folks who irritate us, scare us, make us jealous, and otherwise cause us grief? And aren't families riddled with conflict? What exactly does social contact do for us that tips the scales toward relationships having such a positive impact on us?

First and foremost, other people allow us to love and to be loved. They help us feel secure and cared for; they value us and will step up to the plate for us if we need help. At the same time, loving other people gives us an opportunity to grow and enlarge ourselves. Further, when we take pride in the accomplishments of others, and they take pride in ours, we then share a deep bond.

Relationships matter to our emotional well-being and psychological wealth because our close associates directly help us in a variety of ways. We blossom from children into adults only through the encouragement, support, and mentorship of parents, teachers, coaches, and other influential people. We are able to face tough times largely through the emotional support and compassion of our loved ones. We are able to move from apartment to apartment because we have friends who are willing to help us lug furniture across town.

Other people don't actually have to do anything for us to benefit. The knowledge that there are police officers, air traffic controllers, and firefighters makes life a little more comfortable because such people free up our psychological resources to focus on other concerns. In fact, the mere presence of others can be soothing to us. A variety of studies have found that when people experience a trauma, such as a car accident, they generally fare better if they endured the hardship in the company of others. In the end, people provide us with a psychological (and sometimes physical) safety net that makes life easier to live.

There are many other terrific things about other people. First, there is the wonderful diversity of people. We are not necessarily just talking about ethnic, national, or linguistic differences here, although those can be fascinating and compelling. We mean that people are extraordinarily diverse in their knowledge and ideas. Your friends, colleagues, and family members probably have interesting hobbies, unique areas of expertise, unusual skills, and novel thoughts, and will sometimes surprise you with their actions. Other people can plot the stars' movement through the sky, write *Anna Karenina*, and make us laugh with a witty comeback. This diversity of influences has a profound and beneficial effect on us.

Other people's ideas can challenge us, help us to form our own opinions and ideas, entertain us, and provide the basis for innovation and creativity. Consider how much time you spend absorbing the ideas of others. Every time you watch a film or television show, attend a dance performance or play, see a painting, admire architecture, read a book, shake your head at the letters to the editor, look at photographs in a magazine, listen to talk radio, enjoy music on your iPod, or argue with a friend, you are benefiting from the fact that other folks don't think and know exactly what you think and know. Diverse groups also allow people to specialize. Only by living together in communities can some people become effective farmers while others become experts in medicine. Society as a whole, then, benefits from this diverse pool of skills, knowledge, and creativity.

Another reason we profit from others is that the groups to which we belong help to define who we are and give us a sense of identity. They help us to become something larger than ourselves, and help us define who we are in a large universe. Without other people, we are a speck in the universe. With the people in our nation, religion, political party, and other organizations, we are something larger and more significant.

Finally, people are just good plain fun. Humor and joking, for instance, are the products of social interaction. Have you ever noticed that you can tickle other people but not yourself? The idea of a "party," whether it is a school potluck or drinks on Friday night, is predicated on the idea of getting together in groups. Most folks report that they would rather engage in an activity – whether it is visiting a museum or going out to eat – with other people. Sharing experiences increases our enjoyment of most activities, and many activities, such as most sports, can only be conducted in groups. Sex and emotional intimacy is another arena that is both inherently social and integral to our psychological health. Other people can bring out the best, most playful side in all of us.

Marriage

Although it is clear that social relationships and happiness are important to one another, it is worth considering several specific types of relationships. There are, of course, many types of relationships, including those between parents and children, or supervisors and employees. You have social relationships with colleagues, neighbors, and enemies. Each of these has a different character, and it makes sense that each could have a different bearing on your happiness.

Among the most institutionalized, traditional, and universal relationships is marriage. Every culture on the planet has some form of special union between adults: polygamous marriages in rural Kenya, gay marriages in the Netherlands, arranged marriages in India, and love marriages between a single man and woman. But, in a modern social climate where, at least in the case of many industrialized countries such as the United States, about half the marriages end in divorce, it makes sense to wonder whether marriages add to or detract from happiness. There have been theorists who argue that monogamy is unnatural, and others who tout the commitment of marriage as a moral imperative. What does the research say about the happiness of married folks?

Research shows that married people are on the whole relatively happy. This is something we would expect, given the preponderance of happiness in the world. But the real question is: Are married couples any happier than other folks? Some highly publicized research shows that married people are, indeed, happier than their single counterparts. However, this overlooks the fact that happy people are more likely to get married in the first place. Thus, it could be that marital bliss is less the product of a perfect union and more the result of two people who were pretty happy to begin with. Richard Lucas, a researcher from Michigan State University, examined life satisfaction data from tens of thousands of people across many years of their lives. He found that married people are about as happy as they were before they were married. We have shown his findings in figure 4.1. That is, with the exception of a brief spike in happiness around the time of the wedding itself, marriage – at least in the Germans he studied – didn't seem to make an enormous difference in life satisfaction. How can this be, given that social relationships are so important, and that having a loving, trusting spouse can be so wonderful?

In part, the explanation lies in the fact that researchers usually deal with averages. For some people, marriage is a terrific emotional boon, whereas for others it is a weight that drags happiness down. Consider figure 4.2 below, showing the happiness of three people across the course of their lives. The average of the three (Person B) is roughly as happy as she was before she got married, once the wedding thrill wears off. However, individual C is less satisfied than before, and A is more satisfied. Indeed, Lucas found these three types of individuals. The data suggest an important lesson. Marriage is not, in itself, a guarantee of happiness. Rather, it appears that it matters a great deal

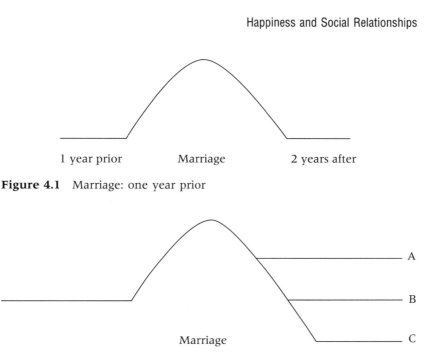

Figure 4.1   Marriage: one year prior

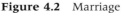

Figure 4.2   Marriage

whether or not your marriage is right for you. Some folks rush into marriage too young, others marry people they are not compatible with, and still others seem to luck onto their soul mate.

It is important to note that although, on average, married people are happier than singles, this is not true of everyone. Whether one will benefit from marriage depends in part on one's personality and in part on the context of one's life. For example, nuns living in a convent don't need marriage to have close, intimate friends. The psychologist Bella DePaulo, in her book *Singled Out: How Singles Are Stereotyped, Stigmatized, and Ignored, and Still Live Happily Ever After*, makes the case that for many individuals the single state may be a happy one. Societies are structured so that deep friendship is often easier to find in marriage, but there are many forms that deep friendship and love can sometimes take. Because 40 percent of adults in the United States are single, divorced, or widowed, and because adults on average now spend more adult years single than married, it is important to know that these individuals can find close friends and a rewarding life; marriage is not the only road to happiness. However, the evidence to date suggests that cohabitating couples are not as happy as the married.

Love

One reason that we believe marriage should lead to happiness is that we associate love with happiness. George Vaillant, in his decades-long study of Harvard graduates, found that happiness is having lots of people whom you love, and who love you in return. Believing in the Golden Rule is not enough; you must experience love. Readers may have heard the old joke "I love humanity; it's people that I can't stand." The line pithily captures the divergence between the belief in love and experiencing it.

Although it would be nice to think that all marriages are built on a foundation of mutual respect and deep, heartfelt love, this is, unfortunately, not the case in reality. Love, so they say, can be a fickle friend. To understand why, it is important to look at love in terms of a timeline, spanning from those thrilling first moments when a couple lays their eyes on one another to the different kind of affection they feel in old age. For humans to meet, get to know one another, and agree to start families together, there has to be an incentive. Fortunately, nature equipped us with flirting and passion. Passion, or romantic love, is the headliner of all the types of love. It is "love at first sight" and infatuation. The love timeline begins with this intense rush of positive feeling that is characterized by enchantment with the other person. This getting-to-know-you phase is associated with the release of dopamine and adrenaline, and infatuated people often are desperate to be with the other person to feel on top of the world.

Unfortunately, or perhaps fortunately, this stage of love does not last. People, as we will see in chapter 9, have an amazing ability to adapt to new circumstances, and even that glamorous new beau can turn old hat. After a few months or a year or two, at most, the fires of romantic love normally die down into embers. Naturally, for the legions of people indoctrinated in the idea of "true love," and exposed to Hollywood images of passion, this less intense period is often mistaken for "falling out of love." When Hollywood passion is mistakenly seen as "true love," we get the brief marriages that often characterize Hollywood, and individuals move from one relationship to the next in search of the high of continuing passion. A surprising number of breakups happen during this transition, which is unfortunate, because the next phase is, in many ways, even better.

Romantic love often gives way to a more companionate and complex relationship. If infatuation is about overlooking a partner's flaws and feeling good, companionate love is readiness to acknowledge and accept some flaws. When people graduate to this type of love, they tend to make sacrifices for one another. Partners with companionate love begin doing things for one another – not because it will make themselves feel better, but because they know their mates will feel better. Consider cleaning up after the dog as he goes through potty training. Nobody likes to do it, but couples in mature love perform such favors even if the other person won't know about it. Not only do people with this type of love become intimate companions who can fully trust one another, but they also experience what Erich Fromm called "being-love," obtaining pleasure from doing things for the other person.

It's true that passion comes and goes during companionate love, and that a spouse can sometimes feel like a friend instead of a lover. This is a sign that the relationship is growing rather than dying, as many people mistakenly believe. When one arrives at the point where it is pleasurable to do things for the other person, even if he or she doesn't realize what you have done, this type of mature love can be an enduring source of happiness. In compassionate love, we also enjoy trusting and sharing our deepest thoughts and feelings with the other person; this is true intimacy.

Yet another kind of affection merits mention here, especially because it has consequences for long-term happiness. "Deficiency-love," as Fromm called it, is based on the idea that we are attracted to people who satisfy our needs. If you are low in self-esteem, you will find attractive a person who gives you many compliments. If you get bored easily, you will be drawn to an entertaining, exciting person. This kind of attraction is not necessarily a bad thing, but does have some hidden dangers. Deficiency-love works only as long as your needs are stable. Unfortunately, for most of us, aging and maturing are usually accompanied by a reordering of personal values and a shifting of needs. As our needs change, we may find that we feel less attracted to our mates because they supply something we no longer need or desire, unless they change as we change.

The type of love you have in your relationships can be a major factor not only in your marital happiness, but also in your overall fulfillment. People's expectations and maturity have a profound impact on how well they can solve problems and communicate with one another. In fact, communication itself is a predictor of marital satisfaction. Negative interactions, such as hurtful arguments or yelling,

Table 4.2

Relationship	Positive	to	Negative
Parents to their children	3	to	1
Bosses to employees	4	to	1
Partners to each other	5	to	1
Friends to each other	8	to	1
Little League coaches to kids	10	to	1
Personnel to customers	20	to	1
Parents to their grown children	100	to	1
Remarks to one's mother-in-law	1,000	to	1

can detract heavily from a marriage, even when equally balanced by positive interactions. In healthy marriages, we call the desirable number of positive to negative interactions the Gottman ratio, after the University of Washington researcher John Gottman. Years of studying couples led Gottman to his understanding of the best ratio: at least five to one in favor of the positive interactions. That is, in satisfying marriages the partners say at least five times as many positive things to each other as negative things, and often more. Compare this to other types of relationships in which the optimal ratio is different (see table 4.2).

Of course, the above ratios are tongue-in-cheek; there is no one exact ratio for each relationship. It will depend on how bad and good the remarks are, and the context and manner in which they are delivered. Telling someone you never loved them is obviously far worse than saying you don't care for the eggs they just cooked. It is important to consider whether negative remarks are framed as constructive criticism, for example, or whether they are hurled at a partner in an attempt to hurt him or her. The point of the table is simply that the ratio may differ across various roles. While we may verbalize more corrections to our children during their formative years, they rarely appreciate this as adults. Regardless of the exact ratio, the point we are making is this: You should become a person with a positive ratio in virtually all of your relationships with others. If you want to be liked and popular, have a positive ratio. This does not mean, of course, that you should fawn over folks you don't like or give compliments you don't believe. Rather, you should be authentic, but remember to mention all the good things others do.

Whether you are a coach, a boss, a spouse, a parent, or simply a friend, dishing out more positive than negative should be an ingrained habit. Of course, there are times when everyone needs to offer some criticism to others. Children, for instance, need advice and discipline to develop into moral and sensible people. But even in the context of discipline there should be an emphasis on the positive when the person is behaving well. You can influence the behavior of others, such as your children, with the positive feedback you give them for desirable behavior, and your occasional corrective comment becomes more powerful against the positive backdrop. If you give out a constant diet of negative comments to others, not only will they avoid and dislike you, but what you say will become less potent. It is also important to understand that love is not contingent – you love your children, for example, even when you are critical of their behavior. Thus, make it clear that you are criticizing their behavior, not them as persons.

Children

What about children? Does the pitter-patter of little feet around the house bring joy to families, or is parenting all about storm and stress? Again, the parent-child relationships are a place where research on happiness paints an interesting portrait. Most happiness studies have not shown children to be an important cause of happiness. Many people are shocked by this finding, and are reluctant to accept it. In fact, for most of us, the idea that our beloved children are not a source of measurable joy for us seems wrong. It is easy to call to mind the school plays, well-written papers, and soccer championships that caused us to beam with pride. But what about those emergency appendectomies, the latenight illnesses, the messes, and all that arguing with teenagers? If we are honest, we admit that there are some downsides to having kids, as well as the high moments.

How, then, are we to weigh the positives and negatives of having children against each other? How do we factor together the hassles of carpools and after-school lessons with the joys of reading a story at bedtime or hearing our kids tell us they love us? Just as we saw in the case of marital happiness, enjoying children is largely a matter of personal preference. Some folks consider having kids a foregone conclusion, and other people don't want the burden of children at all.

For some couples, a newborn might stretch resources in an unhealthy way, while others enjoy sacrificing for the next generation. In terms of maximizing happiness, it becomes critical for people to understand their ability to benefit from children, and in turn benefit the children. People need to take stock of how much they enjoy children, how emotionally prepared they are for parenthood, and how ready they are to sacrifice personal freedoms. If you are an individual who loves talking and playing with children, parenthood may be for you. However, if you are not drawn to children and prefer them at a distance, don't become a parent! More and more couples are choosing to go childless, especially in European nations. We don't know yet how this will affect long-term happiness, but it must be for the better if people who don't want kids don't have them!

There may be sex differences, however, in the way children bear on our happiness. One recent study, conducted by researchers in Denmark, analyzed the happiness of thousands of pairs of twins over time. The researchers found that the birth of a first child made women happier, but not men. It may be that, for men, the primary source of happiness lies in the marital relationship rather than in kids, although children could have an effect to the extent that they keep relationships together. Of course, this may also be a social artifact anchored in traditional sex roles, and may change as norms around work and parenting evolve. And what of multiple children? As shocking as it sounds, additional children beyond the first actually lowered the happiness of parents! Again, these are averages and not descriptions of individuals. In the end, the amount and ways in which children will affect your own happiness is dependent in large part upon your values, resources, relationship, and specific life circumstances. People who don't have kids can find meaning and purpose in other areas, and contribute to future generations through activities other than child rearing. The research literature generally does not indicate that children significantly increase emotional life satisfaction on average, so individuals should choose carefully, with their own values and personalities in mind.

One trend you ought to know about as you embark on marriage is the age trend in marital satisfaction and the apparent adverse effects of teenagers. Researchers have found that marital satisfaction is very high at the beginning, as we might imagine. It is hard to beat sex, romance, and doing fun new things with a person you enjoy. But unfortunately, marital satisfaction dips at the birth of the first child, and continues to move downward, hitting a low when the kids are teenagers. Adolescents can try the patience of even the most loving parents, with their desire for independence, trying new things, and seeming to think their parents are mentally handicapped. Finally, the kids leave home, and marital satisfaction heads back upward, suggesting that the "empty nest" is indeed usually a happy one. Now parents can interact with their grown children as adults, and enjoy parenting on a part-time basis with their grandkids.

The Bad News

We have all been in a variety of relationships. We have been sons and daughters, brothers and sisters. Many of us are parents. We have been classmates, roommates, and love mates. Many of us have been supervisors or employees. We have been students, coaches, and passengers. All of this personal experience tells us that, despite the consistent findings linking happiness to relationships, being social animals is not always rosy. In fact, if you think of the absolute worst experiences you have ever had in your life, it is likely that other folks were implicated. There are instances of outright victimization, such as muggings and robberies. There are cases of harmful carelessness, such as auto accidents. We feel worried for our children if they come down with an illness. Other people are also the targets of our hostility, envy, and jealousy. Thus, our relationships are a mixed bag.

Sara Hodges, a social psychologist at the University of Oregon, studies empathy. Most folks consider empathy a positive skill, and essential for healthy functioning in a relationship or in society. It is clearly beneficial to be able to put yourself in another person's shoes, and understand how she is feeling. Empathy is the bedrock of compassion and altruism. But Hodges cautions that there may be a dark side to empathy. If we have too much empathy, we make ourselves vulnerable to the pain of others. Without regulating our empathy to some degree, intensely negative events, such as genocide or watching a parent undergo cancer treatment, could quickly become overwhelming. Another way empathy can bring pain is in those unfortunate instances when we injure others. If we make a spouse cry or hurt a friend's feelings, it is our empathy, our true understanding of just how they must be feeling, that brings about guilt and sadness. Hodges's work is a cautionary tale that teaches us that relationships come with a price tag. The more heavily we invest in those around us, the more joy they will bring us when things go well, but also the more pain we may feel during the bumpier times.

The psychologist Michael Cunningham maintains that we can even grow allergic to some people, much in the way that we can be allergic to ragweed, cat dander, or peanuts. Although people's obnoxious behaviors are often minor, if they are repeated frequently enough, we may become allergic to these annoying or insensitive habits. Think about a college roommate, or a time you shared a house with your brother. Remember all those tiffs about the dishes, trash, and music on the stereo? Recall how intensely they got on your nerves? This constant grating leads to a reaction that is much stronger than any one annoying remark would suggest. Like an allergen, the annoyance might not bother you at first. In fact, you can probably overlook several small irritations. But, over time, they have a cumulative effect, so that your allergy grows worse. What was once an amiable relationship with a neighbor or mother-in-law can develop into a type of psychological anaphylactic shock in which you itch all over and your airways close up.

We need people, but our relationships, even the best ones, are not completely positive. For most of us, the negative times are in the minority, and we freely accept the costs involved in having close friends, trusted colleagues, and loved family members. You can protect yourself from the down times to some extent. By choosing friends carefully, surrounding yourself with happy people, and communicating well with others, you can avoid unnecessary conflict. Of course, none of us can ever completely avoid life's problems, but then, that's why we have supportive friends.

Increasing Psychological Wealth

For decades, self-help books and gurus have been aimed at helping people increase their happiness, with varying degrees of success. Some readers swear by the clever happiness method advocated in the latest title, while others see little of value between the covers. Only recently have researchers begun to test these ideas to see which ones might actually work. In these studies on happiness remedies, people who want to be happier are randomly assigned to various self-help programs, and their happiness levels are compared to those of a control group. Interestingly, some of the most effective methods are those that involve reaching out to other people in positive ways. For example, subjects might be asked to do five kind acts for others, or to review why they should be grateful to others and how to use active responding to improve relationships and happiness. Or participants might be trained in how to use a type of meditation practice called loving-kindness, in which people focus on how much they love someone, and on doing kind things for them. It is too early to know which interventions produce long-lasting increases in happiness, although each one has produced some initial positive results. What is noteworthy is that many of the interventions being tried involve some form of heightened caring about other people. Practicing positive communication, appreciation, and kindness are likely to boost your happiness, improve your relationships, and add to your portfolio of psychological wealth.

Your Social Relationships Score

If relationships are generally beneficial to happiness, and happiness is beneficial to relationships, it makes sense to take stock of your relationships. How would you rate their quality? Do you have many close intimates that you can be authentic with, share secrets with, and trust that they will not judge you harshly, reject you, or betray your trust? How well do you get along with your family members? How about the folks at the office?

The following survey will help you identify your social strengths, as well as those areas where you might want to improve. In some cases, doing better might require improved interactions with others so that your remarks are more positive. In other cases, a change of social scenery might be indicated, and unreliable acquaintances can be exchanged for more trustworthy companions. Answer yes or no to each of the statements depending on whether or not you feel like they describe you:

1   I give lots of compliments and positive remarks to others.
2   I have someone to whom I can tell my most intimate thoughts and feelings.
3   I rarely or never feel lonely.
4   I am careful about making negative remarks to others.

5   I get along well with my co-workers.
6   I can relax and be myself when I am with friends.
7   I mostly trust my family and friends.
8   There are people I very much love and care about.
9   There are people I could call in the middle of the night if I have an emergency.
10 I have fun when I am with other people.

After reviewing your relationships, consider how much you care about those you love. We should aim for a score of 10, and certainly nothing less than an 8 will do. A psychologically unhealthy person is likely to score a goose egg on this survey.

Imagine that you die and because of some administrative errors in heaven you are sent to hell instead. There, at the fiery gates, you are greeted by Satan who – of course – smiles and offers you a deal. He explains that you have a choice to make that will affect how you spend the rest of eternity. If you choose the three people you love the most to take your place and live with him in hell, you can buy your way out, and be assured of a spot upstairs in heaven. What would you do? Many of us – in fact, most of us – would not take the deal. We would be willing to make the enormous personal sacrifice for the people we hold most dear. Most of us care so much about our loved ones that we would be willing to suffer rather than let them suffer. People matter to most of us an enormous amount. In refusing to turn over our loved ones to Satan, we would of course have earned the right to heaven – because caring for those we love is for most of us at the core of being a good and happy person. People have been called social animals, but the happiest among us are loving and caring angels.

Conclusions

Social relationships and happiness are a two-way street. They serve to reinforce each other. Happy people have better relationships, and good relationships make us happier. Most of us are predisposed to be at least moderately happy because we are social creatures, and being a happy person attracts us to others and them to us. Like food and air, we seem to need social relationships to thrive. When we thrive and are happy, we tend to build stronger social bonds. Cultivating positive relationships is essential to overall psychological wealth. Although people differ in their need for social relationships, and in the types of social relationships they most enjoy, we all need to receive and give social support. We all need to be loved and to love others.

Regardless of whether we choose to get married or have children, we all need close, supportive friends. Lonely people are not only less happy, but their physical health suffers as well. Several of the most severe mental illnesses involve difficulties in relationships. If we don't have good social relationships, we may create them. Little children often have imaginary friends. Such relationships might be the answer to the problems with the Demonians you encountered at the beginning of the chapter. What happened to you in that devilish experiment? After two years of deafening silence and alcoholism, you realized that there were only two options available to you: end the experiment with suicide, or make do with pseudofriends. You allow yourself to go a bit insane, and thereafter have plenty of hallucinated companions. Your new best friend, Poozy, lives in your shoes, Guenevere lives in the attic insulation, and Sham-Pooh lives nearby in the one-acre wood. The four of you have a great time together. You are raving mad, but this is a small price to pay to have friends again.

5

Happiness at Work: It Pays To Be Happy

We have all ordered food at the drive-through window of a fast food restaurant. We are familiar with the script: "May I take your order? Would you like fries with that? Please pull forward and pay." The drive-through concept was successful in streamlining normal conversation to the point that only the bare minimum is needed for completing the transaction. There is no exchange of names and personal backgrounds, no asking about health, family, or the weather, and no other pleasantries. Drive-through clerks get right down to business. The sparse conversation follows a predictable course, regardless of which fast food restaurant you prefer. In fact, this conversational script is so ingrained that it can sometimes be a jolt when an employee deviates from the pattern.

Julie, a worker at a suburban Taco Bell near Seattle, went off script so many times that she frequently had customers getting out of their cars and marching into the store to speak with the manager. The customers, however, were not there to complain; quite the opposite. They were so taken with Julie's friendly personality and authentic approach that they wanted to make sure she was recognized for a job well done. Julie would ask customers how their day had gone. She was friendly and upbeat, and would sometimes relate good things that had happened to her, such as the day she became engaged or the time she received a raise. Julie seemed to be glad to be at work! All of a sudden customers were interacting with a pleasant person, not a robot or surly teenager.

How is it that some people end up loving their jobs like Julie? It doesn't seem to matter whether a person works at Credit Suisse or the Gap; we have all met employees who seem to love what they do from 9 to 5. Likewise, we have all met folks who dread clocking in.

There are unfortunate souls who seem to hate their boss, their uniform, their commute, their paycheck, and us, their customers. Is liking and disliking work merely a matter of a joyful or bleak disposition, or is it a matter of finding a job that is a good personal fit?

Where does work fit into the happiness equation? It is obvious that individuals who are satisfied with their work will – by definition – be enjoying a greater chunk of their lives than people who can't stand their jobs. But there is also the question of whether happiness at work is either beneficial to effectiveness there, or harmful to productivity. Might there be a tendency for happy individuals to overlook what is wrong at the office, and to content themselves with work conditions and labor practices they ought to be fighting to improve? Might happy workers goof off more? Happiness may be good for health and friendships, but is it really something we should bring to work with us as well?

Work as a Calling

You probably know a happy worker – an upbeat person who looks forward to coming to work, is enthusiastic about the job, shows up dependably, performs well, gets along with the staff, covers other people's shifts when necessary, and is working on some side project aimed at improving the workplace, its products, or its services. We do as well. In fact, one professor jumps immediately to mind as a perfect illustration of the many benefits of happiness for workers. This man worked as a psychologist at a prestigious university over the course of his entire career. He did all the usual work of a professor, including conducting research, teaching classes, advising students, serving on committees, taking sabbaticals, and publishing papers. How happy was our colleague with his job? When he retired, he continued to come into the office every day!

The old professor was not merely a case of the driven man who couldn't decide what to do with himself in the golden years of his retirement. He truly loved his work, told anyone who asked that it stimulated him, and – most important of all – believed it was meaningful. Although he did not work at quite the breakneck pace that he had earlier in his career, our colleague still volunteered to teach courses, kept abreast of the cutting-edge research in his field, conducted studies of his own, and wrote articles. Now, as he moves beyond age eighty, this gentleman is a bundle of energy and inspires all who know him. He is physically fit and, weather permitting, rides his bike to the university. Better yet, his mind remains impressive. Perhaps his love for his work and continuing mental stimulation have kept him healthy and happy.

It is interesting to consider what makes the professor so pleased with his occupation, while your accountant is so disgruntled. Amy Wrzesniewski, a researcher at Yale University, suggests that the difference between satisfied and unsatisfied employees is how they view their work. Some employees, people who have a "job orientation," think of their job primarily in terms of its tangible benefits. That is, they clock in each morning so that they can get a paycheck. Job-oriented workers don't particularly anticipate the tasks they do each day, wouldn't necessarily recommend their work to a friend, and look forward to the end of each shift. They see their job simply in instrumental terms as a way to get money.

A second way of thinking about work is "career orientation." These employees like some aspects of their jobs but not others, may or may not recommend it, and certainly look forward to vacation time. Career-oriented people see their work as a stepping stone to something better, as a way of gaining respect, status, and more money. Typically, they are motivated by promotions, making connections, pay raises, increased supervisory responsibility, a bigger office, a closer parking space, and increases in social status. For instance, we know a university professor who received a better parking space when he won a Nobel Prize. For a career-oriented person, winning the Nobel Prize, as well as getting a better parking space, would be the goals behind doing outstanding research, and enjoyment of doing research would be secondary.

And then there is a third group of people, those who have a "calling orientation." People with a calling orientation usually love their jobs. They feel like their work is important, and makes a contribution to the world. They are excited and challenged by their daily work, and you might hear them say, "I would do this work even if I were not paid for it!" Calling-oriented people are not workaholics; they are passionate workers who believe in what they do. They often enjoy vacations, but they also enjoy returning to work. People like the energetic old professor. In table 5.1, we summarize the characteristics of the three types of workers.

Table 5.1 Three work orientations

Job	Career	Calling
1 Leisure more important	1 Might enjoy work	1 Does enjoy work
2 Motivated by money	2 Motivated by advancement	2 Motivated by sense of contributing
3 Would not recommend the work unless required	3 May recommend the work	3 Recommends the work
4 Looks forward to end of each shift	4 Thinks a lot about vacations	4 Thinks about work even off the clock
5 Does what is told	5 Takes initiative to impress supervisors	5 Doing job well is intrinsically rewarding
6 Will work hard for monetary incentives	6 Works hard for possible advancement	6 Works hard because finds job rewarding

The good news is that anyone can have a calling orientation. Callings are not reserved for CEOs of Fortune 500 companies, college professors, or government ministers. Callings can be found in any profession. For example, roughly one-third of hospital administrators fall into each group, and the same is true among hospital janitors. Below, we describe a janitor who has a calling.

Imagine being a janitor in the chronic care wing of a large hospital. This is a section of the hospital where long-term care is given to patients who are in a chronically debilitated state. Janitors sweep the floors, dust, and empty the wastebaskets. But imagine a janitor who goes beyond the requirements of the formal job description and takes it upon herself to rearrange the photographs in patient rooms so that patients have something new to look at from time to time. Perhaps the janitor believes that a little change would bring new cheer to the ward and, perhaps, stimulate the patients in some way. No one has told her to make the changes, and her performance evaluation would not have suffered a bit had she not done so. But still, she wants to contribute to the health of the patients. The janitor is careful to keep things as clean as possible, recognizing the dangers of hospital-borne germs.

If we interview the janitor, we find that she believes her work helps the overburdened nurses, and that she aids patients to get better by making their stay more pleasant. The janitor sees a sense of worth and purpose in her work. Because of her help, the nurses have more time to spend on medical care. Rather than thinking of her job as routine and of low status, the janitor thinks of her job as so important that she always wants to do her best. This mindset helps the hospital, but is also the key to why she loves her job.

According to Wrzesniewski, about one-third of the people in any given occupation are calling oriented. Thus, whether you are a kindergarten teacher, county sheriff, municipal bus driver, financial analyst, or local librarian, you can develop an attitude toward your work that is energetic and positive.

As revealed above, calling-oriented workers differ from the workers in the other two categories in an important way: they engage in what is described as "job crafting," which occurs when people become the architects of their jobs, doing additional tasks, helping other co-workers, and taking initiative in doing tasks in more efficient ways. Take the example of hair stylists. At the most basic level, their work is about washing, cutting, dying, curling, and styling hair. But chances are you have patronized a stylist for whom social contact with clients is also a major aspect of the work. For many men and women in this profession, the opportunity to chat with people is an important element of customer service, even though it has no bearing on the quality of the haircut.

Job crafters are folks who take initiative to make small changes around the office to bring their work in line with their larger vision of what they value in life. We have seen instances of valets who create color-coded organizational systems for car keys to make things simpler for their co-workers, trash collectors who see the job as their opportunity to keep neighborhoods neat and clean, social workers who advocate for their clients in a confusing government system, flight attendants who are friendly and helpful far beyond the list of activities required of them, and police officers who stop to chat with citizens on the street. Each of these is an example of a small act that can make work seem not only more meaningful, but enjoyable as well.

Although having meaningful work is an attractive prospect, many people are wary of investing too heavily in their jobs. After all, isn't too much focus on the office a bit unbalanced? Isn't there a danger of becoming a workaholic and missing out on other enjoyable parts of life? Well, it is true that successful people in general, and calling-oriented workers in particular, often work hard and spend long hours on the job. But it may be reassuring to learn that the people who are happiest at work are also the happiest at home! The happiest people tend to show little difference in their moods whether they are working on a challenging report, making a sale, playing kickball on Saturday, or riding bikes with the kids. Because most of us have to work anyway, it seems clear that a positive approach to your job is a smart choice. Not only will it benefit your employer, it will benefit you as well.

Happy Workers Are Good Workers

Take a moment and think of the factors that lead to success on the job. Your list probably includes intelligence, a good education, hard work, social skills, social connections, trustworthiness, reliability, and ability. Certainly, people who have these qualities *are* likely to be promoted, make more money, and be wonderful workers. Every employer dreams of filling positions with exactly these types of employees. What business wouldn't want energetic, honest, intelligent, hardworking go-getters who have the skills to do the job? But what most CEOs, supervisors, and personnel managers don't consider is whether the person is happy, positive, and optimistic. Worker happiness is a factor that also makes better employees, but is something that is often overlooked by many employers.

One benefit of happiness at work is that happy workers earn more money. In one study, we were interested in analyzing the effects of happiness on success. But we did not want to simply discover that success at work creates happiness; we wanted to explore the influence of happiness on success. So we obtained a measure of happiness taken long before the work began. We obtained cheerfulness data on students entering college in 1976, and then checked on their incomes in the 1990s, when the subjects were nearing middle age. What we found was a clear and surprisingly strong result. Whereas the least cheerful people were earning about $50,000 a year, the most cheerful folks were earning about $65,000 a year – a 30 percent higher salary! Even when we took into account possible complicating factors, such as occupation and parental income, our findings showed that cheerful

18-year-old students were earning higher salaries as they approached age forty. Why might this be the case? It could be that happy workers tend to perform better, and therefore receive more promotions and pay raises, leading to higher incomes over time.

Do happy workers actually perform better? Could it be a bit of positivity really translates to a more efficient, more productive employee? Research shows that both supervisors and customers think so. In one study, supervisor evaluations of workers who had taken a happiness survey several years earlier were obtained. The employees' levels of happiness and unhappiness at the earlier time predicted how well the supervisor evaluated their work, suggesting that positivity on the job gets you a positive nod from the boss. In other studies conducted with both master's of business administration students and corporate employees, it was found that happy students and happy workers were more effective decision makers, received better performance evaluations from teachers and management, and ended up with more pay raises.

Happiness also translates into more creativity at work. Happy workers are better at producing fresh ideas for changing products and services, as well as suggesting clever new procedures that allow their organizations to achieve important goals. One research team studied individuals who were working in seven companies that represented several industries, including high tech and consumer products. These people's jobs included creating new home healthcare products and developing new tracking systems for merchandise sales. In other words, creativity was very important to job success for this group. The researchers asked the participants to keep a diary of daily events, and obtained measures of their emotions as well.

Employees whose diaries included many positive words and those people who scored highly on measures of happiness were scored as highly creative by other team members. The daily diaries also showed that the workers were most creative on their happier days. Creativity has long been linked to happiness because a good mood facilitates broader thinking and the more original thoughts that are fundamental to coming up with new ideas. Laboratory researchers have coaxed people into a good mood and seen that they produce more ideas, and more divergent ideas. The same holds true on the job. Thus, when creativity is needed, happy workers are likely to excel. Google and other information technology companies have been successful, in part, because they build in unstructured time for their employees to play and experiment. It is not too far a stretch to imagine that the happiest workers at these companies will also be the most creative.

Another benefit of happy workers is that they tend to stay in the same job and are far less likely to quit and search for work elsewhere. Because happy workers are more likely to enjoy their jobs and their co-workers, they are less likely to grow discontented and start a job search. Hiring and training new employees is very expensive for companies, and fresh hires tend to be less knowledgeable than workers who have been on the job awhile. Replacing an executive, for instance, can set a company back more than a million dollars. In other words, employee happiness can save companies a lot of money.

One place where researchers have found strong benefits of happiness on the job is in the area of organizational citizenship. Organizational citizenship behaviors are the tasks workers engage in that help the business and co-workers, but which are not formal duties of their job. These include lending a helping hand to co-workers, promoting the organization, and noticing where improvements can be made. Workers who are low in organizational citizenship are more likely to take unnecessary sick days or steal from the workplace. Happy workers are substantially better organizational citizens. They show up to work on time, take fewer sick days, help colleagues, and generally get along better with co-workers and supervisors. Although work satisfaction has a modest effect on productivity, the strong benefits of well-being on organizational citizenship translate to money saved and money earned for businesses. And the small to moderate effects of work happiness on productivity and retention yield an additional competitive edge.

Part of whether you enjoy your job is the attitude you take to it. If you see it as a hardship that must be endured, it will feel that way all day long. If you decide that work is an opportunity to develop your talents, help others, and improve the world, it is more likely to become enjoyable, and you will do those little extra things that make you a better employee. However, your approach to your job is only half the puzzle; some workplaces are better than others.

Best Places to Work

Both of the authors of this book have given talks at conferences hosted by the Gallup Organization, the business that is famous for its national and international polls. When we want to know people's attitudes, Gallup is a Mercedes. We have visited Gallup's headquarters in Omaha, Nebraska, and spent time in their beautiful Washington, DC, building. During our visits, we have had the opportunity to speak with many company employees, and have had candid conversations with them about their work environment. We have been amazed at how enthusiastic most of them are about their jobs. We have heard data analysts brag about how rewarding their work is, secretaries claim to never want to work anywhere else, and administrators talk about a sense of having a worthwhile mission in life. What makes these workers so fond of their jobs when employees at other companies are often complaining around the watercooler every day? The short answer is that Gallup is a good place to work.

Jobs are not just about the specific tasks assigned to us – teaching students, pumping gas, writing reports, making computer chips – they are also about our relationships with our supervisors and co-workers, our commutes, and company policies. Each of these bears directly on your satisfaction with your job and, indirectly, your overall happiness. Good workplaces are those that have policies in place that benefit both the workers and the company, and have mechanisms in place for dealing with internal problems as they arise. Companies like Gallup have policies in place that keep workers happy and save money by reducing turnover. For instance, Gallup has a company policy of focusing on employee strengths. In fact, new hires are given the in-house StrengthsFinder, a measure developed to identify and capitalize on the resources each person brings to his or her work. At the most fundamental level, Gallup management really believes in its workers, so much so that the company is employee owned, the cafeteria is subsidized, the offices are of equal size, the CEO – Jim Clifton – is approachable, and there is no official sick-time policy; workers are expected to take time off as needed. The result is a staff of committed individuals who enjoy their work, make friends at the office, and stay loyal to the company.

Gallup is, of course, a radical departure from the old school of business management, in which workers were viewed as adversaries. Once, many supervisors saw their employees as an obstacle to company growth and profit. Workers, according to the old wisdom, were people who wanted to make a lot of money without having to work particularly hard, and who could not be completely trusted. Workers were seen as lazy, wanting only to goof around if given a chance. The thinking was, if you check on people a lot and give them enough performance incentives, you can usually get them to work hard. The new idea is that if you win people over and make them enthusiastic about their work, seeing it as a personal challenge, you can harness their full energies, beyond the mandatory job requirements. Unfortunately, too many businesses still follow the old-school model.

The specific employee policies of the Gallup Organization may not work with every type and size of business. Still, research shows that there are general indicators of good workplaces. Peter Warr, an organizational psychologist, studies the satisfaction of individual employees and describes the work environment that inspires employees. He has identified the following factors as important to job satisfaction.

Opportunities for Personal Control

We have all experienced the frustration of absurd company policies and demanding bosses. The hilarious movie *Office Space* and the popular comic strip *Dilbert* both point out the many instances in which bureaucracy runs rampant and workers feel pinned down by rules that don't make sense, or that interfere with the job. For example, policies that require unneeded paperwork only slow up the work process. The feelings of frustration that accompany oppressive rules lead to more than just griping employees. Research shows that workers who do not feel they have any control over their jobs suffer more health problems than workers who have some control. Having control over your job means having some discretion in how to best tackle problems, apply skills, and envision outcomes. This flexibility is key to making work feel less routine and the job more rewarding. Although some standardization is needed in all organizations, giving workers some opportunities for personal control over their job will make them more involved with it.

Jobs with a Variety of Tasks

Good workplaces are businesses where workers can engage in a variety of tasks. Offices that allow team members to give presentations, write reports, make sales, participate in meetings, and conduct research are more likely to have employees who feel engaged rather than bored. We once toured a tomato-processing plant where lines of workers stood beside flumes and pulled out stray vines and leaves from the waves of fruit that floated before them. It is hard to imagine a more boring job than long hours of bending over and pulling stems off. The tedium can be alleviated by listening to music or talking to co-workers while doing the job, or by rotating through several different jobs during the course of a day.

Contrast line work with that of a municipal police officer. Cops tend to perform a wide variety of duties, including patrolling the city, attending briefings, giving school presentations, making arrests, processing suspects, working with concerned citizens, and appearing in court. Too much time spent pursuing and arresting criminals might be physically and emotionally taxing, whereas too much time spent completing paperwork might be too routine and frustrating. Instead, police officers can benefit from the variety of tasks. Fortunately, more and more of the truly repetitive work tasks are being done by computers, leaving the remaining jobs with more varied activities.

Supportive Supervisors

The television show *The Office* is a comedy about a small-minded boss who steps all over his workers' rights and emotions in his attempts to be liked by both his staff and the more senior executives. He makes inappropriate jokes, meddles in workers' personal lives, holds ineffectual training sessions, showboats, and interferes just when everything is running smoothly. You may have had a supervisor like this, or know someone who has. Overbearing, closed-minded, or aggressive bosses have a way of sucking enjoyment out of the workday. Good supervisors, on the other hand, are approachable, show interest in their employees, and encourage worker development.

The best managers know just how much freedom to give their workers, and just when to look over their shoulders. They are quick to praise a job well done, but also give periodic feedback about where employees can improve. In fact, good supervisors are interested in continuing employee development and are eager to provide the tools and training necessary to help them do their work better. Perhaps the best aspect of working under a supportive supervisor is that staff members feel relaxed and comfortable, and this allows them to go about their jobs more efficiently. A supervisor who cares about his or her employees and gives them performance feedback is one of the most important resources an organization can have.

Respect and Status

Jobs and workplaces that afford people respect and status are likely to engender feelings of competence and pride. To some extent, this is why being a doctor or judge is appealing. Not only can the work itself be rewarding, but it can also boost a person's self-esteem because these jobs are so highly respected. In short, they are jobs about which people can feel proud. The respect that is inherent in some high-status jobs, however, can be extended to all jobs, even lower status ones, in the best organizations. When customers, co-workers, and management treat you well, it is likely that you feel your work is worthwhile. Good workplaces are those that have opportunities for respect and status built into all jobs.

Perhaps the classic example of respect for workers is the popular employee of the month program. Although being recognized in this way often consists of nothing more than receiving a certificate, having your name engraved on a plaque, or having your photograph posted near the cash register, these programs are nevertheless often effective. Employees whose contributions are recognized report feeling proud of their accomplishments and more enthusiastic about their jobs. The most important aspect of feeling like you receive respect on the job is interpersonal contact. Positive feedback from your boss, praise from a customer, and the respect of co-workers can go a long way toward creating a happy worker. In fact, experts at the Gallup Organization suggest that people need to have good friends at work, colleagues whose opinions, support, and praise they trust and value.

Good Pay and Fringe Benefits

To report on the difficulties of living on a small wage, the writer Barbara Ehrenreich took a number of low-paying jobs, such as working as a waitress and as a clerk at Wal-Mart. In her book *Nickel and Dimed*, Ehrenreich writes about these experiences and comes to the conclusion that it is difficult to eke out a living at minimum wage. Some people, for example, spend almost as much money on dressing for, getting to, and eating at work as they bring in from their jobs. For most of us, work is – at least in part – about making money above and beyond job-related expenses. Regardless of their social class, people need to pay for food, clothes, insurance, transportation, rent or mortgage, childcare, medical services, recreation, and many other common expenses.

There is no getting around it: good workplaces pay their employees a decent wage. This does not mean, of course, that everyone will earn the enormous sums commanded by professional athletes and stars of the silver screen. But it does mean that folks ought to receive a fair wage, one that provides them with the means to afford adequate room and board. Compensation also extends to benefits, ranging from health insurance, to retirement savings, to holiday parties, to maternity leave. The more of these benefits employees receive, the further their pay-check will stretch. But employees have a responsibility in all this too – and that is to develop skills, workplace experience, and productive habits so that their employers can justify paying them a salary well above minimum wage.

Some employers think that take-home pay and benefits are all that workers care about. The truth is, while all workers are concerned with their compensation and prefer to make more than less, healthy paychecks and robust retirement plans by themselves will not produce a happy workforce. Many employees, especially those in typical middle-class jobs, care about an additional thousand dollars much less than they want their work to be challenging, meaningful, and collegial. Even with average pay and benefits, workers may be very happy with their jobs if the other factors are in place.

Clear Requirements and Information on How to Meet Them

When Rebecca graduated from college, she obtained employment as a geologist for a large petroleum company in Houston. The company offered her a handsome paycheck, paid training, the opportunity to travel the world, and an unbelievable benefits package. Rebecca jumped at the job offer and moved to Texas, where she promptly fell into a deep depression. At first, it was difficult for her to identify what was wrong. Her supervisor treated her well, she got along with the people in her work group, she liked her new apartment, and she enjoyed her new city as well. Despite these favorable conditions, Rebecca floundered between 9 in the morning and 6 in the evening. She began dreading going into the office.

It turns out that there were no specific expectations for what Rebecca was supposed to do, how she was supposed to learn it, or a timeline by which to accomplish tasks. She was asked to "shadow" a co-worker, but was unsure of what she was supposed to be learning. When she inquired of her supervisor, he attempted to reassure her by saying, "Don't worry, it will take as long as it will take for you to learn the ropes." Ironically, this panicked Rebecca even more. What Rebecca wanted was a clear set of instructions and the opportunity to complete discrete tasks in a given time.

In fact, clear expectations as well as a solid understanding of how and when to meet them is what we all need. Happiness-promoting workplaces are those that have policies and supervisors in place that facilitate this process. Companies with clear job descriptions, sensible training, and easy-to-understand measures for success are more likely to produce and retain satisfied employees. Businesses with an overly loose structure and too much flexibility in deadlines are often more likely to produce anxiety for workers, and be less successful in general.

There is little that is as stressful at work as being given too much responsibility, or being assigned a task you do not know how to complete. At the Gallup Organization, the management wants to make certain that workers are placed in positions where they can use their best strengths on the job. The hiring process includes interviews and assessments aimed at identifying the right match for workers and the tasks they will perform. Some companies, by contrast, view employees as essentially interchangeable, and ask their workers to bounce from job to job and office to office. But by viewing employees as individuals and recognizing unique talents, as Gallup does, businesses pave the way for workers to feel good about their accomplishments and enjoy their specific jobs.

Consider your own work environment, and ask yourself when, over the past year, you had the chance to shine on the job. When were you able to apply your own particular strengths to a problem, and were you rewarded for it? If so, chances are that it felt great. Also, consider whether you had opportunities to learn and grow. Were there exciting new challenges at work, or did you pick up a useful new skill? If your work is dynamic, and you have the opportunity to use personal resources and talents on tasks that are clear, then there is a high likelihood that you enjoy your job and plan on continuing on with your current employer. The happiest workers are those who are able to use their special strengths every day they are on the job.

Job satisfaction is more than a luck-of-the draw experience. By analyzing the features that good jobs and workplaces have in common, we can identify predictable factors that promote satisfying work, which in turn lead to more benefits for workers and companies alike. So if employees understand their jobs, use their unique skills, get positive feedback, see their work as meaningful, receive social support at work, and possess the tools they need to perform their jobs well, they are likely to be happy and satisfied workers.

Job Fit and Challenge

We described the benefits of happiness in terms of happy workers and happy workplaces, but what about the work itself? It makes sense to wonder whether there are jobs that are more likely to promote happiness and those that might detract from it. Are careers in the military emotionally rewarding or stressful? How about boxing, accounting, dentistry, sex work, or pearl diving? Of course, life would be a lot simpler if it were as easy as identifying a single profession that would guarantee happiness. In real life, however, the issue is more complicated.

The good news is that many jobs promote well-being. You should first look to the experience of others when you are selecting a career. Some professions tend to show high levels of satisfaction, and others do not. These career ratings are associated to some extent with the amount of education required to enter a profession, with jobs requiring more learning and education on average being more satisfying. Don't shortchange yourself in terms of education. Some of the most satisfied workers are clergy, educators, engineers, painters, office supervisors, psychologists, and those working in financial services. Some of the least satisfied workers on average are waitresses, roofers, cashiers, meat cutters, and bartenders. We don't know, however, if the differences in work satisfaction are due to who is drawn to the jobs in the first place, to the pay, or to the nature of the work. Nevertheless, you should ensure that you prepare yourself to be qualified for a rewarding job!

Remember folks who have a calling orientation and engage in job crafting? The research shows that any type of work can be a calling, ranging from secretarial work, to nursing, to being a tour guide. The issue is less about the specific duties of any individual job and more about how well a person fits with the work and commits to it. The detail-oriented work of a tax auditor or a NASA mission control specialist requires a particular personality type, just as the socially demanding work of a tour guide calls for an extroverted disposition. Clearly, not every type of work is for everyone. Finding a job that will make you happy, then, is partly a matter of finding a job that is right for you, one that harnesses your gifts, is interesting to you, and that you find meaningful.

Another aspect of work that can promote well-being is the degree to which it challenges you. Everyone likes some challenge, but the goal is to encounter just the right amount of challenge. Too much and you will feel anxiety. Too little and you will be bored. Think about it: if you were asked to run the world by yourself, the enormity of the task would be discouraging. If you were asked to make peanut butter and jelly sandwiches all day long, you would quickly become restless with this overly easy job. But when the challenge is optimal, that is, when it matches your skill level well, you fall into a state of "flow." Everyone is familiar with flow, that blissful state wherein you become absorbed in your work and lose track of time. It is what athletes refer to as being "in the zone." The psychologist Mihalyi Csikszentmihalyi has investigated this state for three decades. Csikszentmihalyi, a former mountain climber and chess player, became interested in flow as a result of his personal experiences. As it happens, both rock climbing and chess have formal systems for grading the ability of a participant. Csikszentmihalyi noticed that when the ability and the challenge were optimally matched – neither an opponent nor a mountain too hard nor too easy – people fell into flow. His research confirmed his observations and he produced a simple figure to describe this pleasant state (figure 5.1).

Flow arises when skills are matched to the challenge of the activity, and can be especially rewarding when both challenge and skills are high. Consider the sometimes terrifying prospect of teaching your teenager to drive. The first few times you start out, there is likely to be fear, angry words, and a sense of frustration. For the vast majority of teens, the challenge of driving is just too much in the early stages, when they have little or no skills behind the wheel. But with practice, student drivers become adept at turning, signaling, braking, and accelerating. They can become so proficient at these basic tasks, in fact, that if you continue to practice in the safe confines of a parking lot, they will become bored. They are ready for an increase in challenge, to match their new level of ability. Driving on quiet residential streets or main boulevards at nonpeak times is a perfect way to ramp up the

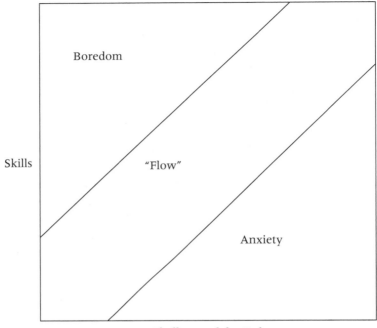

Figure 5.1   Flow: The challenge of the task is matched to the employee's skills. From Csikszentmihalyi (1990)

challenge. But as new drivers master these new tests, they are ready for ever-increasing levels of challenge, such as driving on crowded freeways, in the rain or snow, or through the mountains. So long as a person's skills and the challenge to which she is applying them are matched, she can fall into a state of flow.

When the challenge of work and a person's skill are matched to each other, it is possible to become completely engrossed in an activity, to lose track of time and feel fully engaged, as if nothing else in the world existed. This pleasant state is, ultimately, what we all hope for while on the job. For the most part, finding flow is a matter of knowing your own talents, seeking out opportunities to use them, taking on increasingly challenging tasks as your skills grow, and understanding the reality that you cannot be in flow all the time.

The people who are the most successful at achieving flow are those that look for new ways to grow at work. They are people who are hungry for challenge, mastery, and growth, and rarely like the feeling of "coasting along" on the job. For example, Lisa, an intake coordinator at a neighborhood health clinic in Denver, quickly mastered the computer programs necessary for her job. Within her first month on the job, Lisa was not only competent but skilled at her work. She enjoyed the interpersonal contact and the exactness of data entry, and she believed her work was worthwhile. Lisa also recognized that she risked becoming bored if she ceased growing at work. So, rather than resting on her laurels, Lisa requested further training in more advanced and challenging computer programs. She soon used her knowledge of these more sophisticated programs to reorganize the office's electronic files, making records easier and more user-friendly than ever before. The office staff appreciated the change and the new challenges kept Lisa highly engaged in her work.

Conclusions

Although people have long understood that work can lead to happiness, we now know that happiness can also increase your effectiveness on the job. Happiness at work comes from a variety of factors. First, it is important to find a job that is the right fit for you. This means work that is appropriately challenging, suited to your personality, meaningful, and interesting to you. Don't make the mistake of looking for income only and ignoring the match to your interests and abilities. Look for a job where you can do what you do best on a daily basis. Second, it is better to work for a company that promotes happiness on the job. This means having a happy supervisor, decent compensation, clear expectations for the job, and status and respect. In both cases, having good work and a good workplace can enhance your sense of meaning and satisfaction.

But what about the other side of the coin? What about the benefits of happiness for work? Research shows that positive feelings are related to a variety of desirable outcomes on the job. On average, happy workers make more money, receive more promotions and better supervisor ratings, and are better citizens at work. Why might this be the case? First, happy people are more sociable, and so customers, colleagues, and supervisors resonate well with their warm, friendly attitudes. Also, happy people tend to have more energy and enthusiasm, and are more likely to work hard and confidently.

Happy individuals experience fewer distractions as a result of personal problems, such as marital discord and alcohol abuse. Happy workers are inclined to be more creative than their peers, and are therefore good at generating ideas and solving problems. Finally, happy workers are healthier, and are therefore more likely to show up to work and be fit to work. Taken together, these benefits pave the way for success at work that translates to more money, more friendships, more promotions, and, ultimately, more happiness. Both the worker and the organization profit.

For readers looking for a job, the implications of this chapter are clear. Not only should you inquire about salary, location, and work hours, but you should also ask about the factors that create a happy workforce. Is the job one where you can use your strengths every day? Are the managers supportive? For supervisors, the lessons of this chapter are also clear. Provide workers with support and positive feedback, as well as specific areas where they can improve. Select workers who have the right temperament and strengths for the particular job. And give workers the structure and resources they need to do their jobs well, as well as some personal control over details of how goals are accomplished.

When employers assess candidates for a job, people who tend to be happy and satisfied possess a positive characteristic that is an added factor to consider in their hiring decisions. For organizations, the lesson is clear – it is important to have a happy, satisfied workforce. This is likely to increase productivity, but also helps reduce turnover. Perhaps most important, satisfied workers benefit an organization because they are such good organizational citizens. Happy work does not mean that employees shouldn't be challenged or ever be stressed, of course. Challenge and motivation can be beneficial for enjoyable work. The modern organization that can create calling-oriented workers who are loyal to the company has a clear advantage over its competitors.

Despite individual variability, there are common characteristics that most people like in work – variety, the ability to use complex skills, feedback on how one is doing, and the feeling that the work is meaningful. Few enjoy work that is always simple or repetitive and has little meaningful purpose. It is important to note that complex, challenging, interesting, and meaningful jobs are also those that pay more. Indeed, the pay differential between complex jobs and simple, repetitive jobs is growing. Thus, a major way to obtain a more satisfying job is to gain more education and otherwise qualify yourself for a more challenging occupation. You will kill two birds with a single stone – higher pay and more enjoyable work!

A final point is important to emphasize for readers who want to be happy at work – a lot of job enjoyment is in your own attitudes and behavior. Because most adults have to work, why not decide to love your job, or change to a better one? If you want to love your job, take on the attitudes of someone with a calling. Commit yourself to doing the very best job you can do, to helping your company and other workers, and going beyond the minimal requirements of the job. Be grateful and positive to others at work. Finally, remember that Aristotle defined happiness as activities in pursuit of excellence. If you concentrate on doing your work at a high level of excellence, this will certainly result in your being a better employee. Think about how to craft your job to give it a special fit for you. Within the bounds of your job description, what can you add or subtract to make yourself a more effective employee? How can you help others at your workplace? You might just end up truly enjoying your job.

Many people believe that their work is a drudge and their leisure is fun. But think about it for a moment – some activities are work for some and leisure hobbies for others. When NBA players work, they do what most of us do for fun – play and watch basketball. What farmers do for work, others do as gardeners or hobby farmers. When plumbers fix pipes, they do what some do around the house for leisure. There is no clear line on what is work or leisure. Chefs cook on the job; others cook for fun. One of our family members says there is nothing she loves more than mopping and seeing the spotless floors that result – a leisure activity that could be janitorial work. People travel for vacation, but travel writers do it for their job. Thus, thinking about your job not as an obligation but as something that can be enjoyable is half the battle. Someday we may invent robots that do all the work for us. But we will still be doing many of the same activities we now do as leisure. Thus, if you are not enjoying your job, perhaps you need to change jobs, or change your attitudes to your job.

Depending on whether people love or hate their jobs, this facet of their life can add to their psychological wealth or to their poverty. Because most people spend so much of their adult lives working, it becomes imperative for psychological wealth to enjoy our work and be enriched by it. You will certainly earn money at your job, but it is up to you to ensure that you also earn psychological wealth at work.

Part III
Causes of Happiness and Genuine Wealth

6

Can Money Buy Happiness?

Recently, a journalist from a well-known news magazine contacted us by email to find out the answer to a question that has fascinated people for centuries: Does money buy happiness? He told us that although scientists like to hedge their answers and give convoluted replies full of disclaimers, he wanted a simple yes or no answer. "Does money buy happiness?" he demanded to know, followed by "Please reply immediately." We thought about his question, and then deleted his email. It was a bit like demanding a yes or no answer to the question "Is Chinese food better than Mexican food?"

In the real world, where many processes influence the outcomes we care about, the answer to the burning question of money and happiness is more complex than a simple yes or no. If it were that easy, people wouldn't be asking the question at all; the answer would be obvious to all of us. If, however, we were pressed by a friendly journalist to reduce the answer as simply as possible, we would respond to the question by saying, "Yes, money buys happiness, but there are important exceptions."

When you think of money and happiness, you probably recall all the things money can buy – a nice house and car, fun vacations, and a good education for your kids. More money can help us get better medical care and a more comfortable retirement. There are intangibles, such as status, that wealthy people tend to receive. Therefore, it seems natural to assume that rich people will be happier than others. But money is only one part of psychological wealth, so the picture is complicated. Rich people may sacrifice other types of wealth to get money, and sometimes develop unhappy attitudes on their way to making their fortunes. Money can be a help in attaining psychological wealth, but it must be considered in the bigger picture of what makes people genuinely rich.

The issue of money's influence on happiness is, perhaps, one of the most talked-about and hotly debated in the history of happiness. Some insist that the rich suburbs are sinks of dissatisfaction, while others scoff at the idea that the poor could be anything but miserable. But what does the evidence say about how money affects psychological wealth? Is it a necessity or a curse?

Money Makes the World Go Round

The question of whether money buys happiness is a timely one because there are more rich people alive today than at any other time in history. In the old days, wealth was largely reserved for those with noble blood or in command of large armies. Today, however, riches are more accessible to common people. Newspapers and magazines are full of stories of small-town boys and girls who grow up to be rich movie stars, musicians, television personalities, professional athletes, lottery winners, politicians, business owners, and bestselling novelists.

The number of millionaires is growing rapidly, with more than 8 million in the United States alone. However, poverty is still with us, and the gap between rich and poor is growing in the wealthiest nations. Even in rich Western countries, homelessness and financial marginalization are pressing concerns. As the income gap between rich and poor widens daily, it makes sense to wonder which economic group – the rich or the poor – is the greater inheritor of happiness.

Wealthy People

In the mid-1980s, when Ed's happiness research was starting to gain momentum, he decided to investigate the topic of money and well-being by analyzing the happiness of the superrich. He sent off questionnaires to a hundred of those fabulously wealthy souls who had secured a spot for themselves on the prestigious Forbes list of richest Americans, these people whose net worth was, at the time, $125 million or more. These were people who owned jets, private islands, and large companies. Surprisingly, these economic juggernauts were not too busy to respond to a happiness survey, and forty-nine of them completed and returned it. Some of the wealthy participants even followed up with a phone call. Now, before we get to the punch line, take a moment and make a guess about the results. Were the extremely wealthy happy, or were they anxious and dissatisfied?

It turns out that forty-seven of the forty-nine rich people who responded to Ed's survey were satisfied with their lives, significantly more than a control sample of average Americans taken from the same geographic locations. But, according to the participants in this study, it wasn't money that brought their happiness. None of the Forbes group listed vacation homes, swimming pools, or designer clothing as the major contributor to their emotional well-being. Instead, they mentioned the types of things you might expect from mere financial mortals: pleasing family relationships, helping the world, and fulfillment and pride from their work and accomplishments. The Forbes group wasn't wildly happy, just a bit more satisfied than regular folks.

The notion that money boosts happiness is not a phenomenon confined to people with private jets and impressive mansions. Data collected from everyday citizens in Germany show much the same trend. Our colleagues Richard Lucas and Ulrich Schimmack analyzed many years of happiness data from an enormous German sample and found that life satisfaction increases with income. Figure 6.1 presents these data on a 1–10 scale of life satisfaction. We found in past studies that once an individual is earning a middle-class income, money bought little additional happiness. However, Lucas and Schimmack did not confirm this trend. Folks earning $80,000 a year were more satisfied than their counterparts earning $60,000, and those earning more than $200,000 were significantly more satisfied than the middle class.

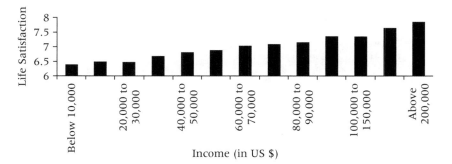

Figure 6.1 Life satisfaction, income. From Lucas and Schimmack (forthcoming)

Wealthy Nations

When we later examine the happiness of nations (chapter 8), we will see that all of the societies with the highest life satisfaction are wealthy ones, such as Ireland and Denmark, and most of the unhappiest nations are extremely poor ones, such as Sierra Leone and Togo. Indeed, the wealth of nations is one of the strongest, if not the strongest, predictors of the life satisfaction in societies.

Figure 6.2 shows the relation between the wealth of nations and the "ladder of life" score from Gallup's 2006 World Survey. The scale asks respondents to say where they currently stand on the steps of a ladder, shown below, which goes from zero, the worst possible life one can imagine for oneself, to ten, the best possible life one can imagine for oneself. As can be seen, there are a few somewhat poor nations with fairly high ladder scores. But all of the extremely poor

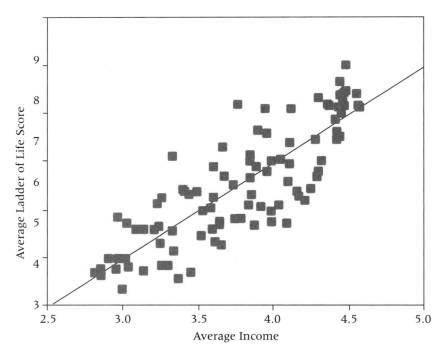

Figure 6.2 The relation between the wealth of nations and the "ladder of Life" score from Gallup's 2006 World Poll: the scales ask respondents to say where they currently stand on the steps of a ladder

nations are low on the ladder, and most of the extremely wealthy nations are high. There is no nation with an average income of less than $2,000 a year that has a life satisfaction as high as any nation with an income of more than $20,000 a year. For those of you who understand statistics, the Pearson correlation between income and happiness is .82, which is about as high as correlations ever get in happiness research! In other words, rich nations are, on average, satisfied, and very poor nations tend not to be. As we will see later, although money matters, other factors also influence the happiness of nations, and this is revealed by the fact that figure 6.2 does not show a perfectly straight line between money and life satisfaction.

Lottery Winners

Rich people and nations are happier than their poor counterparts; don't let anyone tell you differently. But another way to analyze the effect of money on happiness is to examine the emotional well-being of those lucky souls who have won a large lottery. Most of us have heard the horror stories about how a sudden windfall can negatively influence a person's quality of life. At the same time, most of us find the possibilities offered by a lottery win appealing and few of us would turn down such winnings. The lottery is interesting to study because the winners are a random selection of ticket buyers, and so scientists can determine causality and rule out the possibility that happiness led to wealth, rather than the other way around. When we compare the happiness of ticket buyers who won with those who did not win, they are like randomized groups in laboratory experiments.

Winners of large lotteries are often in the news – first for winning, and then later if their life turns sour. Take the highly publicized story of Viv Nicholson. In 1961, Viv Nicholson of Castleford, England, struck it rich. Nicholson became the winner of what – at that time – was the largest lottery pool in Great Britain, totaling (in today's currency) about £3 million (roughly $6 million). Nicholson, as you might well imagine, was euphoric. She told anyone who would listen that she intended to "spend, spend, spend," a phrase that was later immortalized in a musical of that name inspired by Nicholson's life. The sad events that followed will be familiar to many British readers, and may seem predictable to others. Nicholson had a difficult time coping with her new circumstances, and became increasingly estranged from her friends. In a 1999 article in the British newspaper the *Independent*, Nicholson recalled this time: "Even my old friends left me. They didn't want people saying they were going about with me because I had money." Her life became a series of drinking and shopping sprees that, ultimately, landed Nicholson in financial dire straits. At one point, she escaped to Malta, but was deported for assaulting a police officer. Nicholson filed for bankruptcy, was married five times (once for only thirteen weeks), and eventually wound up working as a stripper and drinking heavily.

But the story does not end there. Viv Nicholson found religion, became an active member of the Jehovah's Witnesses, and began a new, more wholesome life. In the same article in the *Independent*, Nicholson described her new state of affairs: "I'm quite happy with my lot. I'm a happy chappy. I can make any situation happy. You don't have to have money to be happy." Whether she learned important lessons, or whether her newfound religion has given her renewed meaning, Nicholson appeared to be living a much more fulfilling life.

As Nicholson's story illustrates, it is a bit difficult to draw firm conclusions about the money-happiness relationship from isolated instances. It might be argued that her lottery wins caused her grief, or it might be said that they ultimately led her to a place of satisfaction. Perhaps we should examine another winner. The American Jack Whittaker won $314 million in the Powerball lottery in 2002, and hoped to make a positive impact on society by starting a charitable foundation. Jack's granddaughter died of a drug overdose after he lavished money on her, and he was sued by a gambling casino for bouncing checks. Like Viv, Jack did not seem to find happiness with his lottery win. Two years later, Jack had two arrests for driving under the influence, had been the victim of multiple burglaries, was estranged from his wife, had been arrested for assault, and had to close down his foundation. The problem with these sensational cases is that they might not represent average lottery winners; the media may find lottery winners newsworthy only when they make a mess of their lives. When lottery winners live happily ever after, we might never hear of them. What does the science say about the average lottery winner? Are lottery winners on average miserable or are our two examples exceptions to the rule that lottery winners are happy? Fortunately, several studies now have been conducted with this fascinating group.

In one study, conducted in Illinois, winners of moderate-size lotteries – those who won about $400,000 on average – were happier than folks in a control group, but the difference was small and not statistically significant. This study is quoted frequently to indicate that money does not help happiness. In a more intensive lottery study, however, the sociologists Stephen Smith and Peter Razzell found that people who had won large lotteries in the United Kingdom were happier than other people. These pools require an individual to guess a large number of soccer game wins for that week. When they were interviewed, the pool winners in the study sometimes mentioned problems that came with the money, such as losing a few of their old friends. But on the whole the winners' happiness was higher than that of a similar group of people who had not won lotteries.

In two other studies, conducted by the economists Jonathan Gardner and Andrew Oswald, the researchers found the same trend: people receiving small to medium windfalls were clearly happier, and this effect persisted over time. In their study, Gardner and Oswald used data from thousands of people who were being questioned time and again over a period of years. From this group, the researchers identified individuals who won lotteries during the course of the study. After analyzing the data, Gardner and Oswald found that two years after winning the lottery, people reported less unhappiness than they had before winning. In a second study, Gardner and Oswald found that those who inherited significant sums of money showed significant increases in happiness.

The Case That Money Does Not Equal Happiness

Despite individual instances where money seems to harm people, with data like the happiness of multimillionaires and lottery winners, as well as the life satisfaction differences between rich and poor, why would anyone doubt that money is on average important to well-being? It turns out that there are also findings that point in other directions. For one thing, people in some poor societies are reasonably happy, at least above the neutral point. For another, it seems that rising desires for goods and services to some degree cancel the effects of greater income. Finally, we know that materialism can be toxic to happiness. We will describe these findings that indicate that money does not always equal happiness, and explore the costs as well as the benefits of money to explain why it is sometimes related to happiness and sometimes not.

City of Joy: The Happiness of the World's Poorest Citizens

The data from samples of rich people and lottery winners paint a positive picture of money and life satisfaction. At the other end of the spectrum, can homeless people and others living in impoverished conditions be satisfied with their lives, or are they doomed to an existence of psychological poverty as well? Some of our most interesting research was conducted with a sample of the poorest citizens in the world. In 2000, one of the authors, Robert, went to Kolkata, formerly known as Calcutta, to learn about the happiness levels of people living in dire poverty. Kolkata is a wonderful city, but is notorious for its widespread poverty, crowding, and noise. By some counts, there are more than a hundred thousand homeless children in the city, and as many as half of the 15 million inhabitants live below the poverty line. Many visitors to the city are overwhelmed by the vast destitution, and on occasions foreigners break down crying on the street. On the other hand, Kolkata has a reputation for inspiring heroism. Mother Teresa, the saintly nun who spent her life caring for the poor and dying, suggested that there is something worthwhile in every corner of life, no matter how humble. Dominique Lapierre wrote the famous novel *City of Joy*, in which the slum-dwelling protagonists fight valiantly against the crush of poverty.

In collecting data in India, Robert spoke with the street people and pavement dwellers of Kolkata. He visited people in make-shift shelters and spoke with women in blackened, windowless kitchens heavy with the smell of kerosene. He posed questions about happiness to sex workers and tea hawkers, to rickshaw pullers and people burdened with leprosy. He heard stories about foraging for scraps of cardboard to light a fire for cooking, and of police harassment. It is easy to imagine that these people were miserable. The data showed, instead, that they were slightly negative to slightly positive on scales of life satisfaction. While this certainly isn't the romantic notion of the joyful poor, it also contradicts the idea of a legion of despondent have-nots with an unmitigated black outlook on life.

We replicated the life satisfaction finding using three samples of homeless people: one from Kolkata; one from Fresno, California; and one from Dignity Village, a tent camp in Portland, Oregon. We collected happiness data from men and women in these locations and found that the two American samples were, on average, slightly dissatisfied with their lives, while their Indian counterparts were mildly satisfied. When we asked about satisfaction with specific life domains such as food, health, intelligence, and friends, we similarly found variation in the amount of satisfaction these people experienced. These results are both informative and reason for optimism. In short, this research indicates that, overall, being extraordinarily poor has a negative influence on happiness, but that some very poor individuals are, in fact, somewhat satisfied, and even extremely poor people are usually not depressed.

Which brings us back to the question: "Does money buy happiness?" How is it that many rich people are not extremely happy, and how can it be that some poor people are happy? The answers lie, in part, in the fact that there are many other influences on happiness, such as a cheery genetic disposition and having supportive relationships. That is, they may have the other components of psychological wealth even if they are missing money. And what of rich people who are unhappy? There are factors that can cancel the beneficial effects of money on happiness if people are not careful.

Wanting it All: Aspirations and Happiness

Money is more than a fixed amount of legal tender. Wealth is, in part, also about your desires. Being satisfied with your paycheck, just like being satisfied with your life, is about your point of view. We have one friend who leads wilderness trips. He lives in a simple cabin, spends much of his time outdoors, and only uses about $5,000 a year. Contrast this with another friend of ours who once spent $30,000 on a single hotel stay. Obviously, money and comfort don't mean the same thing to these two people. To better understand how money adds and subtracts from happiness, and why it does so idiosyncratically from person to person, it is important to consider aspirations. Take the following example.

We know two young couples in which both the wife and husband are professors in universities. One couple, whom we will call the Johnsons, earns a combined income of $90,000 a year, and the other couple, the Thompsons, earns $200,000 a year. The Johnsons are quite satisfied with their income, and feel it is adequate to their wants and needs. The richer Thompsons, making more than twice the money of the first couple, constantly feel strapped for cash and frequently argue over finances. The problem is that the Thompsons want more expensive luxuries and experiences, and thus end up feeling poorer.

This is a perfect illustration of the research findings of the psychologists Wendy Johnson and Robert Krueger. The researchers studied the incomes and happiness of twins, which meant that they could parse out those pesky genetic influences that often contaminate research on happiness. What they found was surprising: the amount of money a person made only modestly predicted whether or not she was satisfied with her income. Some people with a lot of money could not meet their desires, and others with little money were able to do so.

This brings us to the famous formula:

$$\text{Happiness} = \frac{\text{What we have (attainments)}}{\text{What we want (aspirations)}}$$

This formula makes sense. It means that it doesn't matter so much if you make $20,000 a year or $100,000, if you drive a new BMW or an old Chevrolet – what matters more is that your income is sufficient for your desires. Of course, we know from the bulk of the research that it is generally better to have more, rather than less, money. But individual variation in desire helps explain why some poor folks are happy and some wealthy people are not.

Returning to the couples we described earlier, we can see that differences in aspirations lead to very different amounts of happiness. The couple with the middle-class income are quite pleased because they have modest desires. They are content with their large but old home. They drive a Toyota that runs well, and one spouse usually takes the bus to work. If the weather permits, the husband rides his bike to the university. Their leisure time is spent gardening, watching DVDs, driving to see relatives in nearby cities, and attending their children's extracurricular events. By contrast, the wealthier couple pine for expensive trips to Aspen and to Europe, lease new cars every two years, eat at expensive restaurants, dress themselves in the latest fashions, and own an enormous home on which they carry an equally large mortgage. Let's plug the two couples' incomes and aspirations into the happiness formula.

On a scale ranging from zero to ten, here is how the couples stack up in happiness:

Happiness of professors with high income:
_____$200,000_____= .5 or Unhappiness

$400,000 Desires: Foreign travel, luxury cars, expensive house, the latest electronic gadgets, private schools

Happiness of professors with good income:

_____$100,000_____= 2.0 or High Happiness

$50,000 Desires: Modest house and car, some travel, social leisure, health insurance, and inexpensive lessons for their children

The "poorer" example is four times as happy with their money because they have more than their desires require. In contrast, the well-off couple has enough money to meet only half of their desires, and therefore they feel poorer. We saw a perfect illustration of the influence of aspirations when we conducted research with Amish people living in the American Midwest. The Amish are a group of German-speaking Christians who eschew many worldly goods and technologies. They farm without the use of tractors, use horses and buggies instead of automobiles, and choose kerosene lanterns over electricity in their homes. Most do not own televisions, computers, or telephones. The Amish live, in other words, a simple life centered around religion, hard work, and a sense of tight-knit community. They are famous for their frolics, or barn raisings, in which the community joins together to work on a communal building project.

We spent months in Amish country, interviewing the locals and collecting happiness data. Although the Amish live a more technologically simple existence than most readers of this book, they reported being satisfied with their lives. In fact, despite large families and relatively low earnings, the Amish reported being quite satisfied with their income, housing, food, and other material goods. Sophisticated urbanites probably look down their noses at simple Amish pastimes like quilting and donkey basketball, and may prefer instead Dom Pérignon after an evening at the theater. But who is to say which one produces more happiness? It may be that they are both happiness producers for the same reasons – sharing common experiences with friends, in a pursuit that alters the rhythm of everyday life.

Clearly, there are well-off people who feel they don't have enough money, and there are people of modest means who feel that they have enough. The lesson here is that no matter how much money you earn, you can always want more, and feel poor along the way. Even if you make a million dollars a year, you will find that your desires have a way of slowly ballooning over time. You were once pleased with the studio apartment you and a friend shared in college. Then you were proud of your tiny ranch-style house. As you earned more, you graduated to a beautiful turn-of-the-century home in a fashionable part of town. Soon thereafter you found yourself wanting a vacation home at the beach. We see this same pattern of rising desires across the wealthy nations of the world.

Although incomes have increased dramatically since World War II, people are not a lot happier. Why not? As the industrialized world has become more affluent, the average level of aspirations has also risen. What was once seen as luxury – owning two cars, for instance – has become a "necessity" for many in modern times. With this kind of luxury fever, people can always feel poor. Each of us must ask ourselves whether we have become a victim of our rising material desires.

Buyer Beware: The Toxic Effects of Materialism

Having high aspirations is not always bad, especially if they match your level of income. However, when aspirations run out of control, and are too heavily focused on physical comfort and luxury items, we brand this "materialism." Materialism, simply put, is wanting money and material goods more than you want other things, such as love or leisure time. Of course, we all want a good income, but materialistic people think money is the most important thing in life. How happy are materialists? Most studies show that materialistic peopleare less happy than others. That's right: although having money proves to be a boon to happiness, wanting money too much can detract from it!

Take a look at some results from a study on materialism and happiness conducted with college students. In figure 6.3, we show the life satisfaction of people with different levels of income. There are two lines-one for those who said money was not important, and another line for those who said money was extremely important. As can be seen, the materialistic people are less satisfied with their lives at each level of income, except for the highest level of wealth, where they finally catch up.

The happiness of materialists can suffer because their pursuit of money distracts them from other important aspects of life, such as relationships. Huge sums of cash require hard work, and materialists tend to put in extra time at the office and miss out on quality time at home. Although many people enjoy their work, too much of it can

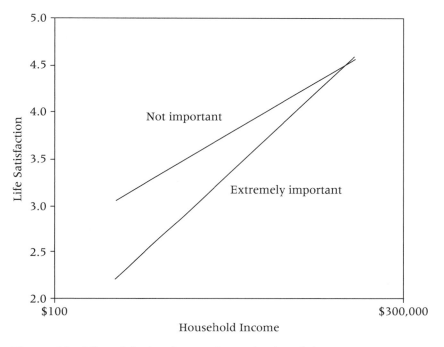

Figure 6.3 Life satisfaction for people varying in valuing money

harm happiness if the person then has little time left for family and friends. In addition, materialists tend to be dissatisfied because their aspirations are so high, and constantly trend higher. In this way, materialism is a neverending pursuit, with one materialistic goal being quickly replaced with another. No matter the income level, there is always a more expensive car, house, vacation, jet, or private island for which a person can strive. Because materialists tend to earn more money than others, some of the toxic effects of materialism on psychological wealth are damped. However, it is harder for materialists on average to be happy at the same level of income as nonmaterialists because they very often feel as though they need more money, no matter how much they have.

Some readers still may not be convinced that heavily valuing money is toxic to happiness. After all, how can a plasma screen television, a PlayStation game console, or a new set of golf clubs be harmful? Aren't these examples of fun recreational pursuits that can be enjoyed with friends? As it turns out, some clever research illustrates both the benefits and downsides of money. Kathleen Vohs and her colleagues were interested to discover how money, and even reminders of money, affects people psychologically. To do this, they primed the concept of money by leaving subtle reminders around the research laboratory. For instance, they placed a flying dollar as the screen saver on a computer screen in the room, or put a framed dollar bill on the wall. Amazingly, research participants who were exposed to these small monetary cues felt more self-confident than those who were not. They also were able to persevere longer at a difficult task without asking for help than folks in the no-money condition. The effects of money, however, were not all positive in Vohs's study. The people in the money-cue condition were also less likely to be sociable later on, preferring to wait for the experimenters alone rather than with others, sitting farther away from others in a waiting room, and opting for solitary rather than group activities when offered the choice. The money-primed participants were also less helpful to a confederate who appeared to accidentally have dropped his belongings, and they donated less of their experimental earnings to charity when given the opportunity to do so. Thus, the merest hint of money led to a tendency for folks to feel confident, but also to feel more distant from others.

Children in Wealthy Families

As industrialized countries grow increasingly rich, there are more children growing up in affluent families than ever before. Although this means that children have access to good schools, lessons, tutors, and other resources in record numbers, kids of wealthy parents also face a number of problems. Many children see too little of their hard-working parents, and modern technologies like BlackBerries and mobile phones have made it easier for jobs to encroach on family evenings and weekends. Another problem is the pressure kids face to achieve – successful and prosperous parents usually hope their children will achieve at the same high levels. Some insist that their children only attend the most elite universities. But the offspring may have less ability, less motivation, or different values. Unfortunately, because many children grow so accustomed to comfort and luxury, they experience extra pressure to excel in pursuits that will allow them to continue in that lifestyle. If a child becomes too accustomed to luxury, his or her freedom can be limited because lower paying but rewarding jobs, such as art and teaching, are psychologically off-limits. Finally, wealthy youths are sometimes given the idea of entitlement, and feel that they are better than others. They feel that their money places them above others, above the "little people."

The fact that children in upper-class and upper-middle-class families face a particular set of challenges does not mean that money corrupts. There are plenty of great parents and wonderful children among this group. For the most part, though, these are kids whose parents did not instill an overly materialist mindset. They are children who grew up in families that emphasized togetherness, taught values other than material ones, were instilled with a sense of responsibility toward others, and who learned that comfort is a privilege rather than a right. We don't mean to exaggerate the difficulties of rich kids – poor kids undoubtedly have more severe challenges. But it would be a mistake not to realize that wealth has its own problems.

It is ironic that as rich nations have increased their wealth, people have not on average become a lot happier. One reason is that material aspirations have continued to rise, so that many people feel short on cash. Another reason is that people who "want it all" often feel stressed and stretched thin. They don't have enough time for family and friends, and need to work longer to make ends meet. As Herbert Hoover reputedly said, "Just when the ends meet, somebody moves the ends." Thus, it is important to remember that as we grow wealthier, happiness will increase only if we keep our material desires well within our incomes.

Benefits of Money (Besides Having Stuff)

In understanding when and why money sometimes helps happiness and sometimes does not, it is important to understand that some of the benefits are not simple purchasing power. Income has benefits that do not depend on how much we spend. These nonmaterial benefits help explain the paradox that the rich on average are happier than the poor, but that people in wealthy nations have not increased much in happiness over the past decades despite the fact that average incomes have risen dramatically.

Earning Money

Although making money is an unpleasant hardship for some people, and is seen as a cost rather than a benefit by some economists, many people derive pleasure from their work. Furthermore, some people absolutely love their work, and this can be especially true of people who own their own businesses or who work in higher status jobs. Quite simply, these individuals might gain some happiness from spending money, but they truly gain enjoyment from making money. The challenges and activities of making more money lead these individuals to want more money, rather than the additional luxury items they might acquire.

Just as some people love their work, others do not. Indeed, some people loathe their jobs. For these individuals, the more they earn – and hence usually the more time they spend working – the less total happy time they experience. Even people who enjoy their jobs might enjoy alternative activities, such as leisure time with family and friends, even more. Hence, higher incomes can relate to either more or less happiness because a major way to earn more money is usually to work more.

Social Status

Although no one wants to own up to having ambitions toward high social status, it is perfectly natural to desire a rung high up on the social ladder. We don't mean being snooty or feeling entitled; we are talking about respect. Rich individuals tend to occupy higher social positions and command more respect than their poorer counterparts. The guy who heads a company with a thousand employees receives far more respect from friends, colleagues, workers, and even strangers than does a homeless man or a cashier in a coffee shop. If you aren't convinced, consider this experiment we once tried. As an experiment, one of the authors, Robert, once went without bathing, dressed in dirty clothes, and stood on a busy street corner with a cup brimming with quarters. He tried to hand out free money to passersby, but after an hour, not a single person had taken money. Most people avoided eye contact or made a wide arc around him, but one person donated money! Now imagine a well-groomed man in an Armani suit with a Rolex watch handing out change on a corner. Although it might raise a few eyebrows, people would more likely approach him, ask questions, and take the money. Money often translates into the respect of others and high social status, and so even those who don't want many worldly goods may want a high income for the respect it brings.

After all, we all want to feel good about ourselves, and other people's respect can be helpful in this regard.

Because of the status factor, the value of money depends in part on social comparison – where we stand relative to others. This is why many people say they would prefer to earn $50,000 in a society where others make $25,000 rather than earn $100,000 in a society where others earn $200,000! H. L. Mencken put it well when he observed that a rich man is one who earns $100 more than his wife's sister's husband. The value of income for happiness is not just the goods and services money can buy, but the respect it can purchase as well.

The researcher Chris Hsee studied the effects of money on satisfaction, sampling respondents from all over China. What he found was that money can have an absolute influence on satisfaction when some basic need, such as food, is involved. But for status items, such as jewelry, the effects of wealth on satisfaction depend on how much a person has compared to how much other people in that area have. This helps explain why rich people are happier, but why, as rich societies have gotten richer, they have not increased much in happiness. Some things money can buy, like food, matter regardless of what others have, whereas other items that confer status have value primarily in reference to how a person stands in relation to others.

Personal Control

Whether we like it or not, money is one of the things that leads to self-reliance and control of our lives. Additional income means that we can pay off debt, engage in more expensive activities, and enjoy more flexibility in our work. Also, when life presents hassles, as is invariably the case, more money means being better able to deal with most crises and unexpected events. For example, both authors of this book have been involved in hit-and-run accidents (on the receiving end!) and, while the price of the insurance deductible stung a bit, it was probably less painful for us than for someone scraping by paycheck to paycheck. If emergencies arise, having money can often help you to overcome them. Things are easier if you are rich when your house burns down, your car is wrecked, or you need special medical treatments. Financial resources can serve as a buffer against life's negative events.

There might be some primal connection between the secure feeling of having resources and the happiness money can deliver. In a set of studies in Belgium, Barbara Biers and her colleagues found that hungry people were less altruistic, donating less money to charity. Furthermore, people who were reminded of money and the things it can buy were hungrier when exposed to a taste test. It appears that money taps into feelings that are related to more basic resources, such as food. Accumulating money might make people feel good because it gives rise to the same feelings as accumulating food did in our ancient past, and there may be good reason for this connection: financial resources can help people overcome at least some of life's difficulties.

Pleasure in Shopping

Besides the consumption of goods, people may enjoy the activity of shopping. We are fearful of bringing this up because many of our friends and colleagues deplore shopping and believe it is a sign of crass materialism. Yet we know a man who loves shopping for tools, another who prizes shopping for food, and many people who are ecstatic about clothes shopping. We know one woman who buys little for herself, but loves buying presents for others. Even among the critics of materialism, we know that one loves buying wine, another prizes purchasing books, and the third enjoys buying music. It is just that they don't care about shoes and clothes, and therefore hate the idea of "shopping."

We believe that shopping and the activities that are required to be a knowledgeable consumer can be a source of pleasure for many people. Maybe this should not be so, and maybe there are better ways to be happy. But let's face it: some people love shopping for clothes! And the good thing about this activity is that it can be afforded to some degree by most people because it can occur at a range of prices, from Wal-Mart to Rodeo Drive. Books such as Robert Frank's *Luxury Fever* and John de Graaf's *Affluenza* point to the detrimental effects of materialism and consumerism, and certainly these exist. However, although shopping is not the royal road to lifelong happiness, it might give many people boosts of pleasure-which is harmless, as long as it is not an addiction.

Ability to Help Others

Of course, not all wealthy people are materialistic, and rich people can do things with their money to help the world. When we think about wealth and happiness, the first thing that comes to mind is that additional income means that we can better obtain the things we want – a new Toyota, that trip to Mexico, or plants for the garden. If you like music, money is what affords you the highest quality sound system or abundant store credit at iTunes. If you enjoy skiing, wealth can get you a season pass on the nearby slopes, a new jacket, or a weekend at Whistler. While there is undoubtedly more to life than buying things, the ability to upgrade your kitchen, take a family vacation, get a dog, or obtain other things you value can sometimes increase your happiness, at least in the short run. But money can also help folks make meaningful contributions to the world.

No matter what your personal, political, or business opinion of Bill Gates, it is amazing to think about the change he is effecting with his billions of dollars in charitable giving to Africa, and those of the cofounder of Microsoft, Paul Allen, who has been donating millions to scientific research. Of course, being rich is no guarantee of a prosocial attitude, but history is full of examples of the amazing generosity of the world's wealthiest citizens. Alfred Nobel left a legacy of promoting important advances in medicine, science, literature, and peace. John D. Rockefeller was instrumental in the preservation of vast amounts of land for national parks in the United States. Because of her wealth, Oprah Winfrey has the ability to experience the enormous satisfaction of starting a girls' school in Africa. The billionaire Warren Buffet has changed the face of philanthropy by donating his fortune to the Bill and Melinda Gates Foundation.

Great satisfaction can lie in creating such a lasting and meaningful legacy. Take the fascinating story of John Robbins, the heir of Iva Robbins, the founder of the immensely successful ice-cream chain Baskin-Robbins. Rather than following in his father's business footsteps or cashing in on his millions, John broke ranks and moved to a simple cabin in Canada. He became disillusioned with the dairy and beef industries and wrote an influential pro-environment book called *Diet for a New America*. In recent times, John has worked with his son, Ocean, to form a large environmental organization for youth, and a program to help wealthy people use their money in meaningful ways. Of course, altruistic giving need not be on the hulking scale of the donations made by billionaires. More modest wealth can be used to help those we love-our parents, our children, or our communities. We can send kids to college, pay for expensive medical care, or help friends in times of need. Money, then, can be more than a crude material concern: it can be a vehicle for helping others and feeling good about yourself.

Making Sense of the Paradox

The important lesson for readers is that money means a lot more than purchasing power. It can mean status, feelings of control, and enjoyable work. At the same time, materialism can be toxic to happiness, and too much work can interfere with other areas, such as family life. Therefore, readers need to carefully pursue income with a keen awareness of how it can help and harm happiness.

Conclusions

It might surprise some readers to learn that, with some important caveats, money can help buy happiness. Many folks want to believe just the opposite. We have heard people claim that wealthy individuals are more stressed out and greedy, and even that they need tranquilizers to sleep at night. In fact, many psychologists believe the myth that income is not related to happiness, perhaps because we would all like to believe that people from every walk of life have an equal chance at fulfillment. Furthermore, the idea that money doesn't increase happiness is consistent with concerns about rising individualism and rampant materialism, as well as with our worries about the environmental problems that economic growth can bring. So we apologize to all those who were positive that money doesn't help happiness. The data from a variety of studies paint a different picture: rich people tend to be happier than poor people, people in wealthy nations are more satisfied with their lives than their less affluent counterparts, and lottery winners are happier than others. It might not seem fair that some folks have not only big bucks but more happiness as well, but rather than begrudging folks their good fortune, consider how money could boost happiness. Additional income can translate to greater social status, feelings of personal control, a sense of security, and unique opportunities to make a lasting contribution to society.

The research linking money to happiness need not be an emotional death sentence for less affluent people. While, on average, poorer individuals take a psychological hit from their living conditions, this does not apply to every individual. We saw, for instance, how most homeless people were dissatisfied with their lives, but some were actually faring well in terms of happiness. And in the study of the Forbes list of millionaires, several were unhappy. This important fact underscores a crucial and often overlooked point in the money-happiness discussion. That is, although money and happiness are linked, the effect of money on happiness is often not large. Income appears to buy happiness, but the exchange rate isn't great. Extra dollars often amount to modest gains in happiness.

More important than the absolute amount of your paycheck or your exact net worth is your attitude toward your money and the ways in which you spend it. Rich people who spend outside their means feel poor, and poor people who live within a careful budget feel secure. Regardless of your actual income, it is your material aspirations that color your mood. The traditional Maasai of Africa are very satisfied with their lives, despite the fact that they have almost no monetary incomes, because material desires are mostly fulfilled and they are doing well in other areas of life. The worst cases are those individuals around the world who have moved to cities and joined the market economy, but have extremely low incomes to meet their needs and developing aspirations. Even for people in wealthy societies, problems can arise when they become too wedded to the idea of striking it rich and accumulating wealth. Materialists are generally less satisfied with their lives than folks who highly value love, friendships, and other worthwhile pursuits.

In the end, it is difficult to sum up with a simplistic yes or no answer the question of whether money causes happiness. However, we can say that the research on this topic tells us that it is generally good for your happiness to *have* money, but toxic to your happiness to *want* money too much. A high income can help happiness, but is no sure path to it. Therefore, readers must determine the motives underlying their desire for money, and not sacrifice too much in the pursuit of wealth. It is important not only to spend money wisely, but to earn it wisely as well.

7

Religion, Spirituality, and Happiness

The Talmud, an important compilation of Jewish writing, is filled with fascinating stories. Among these is the curious tale of the wedding night of Rabbi Akiva's daughter. Astrologers warned the rabbi that on the night of his daughter's wedding, she would be bitten by a snake and die. During the wedding reception, Rabbi Akiva's daughter happened to be holding a long pin, which she stuck into a small opening in the wall. A snake was coiled in the wall, and the pin pierced it in the eye, killing it. The rabbi, greatly relieved but also curious as to how she had avoided her fate, asked his daughter whether she had done anything out of the ordinary. She answered, "A poor man came to the door, but no one heard him over the noise of the reception. I went to the door and gave the man the gift you had given me for my wedding." The rabbi, according to the tale, was delighted to hear how generously his daughter had acted, and from then on, he taught his followers, "Charity delivers from death." Like other stories in the Talmud, this one is meant to be instructive. It is not about how to kill snakes, but rather about the importance and rewards of acting justly and morally. The major religions of the world teach many similar lessons, such as the value of being unselfish. They use entertainment, ritual, prayer, and other methods to help people live good lives. Religions, in some sense, act as how-to manuals for living.

Religion is central to the lives of billions of people. For anyone who has been fortunate enough to travel the world, the importance of religion in everyday life is readily apparent. Cities and villages across the globe are littered with religious architecture, ranging from neighborhood shrines to massive temples and cathedrals. Hundreds of the UNESCO World Heritage sites, for instance, are places of worship, ruins of ancient temples, and places of pilgrimage for religious groups. People wear clothes and jewelry related to their religion, from crucifix necklaces for Christians, to sidelocks for Orthodox Jews, to *bindis* for Hindu women. Hotel rooms in the United States have Bibles in their end tables, while hotel rooms in Islamic nations have arrows pointing toward Mecca.

Religion is one of the activities that most clearly set us apart from the rest of the animals. It should be clear that it is more than just window dressing for many people; it is a deeply personal mindset that can lead to tremendous generosity and, sometimes, intense animosity. If we can learn anything from the charitable giving done and the wars fought in the name of religion, it is that people take their faith seriously.

Many studies have shown small but significant benefits of religion to well-being. Research from a variety of sources provides evidence that churchgoers are a bit healthier, more likely to be forgiving, and, in some circumstances, even more tolerant than their nonreligious counterparts. One study, in particular, bears directly on Rabbi Akiva's message. Neal Krause was interested in the benefits of social support at church. He collected data on social support, financial stress, health, and other variables from more than a thousand elderly Christians in 2001, and then followed up with them in 2004. He found that both receiving and giving support to fellow congregants help alleviate worries about money. Krause also found that more frequent church-goers were significantly more likely to be alive at the three-year follow-up!

Other research shows that religious people are sometimes less likely to use drugs and commit crimes, and are more likely to receive more education, make more money, and live longer. If religion helps people live longer, it makes sense to consider whether there might be other psychological benefits of faith as well. The philosopher Daniel Dennett suggests that religions have been successful, in part, because they help people feel good about themselves and the world in which they live. Whether or not you believe the teachings of a particular religion, it is easy to recognize that religion would not be as widespread as it is today if it primarily made people sad. Which brings us to the question: "Does religion lead to happiness?" Are religious folks happier than their agnostic counterparts?

Happy Are Those . . .

Psychologists who have studied whether religious people are happy or unhappy have often reached a general conclusion – religious people are on the whole happier than the nonreligious. In the vast majority of studies, religious people report higher well-being than their non-believing counterparts. Even when researchers define religiosity in various ways – such as attending church or having self-professed spiritual beliefs – studies show that religious people are, on average, mildly happier. In one study, conducted by one of the authors (Ed) and the Gallup Organization, about a thousand people living in St. Louis were contacted through random-digit telephone dialing and asked to answer a survey related to spiritual beliefs and life satisfaction. It was found that respondents who believed in God and in an afterlife were more likely to be satisfied with their lives.

It makes sense to ask whether these research findings are unique to the United States, a country with fairly high rates of religiosity. Can we extend these findings beyond America, and do they generalize to religious observance, not just to religious belief? When we examined the Gallup World Poll, we noticed that the happiness of people who attend religious services depended on where they lived. In some societies, they were more satisfied with life, and in other societies less so. We are not certain how cultural context plays into the religion-happiness question, but it is possible that there are historical or social factors that add to or detract from the potential power of religion in various nations. Whatever the reason, religion does not seem to equal happiness everywhere.

Varieties of Religious Experience

It is not surprising that the relation between happiness and religiosity varies – across different religions, nations, and individuals – because religion is not a single activity, but includes diverse practices and beliefs. A Scientologist and a Muslim will have few tenets and observances in common. The founder of American psychology, William James, wrote a book titled *The Varieties of Religious Experience*, and the diversity is enormous. For instance, the researchers Adam Cohen and Paul Rozin examined differences between Jews and Protestants in forgiveness and behavior. They found that Jews are more likely than Protestants to forgive *thinking* sinfully, but are more likely to harshly condemn *acting* sinfully. In other words, Protestants place more importance on what a person believes and whether he or she thinks bad things than do Jews. Thus, a married Protestant would likely feel guiltier about feeling lust, whereas a Jew might be most worried about actually being unfaithful to a spouse. Even devoutly religious people probably agree that not all religions may be equivalent when it comes to happiness, because religions differ from each other in so many different ways.

Types of Religious Beliefs and Happiness

When we inquired, we found that people who believe in hell and the devil tend to be slightly less happy than those who believe only in heaven. A view of the afterlife that includes only hell could easily create anxiety in the faithful. Beliefs differ dramatically from religion to religion, and group to group. Consider the Peace Prayer of St. Francis. The language of the prayer is undeniably positive and optimistic, and it is easy to see how such a framework for viewing life would help soldiers in the trenches, as well as clerks working in a grocery store:

The Peace Prayer of St. Francis
Anonymous, c. 1915

Lord, make me an instrument of your peace
Where there is hatred,
Let me sow love;
Where there is injury, pardon;
Where there is error, truth;
Where there is doubt, faith;
Where there is despair, hope;
Where there is darkness, light;
And where there is sadness, joy.
Love, pardon, truth, faith, hope, light, and joy.

O Divine Master grant that I may not so much seek to be consoled
As to console;
To be understood, as to understand;
To be loved, as to love.

For it is in giving that we receive,
It is in pardoning that we are pardoned,
And it is in dying that we are born to eternal life.

It is hard to imagine that people, of whatever religion, who follow the Peace Prayer are not happier because of it. Even the last line about dying can be interpreted metaphorically by the nonreligious to refer to the value of dying to oneself – getting rid of egoism, selfishness, and self-centeredness.

Perhaps at the opposite end of the compassion spectrum from the sentiments expressed in the Peace Prayer are the ideas of the Westboro Baptist Church, in Topeka, Kansas, and the beliefs of its founder, Fred Phelps. Followers of Phelps manage two controversial church-related websites, godhatesfags.com and godhatesamerica.com. They believe in a literal reading of the Christian Bible, and make no bones about condemning the multitudes for not living up to their interpretation of biblical standards.

In a shocking display of insensitivity sure to offend people of almost any religious persuasion, Phelps's followers gather to protest the funerals of people who died of AIDS, as well as those of American soldiers who were killed in combat in Iraq. The flock holds signs bearing slogans such as "Thank God for AIDS." The church's websites profess that the American civil rights activist Martin Luther King, Jr., is "in hell," and – unlikely as it sounds – "God hates Sweden." Although they identify as Baptists, the Christian emphasis on love and forgiveness appears to be largely lost on Phelps's followers. It is difficult to imagine how such a hateful, angry, vengeful view could leave anyone feeling good about the world.

When contacted for an interview, Phelps's wife, Shirley, referred us to two members of the congregation, husband and wife Charles and Rachel Hockenbarger. Charles, who is thirty-two, has been a member of the Westboro church since he was a teenager, as has his wife, who is now forty. The Hockenbargers agreed to be interviewed for this book. When we asked if they had any hope for humanity, the Hockenbargers answered: "The only hope for humanity is God. Given the fact that God hates most of mankind, we have no hope for humanity, in the sense that they will never be anything other than the depraved race of Adam." This point of view differs from that of many Christian denominations, in which God is seen as loving and merciful. When asked whether they thought Americans, on average, are happy, the Hockenbargers replied: "On the average, Americans, like most humans, are not happy. They are angry and miserable. Americans seem more angry and hateful, probably because they can see the blessings of God all around them – in nature, in their history, and in their laws – yet, they do not enjoy the blessings of God in themselves. Our experiences on the mean streets of this country, daily for the last fifteen years, lead us to this opinion. Americans are the meanest, most intolerant, hypocritical people on this earth. They pretend to love everyone, and tolerate all beliefs and opinions; in fact, if you do not agree with them, they hate you, and will try to kill you."

The Hockenbargers illustrate the lessons of this chapter. On the one hand, they might be happy by virtue of being involved in a tight-knit community, and get a boost in self-esteem from believing they are better than others. On the other hand, they view humanity as largely miserable, believe in a hateful God, and view those around them as hypocritical, intolerant, and mean. Such a view seems incompatible with a satisfying and fulfilling life, and could easily lead to feelings of estrangement and victimhood. And indeed, religions that teach that only their religion has merit and can lead to salvation, and that all other religions are to be condemned, tend to produce lower life satisfaction. Thus, religious beliefs may help happiness, but do not inevitably do so; it depends on the particular beliefs.

The Search for the Active Ingredient

In light of this diversity, it makes sense to wonder whether there are psychological processes leading to happiness that are part of only some religions. Are there "active ingredients" contributing to happiness that are more often present in some religions than in others? It turns out that the ways religions differ – in beliefs, practices, morals, and attitudes toward outsiders – each influence whether a religion is helpful or harmful to happiness.

Comforting Beliefs

Ancient Egyptian mummies have long fascinated modern people. The Egyptians, masters of mummification, developed elaborate rituals and practices aimed at shepherding the recently dead from this life to whatever may come after. For the wealthiest citizens of Egypt, attendants worked to preserve the body, the organs, and the earthly possessions for possible use in the afterlife. Imagine how comforting it would be to know that you would not "cross over" empty-handed, but rather would be well-equipped for the life to come. The Egyptians, of course, were not unique in their attention to the afterlife. Nearly every culture, and certainly the major world religions, offer guidance about the "world to come." Many religious people find comfort in their beliefs about the afterlife. Death is a prospect that looms on the horizon for all of us, and most religions provide reassuring answers about our ultimate destination. Whether they believe in reincarnation, a seat in heaven, sex on other planets, or joining deceased loved ones, most religious people have a positive view of the unexplored territory after death.

In a series of studies, the University of British Columbia researchers Ara Norenzayan and Ian Hansen asked participants to write "a paragraph about what will happen when you die." Across four separate studies, they found that simply making mortality salient, bringing it to the forefront of people's minds, made participants later endorse religious beliefs more heavily than those in a control condition. Not only did participants endorse the tenets of their own faith more strongly, but being reminded of death also served to make them open, at least in the short term, to the possibility of supernatural agents in many forms, including shamanistic powers and alien beings. Christians reminded of death were even open to the possibility that Buddha can hear and answer prayers. This last is not to say, of course, that Christians suddenly converted to another faith, but that they were more receptive to the possibilities and comforting beliefs of other faiths when reminded of death. Although we tend not to think much about it in our day-to-day lives, religions offer tremendous psychological comfort by providing answers to questions about death and the afterlife.

The example of our family matriarch, Mary Alice Diener, serves to dramatically illustrate how religious faith can protect us from the fear of death. In her eighties, Mary Alice contracted colon cancer, a disease that had already taken one of her daughters. Rather than fight the disease, she decided to succumb to it so that she could join her departed husband in heaven. As she told her children, although she enjoyed life, death caused her absolutely no fear. Because she had done all the things she wanted to do in life, she was looking forward to joining her husband, Frank, in heaven. Only the emotional pleading of her children and grandchildren led Mary Alice to relent on their behalf, and the surgery gained her another dozen years on this earth. The Christian Bible asks, "O death, where is thy sting?" Mary Alice reveals the power religion can have to erase our biggest existential anxiety.

Talya Miron-Shatz studied what women think about through the day, while at work, shopping, daydreaming, or with family. She noticed one category that was very negative – women thought a lot about their weight, and it was almost always negative when they did so. In contrast, many women also thought frequently about religion, and in this case their feelings were almost always positive. Religion may include ideas such as sin and hell, but apparently women tend to think much more about pleasant religious concepts. This suggests that for women religion is more often connected to ideas like the Peace Prayer than to thoughts of sin and hate.

Social Support

Since the first war that pitted one religion against another, people have debated whether religions do more harm than good. Unquestionably, there has been tremendous animosity and destruction in the name of religion. But so too has there been an outpouring of help and support for friends and strangers alike. An important emotional benefit of organized religion is the social support that frequently comes with being a member of a congregation. Whether you are a member of a synagogue in New York, part of a small Christian congregation in Denmark, or one of the multitudes attending services at the Ramakrishna temple in Kolkata, being a member of a spiritual community provides not only a sense of identity and belonging to a group, but the knowledge that like-minded individuals will help if you fall on hard times. In fact, many religious traditions emphasize social activities.

Several Jewish traditions speak to the group mentality of worship. A common maxim holds that a person cannot study the Torah alone, and Jews gather in minyans, prayer groups of ten or more. Similarly, some Christian denominations have group confession, and Mormons are well known for the amount of time they spend together in church activities. The strong social fabric of most churches offers a safe psychological haven for people. Some theorists believe that the support religion offers is of particular value to socially marginalized people.

Take the example of Father Crispin, a priest from Kenya visiting a Catholic parish in the Pacific Northwest. As anyone who has studied, worked, or lived abroad knows, making the transition to a foreign culture can be difficult, and being welcomed by the local community can feel terrific. Upon arriving at his new parish, Father Crispin was invited to one home after another for meals and conversation. Despite arriving in a new place, the priest had dozens of instant friends. And this type of social support is more than feel-good friendliness. Remember the study we described at the beginning of this chapter-church-related social support actually lowered mortality rates!

Connecting to Something Permanent and Important

When you join a religion, you join something larger than yourself – a social movement with a history, shared by many adherents, and often with connections around the world. The major religions of the world date back a thousand years or more, and the faithful share a connection with individuals of similar beliefs over centuries. When a Muslim bows toward Mecca, he or she can be assured that millions around the world are doing the same, and millions more did so a century earlier. No matter how low a person's status might be, as part of a religion, just as with national identity, he or she becomes something more significant. Furthermore, many religions teach that each person is important and special.

Perhaps most important, religion can give people a sense of meaning. It helps them understand their world, and gives a broad purpose to their lives. More than most human activities, religion can connect people to something larger than themselves. It can give even the most horrible life a sense of deep significance.

Humans enjoy positive feelings when they "belong," when they are part of a cohesive group of supportive people with similar beliefs. At times, we experience this feeling with national loyalty, pride in our company, or allegiance to a local sports team. But few institutions produce the strong feelings of togetherness and group identity that are inherent in many religions. Imagine sitting together with 22,000 other Latter-Day Saints in the conference center in Salt Lake City, listening to the Mormon Tabernacle Choir. Or imagine the experience of togetherness that millions of Muslims making the hajj to Mecca each year must feel. Or the excitement of Catholics as they crowd together in St. Peter's Square awaiting the election of a new pope. Religious experiences connect people not only to others present, but to the entire group, past and current, and sometimes to all of humanity. When we participate in organized religious rituals, we are no longer alone in the world, and our lives gain significance by the connection to something larger than ourselves.

Growing Up Religiously

Another possible "active ingredient" in the religion-happiness connection is being raised religiously, which seems to confer benefits. It turns out that being raised with religious beliefs and attending church services as a child is associated with happiness, even if a person isn't religious as an adult. We found that even people who fall away from their childhood religious beliefs are happier, on average, than those who were brought up without religion and found faith later on. It is possible that a religious upbringing provides a sense of community, a moral foundation, and family unity that continue to benefit people over the course of their lives, regardless of their later spiritual practices. Maybe people who grew up religiously have a more positive view of the world, or maybe they feel more secure and grounded. Or perhaps religious homes had more harmony, stability, and togetherness than the average nonreligious home. Whatever the reasons, growing up religiously might be a help on the road to happiness. With a non-religious upbringing, children must be supplied with other sources of values and stability.

The Experience of Ritual

One of the distinctive features of organized religion, whether it is Buddhism or Christianity, is the beautiful pageantry involved with religious services. Most religions have elaborate rituals steeped in tradition. Religious festivals are frequently marked by music, singing, and colorful displays. Religious buildings, ranging from the impressive rock-hewn churches of Ethiopia, to the massive stupa of Borobudur in Indonesia, to the flying buttresses of Notre Dame Cathedral, are among the crowning achievements of architecture. Much of the world's greatest art and music is religious in nature. The sights, smells, and sounds are an attractive appeal to the senses, and it is easy to get swept away in the beauty and sense of majesty. One of the authors of this book, Ed, had the opportunity to attend the coronation of a new pope at the Vatican. Ed describes his experience:

> The anticipated day of the papal coronation arrived and we made our way toward St. Peter's Square. There, hundreds of thousands of excited pilgrims had come to witness church history in the making. We were assigned bleachers built on top of St. Peter's for the event, from which we had a tremendous view of the throngs below. The square had been cordoned into sections, some holding thousands of priests, and others filled with a sea of nuns. Behind these partitions was an enormous fenced area for lay pilgrims, who had traveled to the event from every corner of the globe. In the very front rows, foreign heads of state gathered and chatted.
>
> Finally, the moment we had all been waiting for arrived. A thousand bishops marched in wearing their splendid robes, followed by eighty cardinals in their striking red vestments. The pope, resplendent in an elaborate white robe, was carried in on a golden chair on a raised dais, waving to the crowd. Singing, incense, and wild applause mingled in the air as the new pope passed slowly up through the crowd. Swiss guards, musicians, and the chair-carriers all were dressed in colorful costumes. Finally, the time came for the pope to be crowned with an enormous beehive-shaped headpiece made of ten pounds of silver, and the crowd was electric with excitement. Hundreds of thousands spontaneously made the sign of the cross in unison. Even the crowning of kings does not match such splendor.

Of course, there is more to Catholicism, or any religion, than mere pageantry. Nonetheless, rituals such as a papal coronation, in which huge crowds turn out, elegant clothes are worn, the music is beautiful, and rituals dating back centuries are performed, help make the religious experience profound. Even though most religious ritual, music, and pageantry are on a much smaller scale than a papal coronation, they are present in most religious observances. What's more, these displays, whether they are bamboo and fabric *pandhals* erected in India during the *puja* season, or little boys and girls singing in the Sunday choir while dressed in their finest clothes, the physical trappings of organized religion can provide an experience set apart from everyday life, which translates to feelings of well-being. It is no accident that music is often an essential part of religion, from the Mormon Tabernacle Choir to the religious masterpieces of Bach and Mozart. Even the "dry toast" religions, without icons or incense, have music, ministerial robes, and rousing sermons.

Spirituality and Positive Emotions

An important part of the overall religious experience, for people of any spiritual persuasion, is contact with the mystical, with something larger than themselves. People go to the gym, read books, take classes, and attend parties to develop their physical, intellectual, and social muscles. But they usually go to church to flex their spiritual muscles. The spiritual feeling, sometimes physical and sometime emotional, is difficult to define, but is universal. Some people arrive at it through prayer, while for others it comes in the form of dreams, charity work, or appreciating nature.

Spiritual feelings can be such powerful experiences that most religious traditions have developed branches of mysticism and practices for achieving this feeling. Chasidic Jews consult the Zohar, dervishes whirl, Catholic monks fast and take vows of silence and celibacy. In fact, the spiritual experience can be so profound and enjoyable that even nonreligious people sometimes seek it out through nonreligious means. For instance, some folks take LSD, hallucinogenic mushrooms, or other psychedelic drugs to try to activate the spiritual experience.

Recently, "spirituality" has become a buzzword for people who are uncomfortable with organized religion. On college campuses, in liberal circles, and among New Age believers, the idea of spirituality – the belief in some higher power that connects all things – is increasingly attractive to many people. Whether a person is a member of a bona fide religion or holds a private set of beliefs, spirituality is an important component of any experience of the divine. Whereas religion connotes institutionalized practices and doctrines, spirituality is usually concerned with personal growth and inspiration. The psychiatrist George Vaillant suggests that the fundamental core of spirituality is the experience of positive emotions such as love, gratitude, and awe that connect people to something larger than themselves. As we saw in chapter 4, positive emotions serve to facilitate relationships, and leave us feeling connected to other people.

When people feel the spiritual emotions that connect them to others, to society, to nature, and to the universe, they are likely to behave in more positive ways, perhaps because they better appreciate the world around them. The psychologist Robert Emmons explored the beneficial effects of gratitude. According to his research, when people feel grateful, they not only focus on the positive aspects of their lives, but they also focus on how others have helped them, and thus the emotion of gratitude fosters a desire to reciprocate and help others. It's not surprising, then, that Emmons's studies show that research participants who practice gratefulness tend to be happier.

One religion that is particularly well known for the open way in which it addresses happiness and other positive emotions is Buddhism. So integral is the understanding, acknowledgment, and maintenance of positive emotion in Buddhism that the religion's most public figure, His Holiness the Dalai Lama, wrote a book on happiness. In fact, it was the Dalai Lama who invited Richard Davidson, the distinguished neuroscientist from the University of Wisconsin, to Dharamsala, India, to interview monks about their emotional and spiritual experiences. Davidson tells friends and colleagues that he himself experienced an exceptional sense of compassion when in the presence of the Dalai Lama.

Davidson and his colleagues tested the power of meditation scientifically. In one study, they attached electrodes to the scalp of a French-born monk, Mathieu Ricard. Ricard has immersed himself in a life of spiritual reflection, logging more than ten thousand hours of meditation and spending years in silence. In their initial trial run, Davidson and his colleagues asked Ricard to voluntarily generate compassion, and then sat back to record the electrical activity of his brain. The activation was so pronounced that the researchers suspected their equipment was malfunctioning. They ran the study again, but with an additional sample of monks, and a sample of local students to act as a control group. In the second trial, not only were the monks' positive brainwave patterns about thirty times as strong as those of the students, but more areas of the brain also appeared to be activated. In particular, the left prefrontal cortex was highly active in the monks. This area of the brain, as it turns out, is also associated with the experience of positive emotions.

It appears, then, that positive emotions and the experience of spiritual contact – of getting in touch with the divine, regardless of your definition – are intimately related. When people attend church services, sing hymns, pray, and engage in other religious activities, they often feel a surge of positive emotions. In fact, the experience of spirituality may be an emotional one, inseparable from good feelings.

Conclusions

In some studies, religious people are on average happier, but the difference is often small, and in some recent data we found that religious people are not happier in all nations. Furthermore, it appears that not all religions equally increase happiness. This led us to try to discover the active ingredients underlying religiosity that more reliably predict feelings of well-being. There are several broad lessons that apply to atheists, nonreligious spiritual individuals, and religious people alike, because the active ingredients that make religious people on average happier can be instructive to both agnostics and the devout. One conclusion is that the major religions of the world capture important ideas about living well, including not being overly selfish and acting morally. These ideas appear to be helpful in living a better, happier life whether one is religious or not.

Second, there appears to be something about growing up religiously that aids happiness. Although we are not yet certain what this entails, it seems prudent for parents to give their children a stable and secure home, a belief system that gives meaning and purpose to life, and a desire to help others and society.

Third, an important aspect of spirituality is the experience of positive emotions that connect us to a world larger than ourselves. A deep spirituality based on broadening positive emotions, such as love, awe, compassion, and transcendence, is an essential part of why religion and happiness are often associated, and is necessary for complete psychological wealth. But we also saw that in some cases people practice a religion that can make others unhappy, and these types of religions clearly are not based on the type of positive spirituality we describe. Religions that broadly condemn others and focus on the negative aspects of people outside of the religion do not have as a core element the idea of broadening positive emotions. Quite frequently, these religions are likely to make outsiders unhappy. Thus, these religions are likely to decrease the total amount of happiness in a society and the world and decrease the person's psychological wealth. In contrast, religions based on prosocial ideas, such as those reflected in the Peace Prayer of St. Francis, are built on broadening positive emotions, and are thus likely to increase the sum of happiness in the world.

A few scholars have accused us of pushing religion, and of not being objective scientists. Our response is that whether people are religious or secular, they can learn something about how to practice happiness from the findings on religion and happiness. We have no wish to convert anyone. Some people find formal religion helpful and some do not, and religiosity is largely a matter of individual faith and practice. We recognize that some religious beliefs and practices have led to genocide, war, and intolerance. But there nonetheless are things we can all learn from what makes some religious people happy, including a supportive social group, meaning in something larger than oneself, and a secure upbringing.

We all need to cultivate within ourselves and our families the emotions of love, compassion, and gratitude. Decentering oneself away from extreme selfishness in service to others and the world can make the individual happier, and also will likely make those around the person happier. For many people, religion can bring positive attitudes – meaning, love, gratitude, security, and hope. It is these attributes that religious and nonreligious individuals alike need to develop, and this is an important lesson that religions can teach us. If you develop a spiritual approach to life that includes positive emotions and not focusing exclusively on oneself, your psychological wealth will increase immeasurably.

8

The Happiest Places on Earth: Culture and Well-Being

Twenty-five years ago, we experienced the adventure of traveling up the Amazon River from Leticia, Colombia, to visit a remote tribe untouched by the modern world. At that time, the region had rarely been visited by outsiders, and our interactions with the locals sparked in Robert, who was eight at the time, a life-long interest in culture. From the travel journal of Ed Diener, 1981:

> We spent the morning heading upriver in a wide-bottomed canoe. There was just enough room for our guide, me, Carol, and the kids if they packed close together. The Amazon was brown and we occasionally saw dolphins and lily pads as wide as the span of my arms. But we were afraid to swim because locals told us of tiny fish that go up your nose and eat your brain, as well as of the horrors of piranhas. Toward noon, we turned up a small tributary, and the river was hardly wider than the boat. We often had to duck under branches. At one o'clock we arrived at the "village."
>
> The Yagua lived in raised stick houses with simple thatch roofs. We could see hammocks stretched from the posts, and a few were swollen with men and women resting in the heat. The children rushed to greet us, mostly naked. The boys had jet-black hair and runny noses that appeared to be ubiquitous. The men, with dried paint on their chests and wearing grass skirts, came next. There was a fair amount of mutual staring and nervous smiling.
>
> Finally, a man stepped forward with a six-foot-long blowgun, eager to demonstrate his skill with the hunting weapon. Our guide translated: we were to fold up a peso note and place it on a faraway tree trunk. If the man could hit the money with a dart, he could keep it. He hit the bill, an impossibly small target, on the first try, and everyone in the crowd laughed. I patted the man on the back and he put his arm around me with a wide grin on his face.

When we asked the guide why the man might want pesos, with no stores anywhere nearby, Daniel offered the explanation. On his last trip to the Yagua, the guide had brought a shotgun along and demonstrated its use to the men. They loved the gun; even better than a blowgun, they said. The guide told the villagers how they could earn money for a future shotgun purchase if they agreed to allow him to visit their village and they performed blowgun demonstrations for the visitors he brought along.

A Yagua elder gave eight-year-old Robert a short blowgun and darts as we were leaving. However, Rob's mom put her foot down to the poisonous curare they offered for the dart tips, afraid that back home a dart might find its way into one of Robert's friends rather than a local squirrel.

These people could not be more different from us. No running water, modern medicine, books, or modern conveniences. Stick homes without walls, and loincloth clothes. They hunt and live in kinship groups. But here they are, laughing and having a good time, seeming similar to us. Are they happy?

Such variation in material wealth, religious values, language, and other cultural factors exists among different national and ethnic groups that it makes sense to wonder if some groups are happier than others. Common sense might suggest that people living in industrial nations are happier than the Yagua because of the modern conveniences they possess. But some believe that happiness is largely a matter of personality and personal choices, and therefore that one's culture or nationality should not matter much. Which is true? Theories of happiness tell us that most people are mildly happy so that we have the energy, creativity, and friendliness to function effectively, while scientific studies reveal that some groups are much happier than others.

A fundamental question is whether happiness really matters to people in all cultures. In table 8.1, we show how important college students from around the globe think happiness and other values are. The respondents everywhere rate happiness as very important, although there are differences in the importance placed on it. As the table reveals, people in some cultures think that there are things more important than happiness, but people in diverse nations all believe happiness is important.

Nations did differ some on how desirable happiness is considered to be. This was confirmed in two studies by Shigehiro Oishi, who studied people's perceptions of Jesus in Korea and the United States.

Table 8.1 Importance ratings of values
1 = not important and 9 = extremely important

Nation	Happiness	Wealth	Love	Looks	Heaven
Brazil	8.7	6.9	8.7	6.4	7.8
Turkey	8.3	7.0	7.9	7.0	7.4
USA	8.1	6.7	8.3	6.2	7.3
Iran	7.8	7.0	8.1	6.6	7.9
India	7.5	7.0	7.5	5.7	6.6
Japan	7.4	6.6	7.8	5.9	6.1
China	7.3	7.0	7.4	6.1	5.0
Overall	*8.0*	*6.8*	*7.9*	*6.3*	*6.7*

He found that Americans rated Jesus as a happier person than did Koreans. They rated themselves as happier and more extroverted than did Koreans as well. If participants saw Jesus as happier, they were more likely to rate themselves as happier. In a second study, Americans rated hypothetical job applicants as most desirable if they were happy extroverts, whereas Koreans showed a preference for the happy introvert. This suggests the possibility that Asians prefer calm and contented happiness, while Westerners prefer more aroused and activated happiness.

Most People Are Mildly Happy

Research shows that most people are mildly happy most of the time. Time and again, this result emerges. Even when different researchers use different samples of people, different methods, and even different definitions of happiness, most research participants report being mildly happy most of the time unless the living conditions are dire. It is common to find that most people are mildly happy, and that only a few are ecstatic or depressed. Some people are incredulous when they learn about this surprising finding. Perhaps you are skeptical. You might wonder if Scandinavians and New Zealanders are happy. Yes, and their suicide rates aren't nearly as high as many people believe. How about Inuit seal hunters in remote corners of the Arctic? Yep. What about Americans? Yes, them too. There are probably strong evolutionary reasons for this: happiness helps people function by keeping them motivated, making them more creative and helpful to others, and helping them persevere. Although widespread happiness seems to be the human default, there is nonetheless cultural variation in the degree of happiness.

Take, for example, a study we conducted with groups around the world. We were interested in gathering happiness data from far-flung groups who lead materially simple lives and have limited exposure to the influences of Western media. We wanted to understand the experience of happiness among people who did not drive automobiles or care which movie stars are dating and divorcing. We interviewed people in traditional Maasai villages in Kenya, hunters in a remote village in northern Greenland, and Amish people in the United States. We stayed with people from these groups over the course of months, talked with them about the quality of their lives, and collected survey data on happiness from them. We sat around campfires and dinner tables, and tried to figure out why they feel the way they do. We asked them about their daily emotions, their overall levels of satisfaction, and how satisfied they were with various aspects of their lives, such as their house and friendships. Members of all three groups reported – on average – that they were moderately, but not perfectly, happy. This is what most groups say (although homeless people and mental patients are notable exceptions). Bear in mind also that these are average scores, and that not every Maasai or Amish person was necessarily happy; just most of them. At the top end, there was no single individual from the hundreds we studied in these groups who was perfectly happy across all of our measures. People on average are moderately happy, but never perfectly happy.

The Happiest Countries on Earth

Given the fact that we have observed regional differences in happiness, many people wonder what the happiest place on earth is. Is it wealthy America? Slow-paced Cambodia? The ultramodern United Arab Emirates? Or possibly upbeat Brazil? The Himalayan kingdom of Bhutan, with its idea of gross domestic happiness rather than gross domestic product? Fortunately, the answer to the question of which cultures are happy need not be a matter of guesswork. We don't have to wonder long about which nations are happy places and which places are not so emotionally shiny.

For this book, we analyzed the World Poll conducted in 2006 and 2007 by the Gallup Organization, the most complete sampling of humanity that has ever been conducted. In this poll, Gallup interviewed over a thousand people in each of about 130 nations, and these individuals were selected in a way to broadly represent each nation. The score we present in table 8.2 is the ladder of life scale invented by Hadley Cantril, in which people place themselves on an eleven-rung ladder, ranging from the best to the worst possible life they can imagine for themselves. It can be seen that the countries with the highest ladder score – with respondents saying they are high on the ladder of life – are economically developed, democratic, high in human rights, and high in equal rights for women. In contrast, the societies with the lowest life satisfaction tend to be extremely poor, are often politically unstable, and experience conflict within and with neighboring nations. The differences between the high and low lists are large, not just statistically significant. What this demonstrates is that not all happiness comes from within, as many pundits claim – to feel satisfied with one's life, it is important to live in secure circumstances where one's needs can be met.

As can be seen, those nations highest on the ladder are all wealthy, and the unsatisfied nations comprise many very poor countries.

Table 8.2 Life satisfaction: the ladder of life (0–10)

Highest		*Lowest*	
8.0	Denmark	3.2	Togo
7.6	Finland	3.4	Chad
7.6	Netherlands	3.5	Benin
7.5	Norway	3.6	Georgia
7.5	Switzerland	3.6	Cambodia
7.4	New Zealand	3.8	Zimbabwe
7.4	Australia	3.8	Haiti
7.4	Canada	3.8	Niger
7.4	Belgium	3.8	Burkina Faso
7.4	Sweden	3.8	Ethiopia

Source: Gallup Organization: Gallup World Survey (2006)

Several societal characteristics are important to happiness, even after controlling for the wealth of nations. For example, longevity correlates with life satisfaction and inversely correlates with negative emotions, even with income controlled. This suggests that health and happiness go together even beyond the fact that people in wealthy societies are healthier. Combining low incomes, political instability, major health concerns, government corruption, and human-rights problems can create a culture in which many people experience very low happiness.

Every society has very happy and unhappy individuals. But in some societies, most people are happy, and in a few societies where conditions are dire, most people are not so happy. Our data demonstrate that societal conditions can and do matter greatly for happiness, and that governments, not just individuals, influence the well-being that people experience. It is often claimed that happiness is an individual matter and not the concern of our governments – but good societies are absolutely necessary for providing the supportive structure in which pursuing happiness can be successful. Living in a well-off, stable, and well-governed society helps happiness.

How Cultures Differ in Happiness

Besides characteristics such as wealth, health, and governance, is there more that can affect national happiness? Can culture influence happiness – the beliefs, values, and traditions that also differentiate groups? Several dimensions of culture influence happiness beyond the stability and wealth of societies.

Prioritizing Groups versus Individuals

When most people consider culture, they think about the most visible aspects, such as language, religion, dress, and food. They think about French and Urdu, crucifixes and the call to prayer, loincloths and tuxedoes, tacos and pasta. And while these elements of culture are interesting, psychologists understand that culture is something deeper. Culture is a set of shared beliefs, attitudes, self-definitions, and values. Researchers analyzing the psychological dimensions of culture tend to examine how people relate to one another, how they understand themselves, their words, and the things they hold most dear.

One way of understanding cultural groups is to divide them into "individualists" and "collectivists." Individualistic societies are those that think of the individual as the most important basic unit. People in individualistic societies are typically seen as separate, unique, and free to make personal choices, even if they conflict with the desires of the larger group. Members of individualistic societies can usually choose their own spouse, profession, and living quarters. Each person is seen as unique and special. Sound familiar? If you are a reader from the United States, Canada, Australia, New Zealand, or Western Europe, you hail from an individualistic society. Collectivistic societies, on the other hand, think of the group as the most important basic unit. People living in collectivist societies are seen as connected to one another through powerful ties of duty and obligation. Collectivists often work to promote group harmony, even if it means sacrificing their individual desires, because the group is seen as more important than the individual. The group, in fact, defines who the individual is. Individualistic societies tend to suffer from more social ills, such as divorce, suicide, and homelessness, whereas people in collectivistic societies can feel frustrated by their personal sacrifices. But it's not all bad news. Individualists tend to feel creative and enjoy more social freedoms, whereas collectivists often enjoy more extended social support.

The subtle influence of individualism and collectivism extends even to our basic concept of self. Take a moment and consider the unfinished sentence "I am . . ." Think about all the different ways you might answer it. Go ahead and provide a few answers for yourself. Write them down if you like. Researchers using this sentence-completion task with people from far-flung countries find that people from different cultures approach it in distinct ways. Chinese people (collectivists), for instance, are more likely than Americans (individualists) to complete the sentence in a way that describes their relationship to others or the role they play in the social fabric ("I am a daughter" or "I am a student"), whereas Americans are more likely to describe personal traits ("I am a hard worker" or "I am beautiful"). Folks from these two types of cultures tend to have different ways of thinking about themselves.

Collectivists, who pay more attention to their roles in each social situation, have a tendency to see the "self" as a more fluid concept. In some situations, a person might be outgoing, and in some he or she might be reserved. In some settings, people might be brave, while in others they might be timid. Contrast this with the individualist sense of self, in which people are likely to see their character traits as stable and internal. To individualists, personal qualities like hot-headedness, intelligence, and dedication to hard work are like personality tattoos, fixed in place even across a wide variety of situations. Because – and this is the kicker – most people believe they are good (or at least better than average), individualists enjoy that sense even across diverse social situations. Even when an individualist is sitting passively watching a funny movie, he or she might still regard her- or himself as brave, even though in that moment he might not exhibit any signs of bravery. The individualist can comfort himself with the knowledge that bravery is like water in a camel's hump, stored for when it is needed. That's a pretty good feeling.

It is worth mentioning that individualists and collectivists derive their happiness from somewhat different sources. Collectivists, focused as they are on group harmony, are more likely to feel good when the group they are a part of is getting along well. An extreme example of this tendency comes from one woman Robert spoke with in a village in South India who refused to give him a direct report of her own happiness. "If my sons are happy," she told Robert, "then I am happy." When he pressed her to tell him how she felt in that exact moment, she replied, "You should go ask my husband how he feels right now, and then you will know how I feel." Collectivists are also more likely to feel good when they are contributing to a sense of peace within the group, even if it means fulfilling obligations that interfere with their own personal agenda. Individualists, on the other hand, are more likely to feel good when their uniqueness is exercised or singled out for praise. Individualists tend to become irritated or frustrated when they are forced to place their own desires on the back burner in favor of the needs of others.

If you are an individualist, what goes on inside you – your feelings – are extremely important. For example, if you fall out of love, you are likely to get divorced because your feelings are seen as sufficient reasons for separating. In contrast, collectivists are likely to value obligations in relationships more, and emotional feelings less, and therefore see feelings of love as less critical for continuing marriage. The psychologist Eunkook Suh of Yonsei University in South Korea showed that individualists weight their happy feelings more when reporting life satisfaction, whereas collectivists weight the quality of their relationships more when thinking about their life satisfaction.

Thus, not only do individualists and collectivists differ in the types of feelings they most value, but they also differ in terms of what makes life most satisfying.

Individualists like to be part of a group – so long as the group is successful. In a study by Shigehiro Oishi, research assistants counted the number of American college students wearing school sweatshirts on a given day. The day after a major win by one of their university's sports teams, the sweatshirts were common. On the days following a crushing athletic defeat, there were almost no sweatshirt-wearers on campus. Although this might sound disloyal at first blush, consider it in terms of happiness. The students in this study saw, at least subconsciously, an opportunity to boost their happiness by taking pride in their school when such pride was appropriate. On the days when there was little to brag about athletically, the students looked for other ways to feel good about themselves. It wasn't that they were unfaithful to their school, but rather that they chose the most promising source of positivity in any given situation. In short, individualists seem to be on the lookout for happiness, paying attention to pleasure and success and able to ignore small influences that might detract from fulfillment. This is, in part, the reason that so many individualistic nations rise to the top of international happiness lists.

Valuing Happiness

Another place in which cultures differ from one another is in the value they put on emotions in general-and happiness in particular. In Western societies, paying attention to the way we feel has become second nature, as is labeling our feelings. But for people in much of the world, feelings are not as important as actions or relationships. One man we spoke to in rural Kenya had difficulty remembering how often he became angry. We tried asking him about his emotions several times. "How often have you been angry this week?" we pried. "Have you felt angry or irritated today?" we asked. He was unable to provide an answer. "I just don't know," he said. "I don't think I have been angry today or this week." Finally, we asked him whether he had ever been in a fistfight. "I was in a fistfight yesterday!" he told us. For this man, events were remembered in terms of actions rather than feelings, and he lacked the habit of labeling his inner states.

Cultures also disagree with one another over which emotions are most desirable. Folks in Western nations, for example, generally think that pride feels good and is appropriate to experience. By pride, we do not mean conceit or putting others down; rather, we mean the feeling of deep satisfaction that comes when a person can claim responsibility for a job well done. Many around the world view this emotion with some condemnation, preferring to shift responsibility, as well as credit, to the larger group. Many Amish people we spoke to during the course of our research, for instance, actively fought against taking personal credit for success in life. Instead, they would grant credit to supportive family, business partners, and God. By contrast, the Maasai often go out of their way to flaunt pride.

If Americans are a society known for our relentless positivity, then the Maasai's favorite emotion is pride. The Maasai tend to be a courageous people with a unique history, and they have much about which to be proud. Their creation myth shows a kind of favoritism common to many world religions, in which their god Ngai gave the Maasai all the cattle in the world for their keeping. (Sorry, dairy farmers in Switzerland and Wisconsin, your cows are on loan from the Maasai.) The Maasai resisted incursions by the British into their territory during the long years of European colonization, despite their obvious military disadvantage. In fact, even today, some Maasai, armed only with primitive spears and bows, execute daring nighttime cattle raids across the Kenyan-Tanzanian border, against tribes wielding modern automatic guns.

The Maasai culture is also one of pain tolerance. They practice ritual branding and adolescent circumcision. After the healing period following the circumcision ceremony, most teenage boys join a group of *morani*, or warriors, the Maasai equivalent to the National Guard. As part of their initiation ritual, the boys head into the bush and fight and kill a lion – with spears, knives, and arrows! Compare that with the rites of passage in industrialized societies – obtaining a driver's license, getting a part-time job, or moving out of mom and dad's house.

We witnessed a stunning display of bravery firsthand. During our research in East Africa, Robert had occasion to attend the circumcision of a 15-year-old boy. On the day of the joyous event, following an age-old custom, the boy went down to the river to wash himself. A half hour later, he returned to the village, wrapped in a brown cow skin decorated with lines of beads. As he drew near, he went into a trance and collapsed on the ground. The women, who stood at the edge of the cattle corral where the ceremony was to take place, screamed and cried and trilled their tongues in a high wail. The men rushed and picked up the boy and laid him on a dried cow skin in the middle of the empty corral. The collective emotion in the air was palpable. The boy appeared limp and unconscious except for the rapid rising and falling of his chest. The men of the village crowded around while his foreskin was systematically cut and peeled from his body with what appeared to be an old steak knife, while he appeared to peacefully rest on the ground. It was surreal. With blood everywhere, we were much more traumatized than the young man. Later on, the boy's father beamed. He confessed that he was extremely proud of his son for being so brave, and that bravery reflected well on the entire family.

There were many cultural differences that made conducting research with the Maasai an uphill battle. When we first arrived in the field, with our clipboards and ready ideas about happiness, the Maasai were largely uninterested. As a tribal people living in a traditional manner, they don't have a lot of time to rate satisfaction with their morality on a one-to-seven scale. Instead, their hours are full of cattle herding, home repairs, cooking, and socializing. To them, we were a naïve folk who lacked any of the basic skills they valued. We could not herd, protect ourselves from predators, build a house, or haggle effectively. The first Maasai we contacted spent more time looking at themselves in the side-view mirror of our car than at our happy-face scales.

One day, early in the research, Robert had the idea that if we participated in activities they valued, the Maasai would pay more attention to us. Not only would we bond through shared experiences, but the Maasai might think better of us. We asked if we could join them for a lion hunt, and they nearly laughed us off the savannah. The idea of *mazungus* stumbling through the bush and trying to figure out how, exactly, to throw a heavy spear while a lion attacks was almost too much for them to bear. After each person in the village took turns making funny comments about us participating in a lion hunt, our translator summed the situation up: "It would be a very good day for the lion."

A few days later, when a group of warriors visited the village, Robert admired the raised scar on the arm of one of the leaders. Many Maasai men and women have a random assortment of scars and burns, another sign of bravery. Robert casually asked if he, too, could be branded in a pain-tolerance ritual. The young warrior smiled and agreed, perhaps trying to call his bluff, and set about making a fire. When the *moran* was sufficiently pleased with the amber glow at the end of his stick, he commanded Robert to take off his shirt. The villagers crowded around and cheered as Robert was branded on his chest over and over in the same spot to make sure the wound was substantial enough to create a scar. When one spot was completed, the warrior moved the burning stick to a second and then a third site, wanting to test whether the bravery persisted even after full knowledge of the pain. In the end, Robert was burned a total of eight times. Although he did not manage the brave face that a Maasai might, neither did he scream out or flee. The ceremony definitely endeared us to the Maasai in the region. In the weeks after that episode, Maasai from other villages came to participate in the research, eager to see the burns and talk to the brave foreigner.

These stories of branding, lion hunting, and circumcising illustrate a point about one way culture can influence happiness. These episodes show how the Maasai, like everyone else, pay attention to the things they value and don't put too much stock in the things they don't. Because they are a culture of courage, honor, and pride, the Maasai spend time paying attention to personal achievements that speak well of them or reflect well on their families. They do not need expensive watches, private planes, a house in the Hamptons, or the material trappings of a modern world to achieve status and enjoy themselves. Instead, they find pleasure and status in the world that is available to them – in lion hunts, cooking, family relations, singing in the evenings, and pain rituals. This might, in part, explain their high happiness scores. They create goals and activities for themselves that are valued within their culture and that can be achieved. What's more, many of the Maasai's goals serve the purpose of enhancing their self-image and leave them feeling good, as well as preparing them mentally for life on the savannah.

Choosing Happiness

The value placed on feeling happy varies across cultures. Asians, on average, are more likely than their Western counterparts to make decisions based on factors other than happiness. For example, they are more likely to sacrifice short-term happiness in exchange for long-term mastery. Practicing scales on the piano today can be seen as a necessary evil en route to virtuoso playing later on. A clever study by Shigehiro Oishi sheds light on the ways culture can affect choices that, in turn, affect happiness.

Research participants arrived for Oishi's study and were asked to shoot some baskets in a miniature basketball hoop mounted on a door. Afterward, they were asked to complete various emotion questionnaires, and told to come back in a week. Oishi, originally from Japan, is particularly interested in cultural differences in happiness between East Asians and North Americans, and the participants in this study came from one or the other of these two groups. A week later, when the research subjects returned to the laboratory, Oishi gave them a choice: they could shoot baskets again, or they could opt for a new activity – throwing darts. Once again, they were asked to complete some surveys, and dismissed from the study. Unbeknownst to the participants, Oishi and his colleagues kept track of how many baskets each person made, and how many they missed.

In the basketball study, Oishi discovered an interesting pattern of cultural differences between Asians and Americans. Most of the Asians who performed well the first week, successfully making many baskets, chose to move on to darts the second week. The Asians who performed poorly at hoops chose to stick with basketball again the second week, in hopes of mastering the skill. If they did well at hoops, they could move on to master a new task. The North Americans, by contrast, chose to stick with basketball if they scored many baskets on week one. They wanted to do well again. If they performed poorly the first time, they opted for darts the second week, perhaps hoping a new activity might bring better luck and more fun. And although the two groups were equally happy during the first round, the Americans enjoyed their task more during the second, because those who did poorly in the first week felt free to choose a new task. According to Oishi, this pattern suggests underlying cultural values: Asians tend to seek mastery first, while Americans have a greater tendency to favor fun and feeling good.

Different Activities for Happiness

Not only do the feelings of happiness vary across cultures, but factors that create happiness vary as well. For instance, Ed Diener and Marissa Diener published a study in 1995 in which they demonstrated that self-esteem is much more important to life satisfaction in some cultures – the most individualistic ones – than in others. Similarly, the Korean professor Eunkook Suh found that Americans use positive emotions more in deciding how satisfied they are, whereas in Korea people tend to rely more heavily on the appraisals of others, and that the activities that lead to happiness also sometimes differ across cultures.

A personal anecdote should shed light on how this pans out in the real world. From the travel journal of Robert Biswas-Diener, Greenland, 2002:

> For five weeks, our research team hunkered down in the cramped weather station overlooking the sea full of airport-sized icebergs and distant islands with rugged cliffs. The sun never set while we were there, and we saw children playing outside at eight in the morning and eleven at night. During the daytime hours, we invited people to talk with us and fill out happiness questionnaires, and during the nighttime hours we tried to avoid the fistfights and howling dogs that plagued the dirt tracks that served as streets. At first, life in Qaanaaq appeared hard, full of difficult labor, strife, and a hostile environment. The locals continued to reassure us that life was pleasant, slow, and meaningful. The Inughuit appeared to be the most happy when they were engaged in traditional activities, such as hunting and fishing. They even recommended we return in the dark and chilly months of winter, when the hunting was at its best. It seemed difficult to imagine fun, meaning, and happiness in such a cold, remote place.
>
> But then we had an experience like the one the hunters described. We were finally exposed to the hidden pleasures of Arctic life. On a research foray to Siorapaluk – the northernmost community in the world – we had the opportunity to hunt for our own dinner. Hunters, farmers, and even gardeners can probably attest to how rewarding it feels to obtain your own food, but as lifelong grocery-store patrons, we had no idea. We took nets mounted on long poles and hiked into the hills outside of town. There, perched high on the scree-strewn cliffs, we hid among the boulders and waited. We anticipated the black and white auks, which flew in enormous flocks and frequently swooped close to the cliffs. Every few minutes, the thunderous drumbeat of wings came closer and thousands of birds would pass within a few meters of the rocks that concealed us. Time and again, we snapped our nets quickly into the air in the hopes of scooping an auk. We missed, laughed, and waited for another chance. We took turns with the net, seeing who might capture the most birds. It was exciting, challenging, and fun, and it was clear that there was much to enjoy in the hunting life.
>
> After two hours, we had succeeded in catching one bird each and began to descend toward the village, toward warmth, and to dinner. We bounded down the slopes, charged with testosterone and the pride of a successful hunt. We carried our birds, like trophies, by their feet. We had used human ingenuity to snatch these animals from the air.

We must have been as large as icebergs by the time we reached the edge of town. There, on the outskirts of the settlement, two children saw our catch and their jaws dropped open. We could only imagine how impressed they were to see these two foreigners, first-time hunters, come back from their successful hunt. Then, the kids started laughing. And they did not stop. Our high spirits fell some, and we continued on toward town.

As we crossed streaming glacial meltwater, we came across a local hunter, a man whom we knew from the happiness interviews and who happened to speak English. "Good!" he smiled, and gave us the thumbs-up. It felt great to be acknowledged, one hunter to another. "Be honest," we asked, "how many auks have you caught in a single day?" We knew he would have caught more than our two, of course. He thought for a moment about his answer and smiled again, shaking his head. When we prodded him he confessed, "Seven hundred." I was embarrassed, but learned a valuable lesson. Catching auks could make this Inughuit gentleman happy for many reasons – because of the pride and respect it afforded, the food for himself and his family it provided, and the enjoyment of flow created by this challenging activity at which one can continually improve with practice. For me, auk hunting was also a happy experience, if a humbling one.

Different Definitions of Feeling Happy

It turns out that people the world over experience happiness as a pleasurable and desirable state. Certain cultures, however, appear to value different aspect of happiness. As mentioned earlier, Americans tend to view happiness as an upbeat and energetic emotion, and value the high-arousal components of happiness. People in India and China, by contrast, view happiness as a state of peace and harmony, and tend to value the low-arousal aspects of happiness. How do we know this?

The Stanford psychologist Jeanne Tsai and her colleagues examined children's books in both the United States and Taiwan to see if there were differences in the way emotions were depicted. The research team analyzed the ten bestselling storybooks for preschoolers in both nations from the beginning of 2005, and another ten books that topped the bestseller list at the end of the year. They created scores for the activity levels shown in the books, how big the smiles were, and the presence or absence of other facial expressions. Tsai found that the American books generally depicted more exciting activities and more exuberant positive emotions. When queried, American pre-schoolers preferred the excited states, and perceived them as happier, compared to the Taiwanese preschoolers. What's more, when children were exposed to the American books, they then preferred to engage in more exciting activities themselves, whereas children shown the relatively calmer Taiwanese books focused on calmer activities.

In another study, Tsai found that ancient Christian classical texts emphasized high-arousal positive emotions, while Buddhist texts emphasized low-arousal pleasant feelings. Following from this, the researchers found that bestselling modern Christian self-help books emphasize more aroused emotions and that Buddhist self-help books emphasize calm and contentment. Thus, for people in Asian cultures, "happiness" means calm and controlled, whereas for Americans it is more likely to mean excited and joyful, and these differences seem to be socialized from early in life. The types of feelings and activities that are most valued differ in various cultures, and different people may find one or the other approach to happiness more attractive.

Conclusions

In an increasingly globalized world, we are left to wonder about the nature of cultural differences and similarities. Are societies growing more homogeneous, with international businesses as likely to crop up in Kansas City as Kandahar? How might cultures differ where happiness is concerned? Research from the science of happiness shows us that there are some important cultural universals in well-being, as well as some fascinating differences. Understanding what these are can help you set realistic expectations for your own happiness, and help you benefit from the wisdom of people in other cultures.

Perhaps the most consistent finding in well-being research is that most people are mildly happy, except where poverty and disruption are extreme. Rich people and poor people can both be happy, as can Canadians and Serbians, high school graduates and illiterate people. In study after study, using large samples from the far ends of the earth, the majority of people report that they are, on the whole, mildly happy, except for those who live in terrible conditions. This makes sense because happiness can give us a boost of energy and friendliness that we need to function effectively in families, at work, and in society. Not only are most people happy, but most people think that being happy is desirable, and that the experience of happiness itself is pleasurable. It doesn't matter if you live in South Korea or South Carolina: happiness feels good to everyone.

There are other apparent universals in happiness. Everywhere, people want friends and to be respected by others. Everywhere, people want to be proficient at the activities valued in that culture. In all cultures, people can find pleasure in activities that capture their interest. It is, of course, the specifics of how people achieve flow, respect, and competence that vary dramatically across the globe.

Despite the universals, there are also cultural differences. Although happiness is widely seen as pleasurable, people from different cultures define this feeling in varying ways. Folks from Asian and Pacific Rim cultures are more likely to promote calm happiness, while North Americans are more likely to value upbeat, enthusiastic, and energetic positive emotions. Thus, Asians looking for happiness are generally more likely to seek out calm, harmony-producing activities. Westerners have a tendency to seek out exciting, pleasurable experiences to produce arousing feelings of happiness. Furthermore, the cultural psychologist Shinobu Kitayama and his colleagues found that pride predicts happiness more among Americans and feelings of friendliness predict happiness more among Japanese. Thus, the positive feelings that are most prized vary across societies. The differences in what people value, how they believe they should feel, and how they go about the business of pursuing happiness depend to some extent on culture.

In the end, people around the globe are probably more similar than they are different where emotions, including happiness, are concerned. Friends and family, being able to meet basic physical needs, receiving respect, and having valued goals are important everywhere.

Postscript from Ed

After reading the chapter, you can see why Robert has been called the "Indiana Jones of psychology." Whether it is sex workers in the slums of Kolkata, peasants in southern India, the homeless in California, or the Amish, Robert has surveyed them with gusto – and often lived with them. He has gone far beyond duty in his work, and has been branded, has risked his life kayaking across glacier-strewn water to collect data, and has been harassed by police on several occasions when they were suspicious of his activities. He has eaten dinners in Amish homes and has eaten capybara (a giant rodent) and grubs in the wild. Once when we were interviewing Maasai together, a large cobra brushed his boot as it slithered by in the grass. I have had adventurous research assistants in the past, but none the equal of Robert, and for him I am very grateful – and proud.

9

Nature and Nurture: Is There a Happiness Set Point, and Can You Change It?

Nowadays many people are concerned about, if not obsessed with, their weight. Some folks are petite while others are a bit . . . ahem . . . stockier. One of the authors of this book, Ed, comes from a family of – shall we say – "big-boned individuals." These Dieners are the types of folks who are a whopping ten pounds at birth, and keep expanding through adulthood right up to three hundred pounds. At family reunions, there are no exceptionally skinny people, unless they married into the family or were adopted. The relatives are more likely to spend time shopping at the Big and Tall store rather than at Petite Sophisticate. Like many of his family members, Ed struggled with his weight, trying to stay in the same pants size year after year. He dieted and exercised, but it took a lot of effort.

Then Ed read about "weight set point" – the idea that your genetics are the major determinant of your weight. Some lucky people are born to be thin and others are born to be heavier. With this idea in mind, Ed set about trying to discover his personal weight set point. He ate whatever he wanted, whenever he wanted, and in whatever quantity he wanted. He ate salads, pie, steak, pasta, mustard, ice cream, bread, Chinese and Mexican food, and anything that happened to be appealing. And then some more. Being a carnivore, he avoided vegetables. After all, this gastronomic adventure was his genetic code ringing the dinner bell. During the year of this culinary experiment, Ed gained a pound a week, and ballooned from 208 pounds to 260 pounds! Figure 9.1, below, shows Ed's projected weight, had he not made the very sensible decision to stop the set point experiment.

Ed continued to put on pounds, and there seemed to be no end in sight. His pants, which a tailor had let out, were getting very tight,

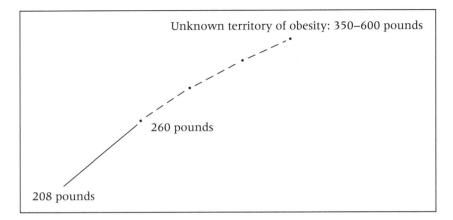

Unknown territory of obesity: 350–600 pounds

260 pounds

208 pounds

Figure 9.1   Ed's weight

and he was worried that he would have to buy a larger bed. Ed took a new tack. He changed his diet and began exercising again, and in two short years he was able to drop back down to his pre-experiment weight, so that he no longer had to wear pants with elastic waistbands.

Although you should not try to follow in Ed's footsteps and divine your own weight set point by eating cookies and hamburgers at midnight, there may be an element of truth to the idea of a genetic influence on weight. Certainly, people are born with natural predispositions toward body type, and you can see that some families are muscular, others are lithe, and still others are round. There is some leeway – dictated by diet, exercise, and life circumstances – in how much you weigh, but there are some absolute limits you cannot cross no matter how hard you try. You will never, for instance, weigh as little as an infant or as much as a Volkswagen. Happiness works in much the same way. For years researchers have theorized that there is a happiness set point, some genetically determined level of positivity. No doubt you have heard of the genetic links to depression and how mood disorders are, in part, inherited. Just as our DNA holds the key to a predisposition to sadness and anxiety, scientists have been fascinated by the possibility that there is also a genetic code for happiness. In fact, there are data to support this notion, and the idea of a happiness set point is in vogue.

You can see emotional set points all around you. When you attend your twenty-year high school reunion, your old classmates seem about

146

as happy as they were back when you walked the hallways together. That enthusiastic, upbeat girl you once had a crush on may have dyed her hair, but she is likely just as positive decades later. And those melancholy kids who lurked in the social shadows tend to grow up to be reserved adults. Even though the lives of your former class-mates are very different – they make more money, enjoy the freedoms and responsibilities of adulthood, have children, own a home, work full time, and take vacations – the emotions of your high school alumni are usually about the same as they were back when you were students.

The idea of a happiness set point is immensely important because it raises so many questions about the pursuit of happiness. If our smiles and optimism are simply a part of our natural physiology, then why should we waste the effort to try to achieve more happiness? Is a genetic basis to happiness a type of emotional fate that none of us can escape? It makes sense to stop and ask whether happiness is genetic-ally determined so that it can resist even our best attempts to live a rosier emotional life.

The Minnesota Twins and Genetic Happiness

Minneapolis, Minnesota, is famous for twins. Minneapolis itself is a twin city, sidled up as it is with its sister, St. Paul. Also, the local professional baseball team is called the Twins, and the sidewalks and cafés of the city are full of hats and sweatshirts emblazoned with this single word. But there is another group of twins, perhaps less well known, but certainly no less important. A group of researchers at the University of Minnesota was able, over several decades, to locate and study a large group of twins – some of whom were separated at birth and raised in different households. The twins raised apart offer crucial insights into human nature because they help to answer the difficult question of how much of our personality is the result of life cir-cumstances and how much is the product of genetic inheritance. The researchers studied monozygotic (identical) twins, those who share virtually all of their genes in common, and dizygotic (fraternal) twins, who share about half of their genes. By looking at twins who shared different amounts of genes, as well as similar or different family environments during their upbringing, the researchers were able to identify how much happiness is inborn.

You may have come across interesting stories about how similar identical twins can be. You may have read accounts of shared hobbies, dressing alike, and even spooky instances of being able to feel each other's pain. You may have heard how even twins who grew up apart marry people with the same name, and wear the same jewelry. We have twin daughters in our family, and it is truly surprising how similar they can be. Not only do they look alike, but they both chose to enter the same profession, both married men named Frank, and often send each other and their parents the exact same birthday cards. When they took classes together in school, they received nearly identical grades on all tests and assignments. Although these examples are possibly just coincidences, compelling data indicate that twins are, in fact, similar in many ways. For instance, twins show impressive similarity on standardized tests of personality, intelligence, and emotion, which cannot be due to coincidence.

The research team in Minnesota found a number of striking findings in their study of twins. They found genetic links to a variety of surprising behaviors, ranging from church attendance to a preference for recreational hunting! But some of the most compelling data concerned the twins' emotions. The genetic factor turned out to be so powerful that the identical twins who were raised in different households were more similar in their emotions than were fraternal twins who were raised together! If one identical twin was generally positive, the researchers found that there was a high likelihood that the sibling on the other side of the country would be as well. These findings point to the importance of genes in how happy we are, and other researchers have replicated this finding. For example, a Danish team used twins as participants in their research to analyze how variable happiness is over time. They were interested in how much people's moods naturally bounce up and fall down from their own personal happiness average. The Danish researchers estimated that about a quarter of variability in happiness is based on direct genetic factors.

Additional support for a genetic link to happiness comes from the study of personality. Take the example of personality types, which have been shown to be substantially inherited. Some folks are natural social butterflies and others are wallflowers. Some people are imperturbable while others are hotheaded. Two personality factors that have received focused research attention are extroversion and neuroticism. Extroverts are reward-seeking, sociable people, while neurotics are more prone to worry, guilt, and sadness. Neurotic people, almost by definition, score lower on measures of happiness. The research psychologist Richard Lucas has studied personality and emotion and concluded that, in cultures around the world, extroverts tend to experience more positive feelings, as though they are prone to this by biology. Even in controlled confines of laboratory studies, researchers find that extroverts tend to report more positive reactions to experimental stimuli, but mostly they are just a bit happier even when they arrive at the lab. It is not that introverts are unhappy – many of them are happy – it's just that, on average, they feel fewer positive emotions, and feel them less intensely than extroverts.

If your happiness is, in part, a product of your genes, it makes sense to ask what is happening at the biological level that affects your positivity. Neuroscientists, physiologists, and other researchers are beginning to identify specific genes that can influence good moods. For example, a research team at London's King's College followed kids over the course of many years from childhood to adulthood. The scientists tracked the kids' DNA, as well as their life circumstances and social backgrounds. The researchers were able to isolate a single gene, 5-HTP, and identified one of the variations of this gene as a factor in depression. The gene influences how serotonin – a neurotransmitter – is processed by the brain. Serotonin is the same brain chemical that is acted upon by common antidepressants, such as Prozac. Completing the scientific loop, researchers have shown that people with the specific allele of the 5-HTP gene react more in emotional areas of the brain, such as the amygdala, when they are shown disturbing pictures, and ruminate more in response to stress. Thus, one likely reason that there is a substantial influence of your genetic blueprint on your happiness is that genes influence how the brain processes mood-related hormones in emotion areas of the brain.

There is a connection between our DNA and our levels of happiness, and we even have some insight into the specific mechanisms of that connection, such as 5-HTP. How strong is the relationship of genes to happiness? Does your genetic code entirely determine your happiness? How much of your well-being can be chalked up to chance factors and your personal choices? The Danish research team gave an estimate of 22 percent, while the Minnesota team says as much as 50 percent of happiness could be inborn. You may have heard these types of percentages thrown around by experts talking about the nature versus nurture debate. One common story is that about half of our moods, choices, values, and behaviors are due to environmental influences, and half can be chalked up to genetic inheritance.

The truth is, there is no easy way to give a simple percentage when talking about what makes humans feel, think, and act the way they do. In the London study, the 5-HTP gene and a difficult environment were needed in combination to produce depression. To complicate matters further, life circumstances (nurture) and genetics (nature) affect one another. If you inherit your grandfather's foul temper, your father's good looks, or your mother's fantastic memory, these inborn qualities will influence your relationships, job, education, and interactions with strangers. On the other hand, our environment can also affect our genes. The emerging field of epigenetics shows that the expression of our DNA codes is affected by our environments in producing who we are.

Some specific genes only get expressed under the right environmental circumstances; otherwise they lie dormant. In a study of mice, for example, exposure to toxins during pregnancy affected not only the fertility rates of male offspring, but also their descendants down through four generations. In one study of life satisfaction, genes predicted more about the happiness of rich people, whereas for poor people, variations in environment had a bigger influence. If the impact of the environment varies depending on life circumstances, then the percent due to genetics also varies. Thus, genes and environments interact to affect important bodily processes, including those related to happiness. It is not possible to pin a universal percentage on genetic influences, because genes and environment influence each other, with the environment sometimes switching on or off the expression of particular genes. Although there is no such thing as a true number indicating the amount of happiness due to genes, we can say with confidence that both genes and environment are important.

Despite the exact figures or proportions, it is still important to understand the extent to which genetics matters to happiness. Genes do seem to be a powerful influence on emotion, but surely, there must be limits to the power of our DNA. After all, even a happy temperament can be unhappy in a bad situation. Even the most naturally upbeat person can get irritated over an insult, disappointed when her team loses the World Cup, or sad when his child has an emergency appendectomy. So why aren't people in terrible neighborhoods chronically depressed and people in the affluent suburbs routinely positive? The answer lies in the amazing human capacity for adaptation.

Adaptation: The Force Pulling Us Back to Baseline

Chris Ware, the creator of the popular *Jimmy Corrigan* comic series, has a superpower. Or at least he thinks he does. Ware, who was interviewed on the Chicago-based radio show *This American Life*, admitted that when he was a kid, he desperately wanted to be a superhero, and was vigilant for signs of developing powers, such as flight or invisibility. Then, one day, his dream came true. He was taking a shower in warm water, and noticed that, as the shower continued, he was able to turn the handle and make the water hotter and hotter. He was amazed to see, by the end of the shower, that he could withstand even the hottest temperatures. He appeared to be nearly invulnerable, able to withstand even scorching heat. He was delighted!

Of course, you and I (and hopefully, Chris) know that there was nothing extraordinary about that shower. The hot water simply ran down while Ware's body adjusted to the warmer temperatures. The same process happens in the first few minutes in a swimming pool, which can feel torturously cold at first, but later feels fine. Happiness works in much the same way. People are built with the natural ability to adapt to new levels of joy. All of us can experience the emotional highs that come with buying a new car or reading a child's outstanding report card, and each of us is familiar with the emotional troughs that come with chronic illness, remodeling the house, or getting arrested (okay, well maybe only a few of us are familiar with getting arrested). But ask yourself: Why don't you stay that way? Why aren't you as happy today as you were on the day of your promotion at work, or as sad as you were on the day your grandmother died? It is not simply because new events – both happy and sad – have occurred in your life. It is because you adapt to the new conditions over time. This is why so many folks seek out novel experiences, look forward to a change of pace, or develop new goals once old ones have been met. We tend to react to changes, and then quickly adjust to the new circumstances.

The influence of adaptation on happiness was identified by well-being researchers in the 1970s. In their classic article on the subject, Phillip Brickman and his colleagues suggested that most people experience "hedonic" neutrality over the years, with only occasional emotional spikes and valleys. That is, with the exception of a few potent events that temporarily raise and lower happiness, people tend to be relatively even-keeled where happiness is concerned. Tough times bring us down and joyous occasions are uplifting, but we quickly adapt to both.

This means, in essence, that people who try to make themselves really happy – those folks who chase excitement in relationships, a big paycheck at work, and intense thrills in their leisure time – are a bit like rats on a treadmill, running and running, but not really getting anywhere. You probably know people like this. These are the kind of people who thrive on pressing deadlines, social crises, constant novelty, and thrill seeking. The problem is that pay raises, new lovers, new jewelry, and new jobs can all seem exciting and rewarding at first, but over time you adjust, and their emotional luster dims. What was once thrilling eventually seems no more than mildly pleasant. Brickman called this phenomenon – the idea that people can chase emotional highs but adaptation will drag them back to a neutral mood – the "hedonic treadmill."

When they first introduced their theory of the hedonic treadmill, Brickman and his colleagues thought that people adjust back to neutral, emotionally speaking. Later research showed that this was not the case. Closer to the truth is that people adapt idiosyncratically, with each individual adjusting back to a unique set point. Some folks are exuberant extroverts and others are more morose. Most of our set points are somewhere in the mildly positive range, and this is the place to which we will naturally return when there are no extraordinarily positive or negative events taking place in our lives. Mildly pleasant happiness is like our resting heart rate or blood pressure. This makes good evolutionary sense. Mild feelings of positivity give us just the boost we need to be motivated, seek out friends, take appropriate risks, and persevere at difficult tasks. But seeking out the Shangrila of continual intense happiness is a prospect doomed by adaptation.

Individual genetic emotional set points and the potent process of adaptation can be so powerful that they are able to temper even very strong positive events. Several years ago, our friend Daniel Kahneman won the Nobel Prize in Economics, an incredibly celebrated award. In the wake of the Nobel awards ceremony in Sweden, Danny – like all Nobel laureates – received intense media attention, attractive offers for book contracts, and honorary doctoral degrees from prestigious universities around the world. It was, as you might imagine, a rush, the type of career high point all of us envy and only very few achieve. How long do you think this period of intense euphoria lasted? When we asked Danny about the duration of the emotional glow of the Nobel Prize, he confided that it was good fun for about a year, primarily because of all the social invitations, and then it was back to business as usual in his research laboratory at Princeton.

What about adaptation to circumstances that are even better than winning the Nobel Prize? What could be better than winning the world's most prestigious award, you ask? How about recovering from cancer? In one mood-related study we conducted in Illinois, research participants completed daily mood questionnaires over the span of several months. We happened to collect happiness data from a 21-year-old student, whom we will call Henry, during eighty of the most important days of his life. Henry was afflicted with Hodgkin's disease. As chance would have it, we collected happiness data from Henry while he was being treated for cancer, on the day he learned that the treatment was effective in wiping out his cancer, and in the days that followed. Picture how overjoyed you would be if you learned that your cancer was in full remission! Imagine what a profound and life-changing event that would be. Wouldn't people after recovering from cancer have a new lease on life, a new ability to experience intensely in the moment? We show Henry's happiness data in figure 9.2.

As you can clearly see from the figure, Henry's moods fluctuated daily, sometimes bouncing into joyous feelings and sometimes spilling

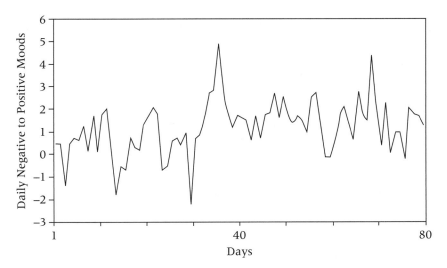

Figure 9.2 Henry's happiness

into the blues. And then, almost halfway through the study, Henry received the news that his latest treatments had been successful, and that the cancer was, for all intents and purposes, gone. As you can see, and as you might expect, Henry showed a huge spike in happiness on that day, day 38. What is far more surprising is that Henry's happiness quickly dropped back to his mildly happy average. In Henry's case, adaptation was so strong that the euphoria of beating cancer lasted only a day or two! Of course, there were some happiness benefits for this lucky young man. You can see that during the remainder of the study Henry had many fewer days of sadness, so that his overall happiness average went up some. Henry's case provides an emotionally moving illustration of the power of adaptation.

At first glance, Henry's story can be alarming. Adaptation sounds like a helpful process, but how good can it be if it does not let us bask for a while in the glow of recovering from cancer? What function might adaptation serve if it keeps you from enjoying your Nobel Prize, your health, or your other life successes? Adaptation has a remarkable upside. Just as it acts as an emotional ceiling that keeps us from experiencing nonstop joy, it also protects us from being dragged into emotional pits. When we fall on tough times, adaptation is there like a trusted friend to make sure the negative feelings don't last forever.

The two-directional nature of adaptation can be easily seen in the case of marriage. In one study, we were interested in how happy people are across the span of their marriages. This is a tough question to answer. We needed to gather data by the wheelbarrow, essentially asking the same people how happy they were, over and over, year after year. In this way we were able to chart people's emotional highs and lows over the course of their relationships. We could use this information to look at their happiness before they were married, when they married, a year after they were married, and years later. Fortunately, we were able to obtain exactly these kinds of data from Germany, where they had been tracking this type of information for over two decades. We obtained twenty-one years of happiness data on thousands of people, and you can see the results in figure 9.3.

Figure 9.3 shows the life satisfaction over the years of a group who married during the study, and of another group who divorced during the study. The top line is the life satisfaction of those who got married, at year 0. The figure shows that people were, on average, pretty satisfied with their lives, but became more so in the year or two

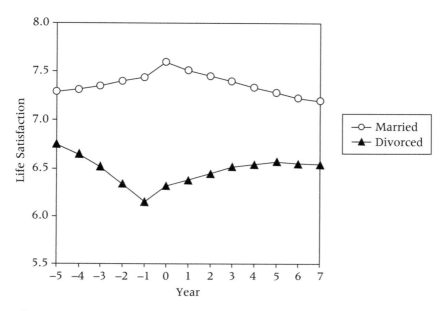

Figure 9.3 Marriage and divorce

before their wedding. Perhaps they had finally found that special some-one and were enjoying the flirting, infatuation, and anticipation of their new, serious relationship. Then, in the year of their marriages, the Germans had a peak in satisfaction. They had finally found their mate, and it was a time of family gatherings, intense support from friends, and celebration. Even in the year after the wedding – think of all those gifts, the honeymoon, the new apartment, the joint bank account – people still enjoyed elevated levels of satisfaction. But then, if you look at the years after their marriage in the figure, you can see that the Germans dropped to their earlier prewedding levels of satisfaction. The data provide clear evidence of adaptation. In short, falling in love and getting married pay off emotionally, but kick out dividends for only so long.

You can also observe the protective side of adaptation in this figure. The bottom line shows the life satisfaction of those who divorced, again shown at year 0. You can see that the years leading up to the divorce were tough, with each successive year being accompanied by a further drop in satisfaction. This makes sense: you can probably imagine the arguing, yelling, periods of silence, frustration, and fuming.

It is easy to picture the marriage growing worse by the year, with communication difficulties, and anger slowly driving the couples apart. Then, during the year of the divorce itself, the couples were at their well-being low point. Splitting up takes a heavy emotional toll, and the stress of losing a lover, moving, wrangling over custody of the children, and dividing assets can be particularly unpleasant.

You can also see that as quickly as a year after the divorce, people's life satisfaction levels began to climb. They did not shoot quickly back up, but over the course of the years following the split, the people in the study became more and more satisfied. Perhaps they began enjoying the freedoms of singlehood, felt relieved at being out of such intense conflict, began dating and forging new lives for themselves. In short, they began to adjust. Adaptation, even to tough times, helped them to dig themselves out of an emotional hole and enjoy life again.

Perhaps the most amazing illustration of adaptation and positive coping is among survivors of the Holocaust. Israeli psychologists studied several groups of Holocaust survivors, individuals who had undergone terrible experiences in Nazi Germany and had frequently lost some or all of their families. They found that many of the survivors had high subjective well-being. For example, many of the survivors reported high levels of positive emotions. The study was many decades after the Holocaust, and we don't know how long it took the survivors to cope and adapt. Nonetheless, many of the survivors were quite happy and obviously resilient. Rather than allowing themselves to be lifelong victims of the Nazis, they rebounded to create positive, happy lives for themselves. They should be a model of positive coping for all of us!

Limits to Adaptation and Set Point Change

If you have ever read a book on happiness or come across a magazine article or television show on the topic, then you may have already heard about this protective aspect of adaptation. The popular media are full of uplifting stories about cancer patients, divorcees, and other star-crossed folks who have courageously overcome misfortune to return to their former high levels of wellbeing. Take, for instance, the common yarn about people who have handicaps. According to this often-told story, people who suffer from serious spinal cord injuries – severe enough to leave them wheelchair-bound – bounce back emotionally. Not only do paraplegics adjust to their new circumstances, according to the legend, but they also adapt back to pre-accident levels of happiness within two months! Who wouldn't want to hear a comforting story like that? The rapid and complete adaptation of spinal cord injury victims is like a psychological insurance policy for the rest of us, in case we ever suffer a terrible accident.

Unfortunately, as inspiring as the tale is, the rapid emotional recovery of spinal cord injury victims may be exaggerated in the popular imagination. There is a kernel of truth here, in that a famous study was conducted in which the researchers found that injury victims were less unhappy than expected, and that they actually scored in the positive range on a measure of pleasures of everyday life (like enjoying eating breakfast). And in another study, accident victims showed more happiness than specific negative emotions by eight weeks after injury. However, research shows there is more to adaptation than meets the eye. Just as there are some folks who adapt better than others, and there are conditions we adapt to better than others, there are limits to adaptation. There are instances to which we do not adapt completely. On the positive side, we may not adapt that much to sexual pleasure – the thousandth time can still be very good. On the negative side, loud music is a condition that is tough to adjust to, as any parent of a teenager can attest. This is why police tactical teams sometimes blare rock and roll music during hostage situations. People living in the landing paths of major airports often don't seem to completely adapt to the noise.

One study looking at the happiness of sex workers in Detroit found that these women were extremely dissatisfied with their lives. In fact, the health issues, social stigma, drug use, violence, and other problems for women living on the street are so severe that the sex workers were among the least happy people ever studied. They probably had adapted to their terrible conditions to some extent, but they were still very dissatisfied.

As for those inspiring cases of spinal cord injury victims who bounced back heroically, the psychologist Richard Lucas analyzed the happiness levels of individuals with disabilities in huge British and German samples, and found that not only do people take an emotional hit around the time of their severe disability, but their life satisfaction tends to stay lower than before. In fact, people with 100 percent disability, those that are severely challenged and unable to work at all, had little emotional recovery. This does not mean that disabled people are doomed to a life of misery. Certainly, many individuals who suffer through painful injuries and long periods of rehabilitation resume lives rich with meaning and rewarding relationships. In fact, for anyone who has gone to dinner with a friend with a disability or had the pleasure of watching wheelchair athletes compete, it is obvious how full their lives can be. But the statistical averages suggest that severe disability is an extreme life circumstance that is difficult to fully adapt to for the average person. People with disabilities very often reach a positive state again, although usually it is not quite as satisfying as before. Despite the widespread capacity for adjustment, adaptation is not a process that completely frees us from our circumstances.

The idea of a limit to adaptation is important, but perhaps not as important as the recent findings about set point. Exciting new evidence suggests that the happiness set point can change! Genetically determined happiness and adaptation need not be an emotional cage from which there is no hope of escape. Increasingly, research on genetics is showing that our DNA is not akin to an inherited fate, but rather gives us a range of possibilities. For example, differences in intelligence are partly inherited, but IQ scores have gone up as schooling became universal and nutrition improved. Where happiness is concerned, there is now the prospect of increasing your inborn tendency for happiness. Of course, it is not usually possible to turn natural worriers into carefree adventurers, but small to moderate changes are certainly possible.

Some of the fascinating new evidence for set point change comes from the huge German sample used to evaluate marital happiness, as well as thousands of British citizens studied over fourteen years. Over the course of the research, the happiness of most people remained fairly stable – their positivity would bounce up or fall down in reaction to life events, but not change much for long from its earlier levels. Despite the year-to-year fluctuations in happiness that are familiar to all of us, most folks showed a fairly consistent average level of happiness over time. However, the happiness of about one-fourth of the people did change. Their levels of happiness changed significantly and substantially from the first five years to the last five years. That is, their emotional set point actually moved. Why might this be the case? What is so unique or special about this group? What might have happened in their lives that can provide us with lessons about changing our own happiness?

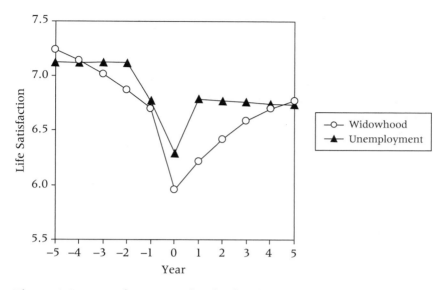

Figure 9.4 Unemployment and widowhood

Careful analyses reveal that some powerful events can change our baselines. Not only did some of the participants in the study get married and divorced over the course of the research, but some of them also lost their jobs or their spouses. You can see the data on unemployment and widowhood in figure 9.4. Look at unemployment first. No one likes to get fired from a job, and the process of unsuccessfully searching for work can be just as disheartening. As you can see in the figure, people who are about to lose their jobs experience a drop in life satisfaction. Perhaps they know that layoffs are looming on the horizon, or maybe they are aware of their own poor performance on the job. In any event, their satisfaction bottoms out at the time they lose their job.

The unfortunate folks who lose their jobs adapt somewhat to their new circumstances, in that their happiness climbs during the post-unemployment period. But the adaptation is not complete, perhaps because there is a cascade of bad events after losing one's job, such as marital discord and loss of friends. Sad to say, there was a kind of "emotional scarring," in that the people in this sample did not fully return to their preunemployment levels of happiness. Even after they found a new job and earned almost the same income as before, they were lower in life satisfaction – perhaps because of the feelings of insecurity and the blow to self-esteem they experienced from their layoff. Of course, these are broad averages, and not everyone will react to unemployment in the same way. Other factors, such as the length of unemployment, almost certainly also play a role in how adversely it will affect an individual. Regardless of individual variation, however, unemployment is one instance of an event that can actually change the happiness set point of some people.

The case of widowhood presents another illustration of a possible change in emotional baseline. Figure 9.4 clearly shows how people's life satisfaction falls over time, presumably mirroring their spouse's declining health. Then, in the year the spouse passes away, there is a precipitous drop in happiness. This is, of course, more than understandable. We invest so much in our beloved partners that the loss can be traumatic and overwhelming. As with divorce and unemployment, the process of adaptation kicks in as the bereaved begin the slow process of learning to live life without their spouses. You can see that widows, who make up most of the sample, do grow more satisfied as times goes on, but adjustment takes a long time in the case of widowhood. Even five years later, most spouses have not completely returned to their former levels of life satisfaction. In fact, on average, it takes eight years to regain those old feelings of well-being! It is still important to recognize, however, that on average even the unemployed and widowed were in the slightly satisfied zone, about the neutral midpoint of the scale.

Although these findings may appear to be a bit depressing, there is good news as well. For one thing, it is essential to remember that the life satisfaction scores of the unemployed and widowed are still above neutral in the satisfied zone, even though they are lower than before. Furthermore, it is important to understand that the happiness set point can be raised as well as lowered. Some of the most compelling evidence for this comes from the medical treatment of depression. For folks who suffer from the guilt, lethargy, sadness, and hopelessness of depression, it can be heartening to remember that there are a number of effective treatments.

Several types of psychotherapy have been shown to work well for many people, and, of course, there are psychopharmacological treatments. Antidepressant medication isn't big business just because of widespread marketing; the use of medications can be effective. Recent research has shown that many folks who take certain types of depression-fighting medications, such as those that affect the way that the brain processes serotonin and norepinephrine, and simultaneously receive "talking therapy" can experience long-term gains in well-being even after they quit taking the pills. Although every detail of the mechanisms by which antidepressants work is not known, it is possible that their use causes structural changes in neural networks and neuro-transmitter processing.

Chronically engaging in pleasurable activities, surrounding yourself with upbeat friends, and experiencing successes at work can result in gains in your happiness baseline. As noted in chapter 3, some individuals end up happier after marriage than they were before, even after adaptation takes place. While everyone experiences the occasional tiff with a spouse or frustrating day at the office, people who regularly have successes may find that positivity begets more positivity. Initial research shows that people can become more optimistic, hardier, and even happier over time.

New brain imaging technologies, the mapping of the human genome, and other recent advances have led to increased understanding about how genes and physiology affect our feelings, decisions, and behaviors. The case of happiness is no exception. We have progressed from ancient accounts of bodily humors and laypersons' guesses about the causes of happiness to an understanding of the complex ways in which our inborn temperaments do, and do not, affect our happiness. We now know, for instance, that our DNA does play an important role in our happiness. At the physiological level, your genetic code determines how your brain uses hormones that are vital to a positive outlook on life. We know that certain environmental factors, such as nutrition, can also affect our moods. Our findings about the happiness set point provide several fascinating insights into some of the processes that underlie happiness.

The Natural Process of Adaptation is a Vital Component of Psychological Wealth

Adaptation is the psychological mechanism that is responsible for governing the emotional baseline. Adjusting to new circumstances allows us to learn new skills, tolerate change, and seek improvement. Adaptation also acts as a buffer against the bad events in our lives, and prevents us from permanently succumbing to negativity. It is intuitively obvious that adaptation to tough times is desirable, but what about the usefulness of adapting to good times? Even this serves an important function. Returning to our mildly pleasant baseline allows us the room to experience the emotional highs and euphoria of exceptional events when they come along. If we did not have some room for growth in happiness, we would not care about personal growth, new goals, or exciting surprises. Adaptation is the reason you feel particularly great when your daughter graduates from college, instead of experiencing it as just another good day. Psychological wealth includes the ability to cope with bad events, but many fail to realize that it also means understanding that continual euphoria is not a desirable goal.

The Set Point Can Change

The happiness set point is not really a set point at all, but a "set range." Although there are genetic influences on our happiness, with some fortunate folks being born a bit happier than others, change is possible for all people. Like losing weight, lasting emotional change requires sustained effort to modify the ways you think and behave. In addition, if your circumstances improve substantially – such as benefiting from newfound social support or experiencing financial security for the first time – you can probably raise your well-being. Even for some of the folks who seem to have such a low set point that they require medications or therapy, treatment can usually be effective.

Conclusions

In the end, you cannot blame your current level of happiness on your parents and the genes they passed along to you. Yes, emotions – like intelligence, height, and weight – have a genetic component. But just as you can use your intelligence in different ways, for example to invent new life-saving medical technologies or to remember every telephone number of every girlfriend you ever dated, there are also choices you can make and habits you can form that will raise or lower your happiness. Thinking positively, surrounding yourself with upbeat friends, and not giving in to pessimistic thinking are all strategies that can temper a depressive disposition or enhance a happy one. In the following chapters, we will examine how to make better decisions about your happiness and avoid common "happiness forecasting" errors. Later, we will describe the mental strategies that can raise your happiness.

Although adaptation to certain powerful circumstances is often not complete, we do adapt to some degree to virtually all circumstances. You must learn to use the natural tendency toward adaptation to your advantage – to maximize feelings of well-being, but also to accomplish your goals. If you can think ahead to your future circumstances, and understand to which events and transitions you will easily adapt, it can help you plan goals and take appropriate risks. If, for instance, you are the type of person who does not need intense stability, you can likely predict that a move to a new city, while difficult, will be something you can handle psychologically. Instead of focusing on the tough aspects of the move, you can look down the emotional road and reassure yourself that in several months your new town will feel like home. Similarly, it will be helpful to identify areas that are tough for you to get used to. Each of us can adapt to certain types of changes more easily than to others.

Even if you fall on hard times, and even the luckiest of us do occasionally, you will be able to anticipate coping strategies, such as learning a new skill, meeting new people, using humor and prayer, and surrounding yourself with supportive friends, which will likely help you bounce back quicker than you otherwise would. For people who struggle through the pain of a divorce and similar negative events, it is helpful to understand that adaptation will occur, and there are personal coping strategies that can help the transition be more successful. In the darkest days of her bereavement, the author Joan Didion found hope in our findings that things do slowly get better for widows.

In a way, the scientific findings on adaptation are the best of all worlds. We can take heart in the knowledge that we can cope and adapt to even bad events, at least over time. We suffer pain when things go bad, and this can help us adjust and grow, but adapting back to normal and not staying chronically unhappy is the goal. We also adapt to life's better moments. At first, it might seem unfortunate to adapt to good things, but this is what allows us to continue growing, to react afresh to new rewards, and to develop new goals. When very good circumstances in our lives occur, such as a wonderful marriage, our life satisfaction can increase, even after the initial high is over. But our life satisfaction is unlikely to increase to perfection because we want other goals and future events to be rewarding – we do not want to remain in a euphoric state. People who seek ongoing ecstasy are impoverished in a psychological sense because they are chasing the impossible, often with behaviors that are destructive.

Although continuous euphoria is not the goal, raising your set point will be a desirable goal for many readers. The search is on, both for you and for scientists, to seek out those things that don't just produce temporary increases in happiness, but can actually raise your emotional set point. It is also important to set realistic expectations about adapting to emotional highs. You must realize that occasional euphoria and intense happiness, while enjoyable, will not last. You profit from these occasional emotional spikes that come with successes, but don't lament the fact that these states are temporary. Adaptation to both good and bad events is part of our psychological wealth because it helps us move forward in life. To be stuck in either a depressed or euphoric world would be detrimental because we could not function well. Thus, people who adapt to some degree, even to good events, are psychologically wealthier than those who do not.

10

Our Crystal Balls: Happiness Forecasting

We all would like to know the future. For as long as humans have roamed the planet and for as long as we will remain here, we will be – to some extent – preoccupied with the future. We are curious to know if the dinner party will go well, if our mothers will like their birthday presents, which stocks will perform well, and whether our flights will arrive on time.

By trying to gather information and speculate with acumen about things to come, we maximize our chances of achieving our goals, whether they are making a connecting flight or being promoted to sales manager. If the future doesn't pique your curiosity, nothing will. Unfortunately, the future remains, at best, a guessing game – one that has gone on since humans developed an advanced brain with a frontal cortex capable of thinking about tomorrow. Our pets pretty much live in the here and now, but we spend a lot of time contemplating what's ahead.

Humans have long employed experts – like weather forecasters – in predicting the future. The Hebrews had prophets, the ancient Greeks had soothsayers and oracles, European kings were served by astrologers and wise men, and powerful generals had their strategists. In each instance, people in these specialized crafts tried to gather information and cobble together some good guesses about what might happen tomorrow, next week, or further down the road. They tried to predict the likely outcomes of battles, the course of illnesses, the end of a risky journey, or the fate of a people.

Even in modern times, we turn to pollsters, financial analysts, and economists to know what might happen in the future. While we might not have an actual crystal ball telling us what will happen to us, we often go about our lives as if we did. We make decisions all the time based on what we think will happen. We choose jobs, boyfriends, and homes all because we can, to some degree, imagine how these will work out for us in months or years to come.

How do we do at predicting what will make us happy? Over time, we become experts at our own emotions, and are able not only to experience our current moods, but to predict how we might feel in the future. We are good at guessing the valence, or direction, of our emotions. That is, we can accurately predict when we will feel generally good, and when we will feel rotten. We don't need to be tortured to know that it will be unpleasant, and you probably need little convincing that sex tomorrow would be pleasurable. The same holds true for other feelings. It is a good bet that you will feel proud on the day your daughter graduates from law school, and that you will feel sad on the day you learn your father has passed away. These predictions, which often occur subconsciously, are important because they factor into the decisions we make. They are part of the mental algebra of buying a new home or deciding to marry.

How accurate are we at making emotional predictions? Well, if you were a worker at a carnival, and predicting your happiness was like guessing everyone's weight, you would be pretty darn good at it. Sure, you might purposefully overestimate the men's weight by an average of nine pounds, and underestimate the women's by fourteen, but you would still be in the close vicinity of the correct weights. In fact, it is important, from a functional point of view, that people are good at knowing what will make them happy and what will make them feel sad or afraid. If we couldn't rely at all on our emotional foresight, our feelings would lose much of their usefulness to us.

At this point, you may be asking yourself, "If folks are so good at predicting how we are going to feel in the future, how come so many people end up regretting poor choices?" It is easy to call to mind a friend who is dating a guy who clearly makes her unhappy, or a nephew who accepted an offer to a prestigious university only to find himself miserable midway through winter term. Our lives and those of our friends are replete with stories of bad decisions, instances of self-perpetrated unhappiness, and I-should-have-known-betters. People sometimes choose jobs they hate and buy homes they can't afford. Is it just a matter of ignoring the emotional warning signs? Is it a case of their emotional tracking systems being broken?

The ability of people to try to predict how they will feel in the future is called happiness forecasting, and research on the topic shows that folks make some fascinating, and predictable, mistakes when guessing their own feelings. For instance, the psychologists Daniel Gilbert and Tim Wilson conducted a study in which they asked young professors to predict how obtaining tenure or not might affect them emotionally. As you might expect, the young professors reported that they would feel elated if they were awarded tenure and would feel crushed if it were denied to them. Interestingly, this is not what Gilbert and Wilson found to be true once tenure decisions were actually made. Those who received tenure felt relieved and excited for a short time, but they soon adjusted and it was business as usual. Those unfortunate professors who did not receive tenure felt a stab of emotional pain, but it was much less painful than they expected. Thus, they were able to predict in the correct direction – receiving tenure would be pleasant and being denied tenure would be unpleasant – but they incorrectly predicted the duration and intensity of these feelings.

New research on happiness forecasting is showing results similar to Gilbert and Wilson's. There is now evidence that it is not only newly minted university professors who make affective forecasting errors, but that the phenomenon is widespread. For instance, researchers found that people incorrectly predicted the extent to which they will experience distress when learning the results of their HIV tests, with people believing a positive result would be emotionally devastating and a negative result would be like a new emotional lease on life. It was found that people consistently overestimated the impact both for the pleasant and unpleasant outcomes. That is, people predicted they would be in greater distress five weeks after learning they were HIV-positive than those who got positive results actually were. This is not to say that those unfortunate people who acquired HIV were not upset. Of course they were. Rather, it is testimony to the ability to adapt that they were not as upset as we would expect.

The good news is that researchers have discovered an easily identifiable set of reasons why people make happiness forecasting errors. We now understand a lot about the way people think, arrive at judgments, and make decisions, and we know where individuals systematically go wrong in their mental calculus. After you read this chapter, you should know where you are likely to go wrong in anticipating your own happiness, and correct the thinking errors to which you are likely to fall victim.

Reasons People Incorrectly Predict Their Future Happiness

The human mind is built to think efficiently. We are able to make very quick and accurate judgments about the speed of oncoming traffic, how threatening we think a stranger is, and how much we like the teacher of our evening class. The capacity to make judgments and identify personal preferences helps us survive and function in a complex world. Take the example of assumptions. Common wisdom tells us that assumptions are presumptuous and mistaken. The fact is, just the reverse is true. All of us make hundreds, if not thousands, of assumptions every day that enable us to get by in the world. Think of a simple trip to the post office. Chances are, you do not begin an exchange with the postal worker by asking, "Excuse me, do you speak English?" or "Are you selling stamps today?" You assume she does, and proceed from there. It saves time and embarrassing awkward moments. However, as we all know, assumptions occasionally can be wrong. Have you ever asked a store clerk for a price on an item only to find out you were talking with a fellow shopper? In all likelihood you misinterpreted some piece of information-perhaps the other customer was wearing a shirt similar to that of employees. Although humans are, by and large, quick and efficient thinkers, we also make some systematic errors. Some of these predictable errors lead us to incorrectly predict our own future happiness.

Not Seeing the Big Picture: The Focusing Illusion

In the early 1980s, our family moved to St. Thomas, in the US Virgin Islands. We rented a house and bought a car. It was a sabbatical year for Ed, and his wife was a professor at the local college. The kids were enrolled in school and a new, more tropical life was under way. Our time there was fantastic, with lovely weather, interesting culture, fresh food, and beaches. We sailed, swam, scuba dived, and read in the hammock on the porch. During the course of our tenure on the island, we met a slew of people from the mainland who visited on a cruise or vacation, fell in love with the place, and decided to move there. Most of them lasted about six months before figuring out that island life was not for them. A few lasted only weeks!

Why couldn't people accurately predict how happy they would be living in St. Thomas? In part, they never took the whole picture into consideration. Sure, the island boasts what is reported to be one of the ten most beautiful beaches in the world; the sun is unfailing, and the water inviting. But what most visitors overlooked was the rest of the details once the day at the beach comes to a close. At that time, frequent blackouts threw whole portions of St. Thomas into darkness for hours. There was no regular garbage collection, and some inhabitants tossed their waste out on the side of the road. Driving was dangerous and wrecks were common. Food was expensive. Other than water sports, leisure activities were limited. In other words, many of the people we met seemed to focus on the beach and water sports while ignoring the bills, traffic, and living conditions.

This common mental trap is called the "focusing illusion," and occurs when one fact about a choice particularly stands out in our minds, so much so that we tend to overlook other important characteristics. If we were to ask you to rate the happiness of a newly divorced woman, chances are you would give us a somewhat low rating. After all, she is newly divorced. But the divorce can cast such a large shadow in her mind that she might be overlooking other possible positive aspects of her life: more free time, fewer fights with her husband, the ability to pursue her career in the way she always wanted, the freedom to date, and so forth. Further, much of the time, in her own mind, she is not a divorced woman, because she is attending to being a shopper, an employee, and a friend. In a sense, she is only a part-time divorced person, when her attention is drawn to that fact, or she chooses to dwell on it.

The Nobel Prize-winning psychologist Daniel Kahneman and his colleague David Schkade studied the focusing illusion and discovered when we are most likely to make these types of errors. The focusing illusion occurs when people focus on a distinctive feature of a possible choice (for example, St. Thomas has beaches and Cheyenne does not). In one study, the researchers asked university students in the Midwest and in California which of the two groups was happier. Both predicted the Californians would be more positive – after all, they have an enviable climate – when in fact both groups reported about equal levels of life satisfaction. By focusing on the weather, respondents forgot about other important aspects of the two locations, such as traffic and the trustworthiness of one's neighbors.

This same focusing illusion can be seen in the instance of purchasing a new home. Most prospective buyers tour the house and imagine how they will decorate, where the kids will sleep, and what they might do with the yard. It is easy to picture these things because the physical details of the house easily stand out. What we tend to overlook is how friendly the neighbors are, how well the basement drains in the rainy season, how bad the traffic will be when we drive to work, whether the shops we frequent are nearby, and whether the train on the tracks a half mile away will keep us awake at night.

You are particularly likely to be biased by the focusing illusion when you are paying attention to or evaluating something that is obviously positive or negative. Take, for example, folks living in the slums of Kolkata. Their lives, filled as they are with hunger, police harassment, poor healthcare, and unemployment, are bound to stand out in your mind as miserable. Our research shows that, on average, people living in the slums of Kolkata rate their life satisfaction as about neutral, and some feel slightly positive! If this sounds surprising to you, it is because you, like us, overlooked the close family relationships, soccer games, religious celebrations, new babies, weddings, card games, and many other positive events that are a daily part of slum life. We term this the "pathetic fallacy," and it is the cousin of the "paradise fallacy."

The paradise fallacy is the tendency to be so taken with a positive feature that you overlook the negatives. Love at first sight can sometimes be an example of the paradise fallacy. That dashing Romeo with clever stories, wit, and good looks can seem like a lucky catch at first. Down the road, though, the luster can fade as you learn about his insincerity, excessive drinking, and selfishness. Admittedly, good looks are attractive, but can be distracting from good character and other personal qualities that are important to long-term relationships.

Another place the focusing illusion rears its ugly head is when we make choices between alternatives. Typically, when we are trying to decide between two things – say, flat panel televisions made by two different manufacturers – we tend to evaluate them based on differences that are apparent at the moment. The researcher Chris Hsee calls this mental tendency "joint evaluation." Stores take advantage of this by displaying their merchandise side by side. Your local electronics emporium, for instance, probably has a wall of flat panel televisions from which you can choose. As you stand there on the salesroom floor, the differences are readily apparent. This model has a larger screen, and this one is smaller. This type has brighter projection, and this one doesn't. This screen is ever-so-slightly clearer when figures move quickly. As you go about the mental arithmetic of deciding which one to buy, you are swayed by the differences between models. The important thing to note is that once you buy the larger, brighter, more expensive television and take it home, the comparisons you made back at the store no longer matter much.

When the television is in your living room, you won't think of it as "larger" or "brighter" – you will evaluate it on its own merits, irrespective of what other manufacturers might produce. That is, you will just experience your television. Do you like the sound quality? Is the remote control easy to use? Does it fit well with the aesthetics of your house? Is it bright enough for the location you choose? Hsee's research shows that, in terms of our long-term satisfaction, *experiencing* products is more important than *choosing*, even though we tend to decide based on the latter. We may have paid much more for that television because it compared well with the ones next to it, whereas in fact the differences between them make no difference to our experience once we get it home.

One place to be wary of the focalism trap is in the case of novel experiences. If New York City seems so exciting to you on your first visit that you are tempted to trade your home in St. Louis for an apartment in the East Village, you might want to take it slow. People are often taken in by novelty because it is, by definition, fresh, new, and exciting. But it is important to remember the amazing human capacity for adaptation, and how, three months down the road, the thrill is certain to wear off. If you feel trapped in the drudgery of your daily commute, predictable work assignments, and weekly trips to the grocery store, it may be worth considering that life in New York might acquire these same features.

A friend of ours, Heidi, had a tough time making a major life decision: Should she move to Los Angeles or stay in Chicago? Heidi was finishing her graduate study at Northwestern University, and was beginning to think about life after school. She had grown up in Chicago, knew the city well, and had plenty of family and friends in the area. But Heidi longed to move away to the West Coast, and had always dreamed of an LA lifestyle. Fortunately for her, she was offered a two-year position in a Los Angeles suburb, a job offer that could make her dream a reality. The problem was, Heidi wasn't certain about the move. When she thought of it, a host of problems jumped to mind. She wouldn't have a social network. Apartment hunting sounded like a drag. She didn't know her way around and imagined getting lost in the city. She didn't own a car, and felt that an automobile would be a vital asset in Southern California.

Interestingly, every one of Heidi's complaints was a short-term gripe that had to do with the transition period. She was focusing exclusively on the two or three months after the move. When we asked her to picture her life eight months or one year down the road, her attitude changed. She admitted she would know her way around the city and would certainly have friends. She would be moved into her apartment and would have bought a car. Widening her view beyond the transition period helped give Heidi the confidence to make the decision to move to LA.

The good news is that the focusing illusion is predictable, and therefore can be – if not avoided altogether – tempered. Like Heidi, we can overcome this bias. When making decisions like choosing a telephone plan, a job offer, a new apartment, or a prospective girlfriend, it can be helpful to take a step back and try to look at the bigger picture. Consider all the qualities and don't let yourself be swayed by a single flashy detail. Try to gather more information beyond the features that stick out to you in the current moment. Ask yourself if Mr. Right will be as nice to your children from your former marriage as he is to you on a Friday night date. Imagine what things will be like a year down the road, after you have grown accustomed to the new situation and the novelty has worn off.

If possible, take time to make important decisions, so that you have the opportunity to experience as well as compare. Look beyond the initial excitement and novelty to the time when the choice will be a routine part of everyday living; will the choice look as attractive when the initial thrill has worn off? No doubt, you – and we – will fall prey to the focusing illusion from time to time. It is natural. But knowing about the human tendency to focus on one detail while overlooking others can be the first step in avoiding that trap.

Impact Bias: Forgetting About Adaptation

In November 2000, the world watched as Americans went to the polls to decide the fate of the president in what was a highly controversial election. Chances are, if you would have asked any voters how they would feel if Bush were re-elected, they would have had a strong answer. Supporters would have told you they would be swept with enthusiasm and opponents might have mentioned emotional devastation. In the end, Bush prevailed. The interesting question, psychologically speaking, is whether people actually felt relief and depression at the level they predicted.

Research by Tim Wilson, Daniel Gilbert, and their colleagues suggests that people are far less emotionally affected by events than most of us typically predict. In fact, they collected relevant data from the George Bush-Al Gore presidential election in 2000. Gore voters predicted they would be unhappy after a Bush win, and Bush voters predicted the opposite. When Gilbert surveyed voters later, they were far less happy (in the case of the Bush voters) and far less unhappy (in the case of the Gore voters) than they had predicted. The truth is, while electing a Commander-in-Chief is important, it has less bearing on our everyday lives than most folks think. Regardless of who sits in the White House, you probably go to the same office, take your kids to the same school, and come home to the same house each evening. Gilbert and Wilson's research group came upon the same findings when they asked study participants how affected they would be by the win or loss of their favorite sports team. People predicted that a win or loss would affect their moods longer than either actually did.

Psychologists call this phenomenon "impact bias," and it is our tendency to overestimate the emotional impact an event will have on us, either positively or negatively. We sometimes think a visit from a mother-in-law will be catastrophic and a vacation to Fiji will be life-changing. Nine times out of ten, the events of our lives are neither catastrophic nor life-changing. Rather, these daily successes and failures are usually emotional blips that don't change our long-term happiness much.

Research points to the fact that we consistently incorrectly predict the effect of births and deaths, summer blockbusters, and fender benders. Does this mean that people are just slow learners? Why don't we use our past experience to predict our future emotions? Why can't we just remember the last time our favorite hockey team lost and say to ourselves, "Oh yeah, a loss won't be that bad. It will only last a day or so"? Why can't we easily recall how we felt a month after the last election, and reassure ourselves that this election will be no different?

A major reason we *overestimate* the impact of the things that will happen to us just around the bend is that we *underestimate* our own resilience. Most of us discount our ability to bounce back from hard times and cope with problems. Even though we have overcome difficulties in the past, we sometimes forget that we are likely to struggle through in the future as well. It is tempting to think that we could never get through something as horrible as the death of a spouse or child – and, indeed, these are traumatic and trying events for everyone – and yet people work through them every day.

You can probably imagine the intense sorrow you would feel if your spouse died. You can picture the numbness, the crying, the funeral, the friends comforting you, the loss of enjoyment in life, and maybe even the period of medication. It would be horrible. And yet the world is full of examples of folks who are happy years and decades after the loss of a spouse. There are men and women who return to their work and their hobbies, continue to take vacations and visit children and grandchildren, and who once again find meaning in life. Even if you take a big emotional hit from such an extreme loss – and you inevitably will at some time – it is highly likely that you will recover over time, and that the experience will be less devastating than you would predict.

Not Using Personal Experience

If you know any college students, you may have noticed the same surprising trend we have. As instructors of psychology courses, we often ask our students why they are interested in the field, and what professional plans they have for the future. In the last ten years, the number of students who want to be forensic investigators for the FBI has skyrocketed. In nearly every class, there are hopeful students who watch *CSI*, *The X-Files*, and *Law & Order: Criminal Intent*, and are carried away by fantasies of the exciting work they see there. They imagine the rush of being a hostage negotiator or the thrill of being a criminal profiler. But because much of what they know about the actual work of forensic detectives comes from television, there is a natural temptation to focus on other people's experiences rather than their own. We are likely to incorrectly predict our future happiness when we overlook our own experience in favor of others. And the experience of others, even when more realistic than that portrayed on television, is not necessarily a good guide for our own feelings.

We are as guilty of this as anyone. Throughout his years at college, Ed wanted to become a psychotherapist. He thought being a therapist would be rewarding because it is a helping profession and because he was interested in all the classes on psychology he had taken at school. Then, after graduation, Ed took a job at a mental hospital, hoping the references would look good on an application to graduate school. It didn't take long for Ed to figure out that he hated working in that environment. He didn't particularly like interacting with patients, and he felt frustrated with the cases that showed little progress. It turns out that Ed was interested in the ideas of psychology and in understanding the mind, but he was not particularly happy working with people in a clinical context or focusing on psychological problems. It took personal experience, rather than just vague ideas or other people's testimonials, for Ed to learn what occupation would make him happy.

You can avoid falling into the wrong job or relationship by drawing on your own experience or finding out what it will really be like in the long run. Some kids want to go to Yale to please their parents – and this is admirable – without considering whether it is a good fit for them. Some folks want to be paramedics because of the fast pace of the work, but overlook the fact that most in this occupation spend many endless hours of downtime between calls. Some people want to be university professors because they think the academic calendar and teaching classes would be great fun, but aren't aware of the pressure to publish, obligatory committee meetings, difficult students, and weekend work. You can get around not seeing the full picture by talking to others and benefiting from their experience. Ask a paramedic what a typical shift is like. Find out from a professor what she likes best and least about her job. But in the end, there is no substitute for personal experience. Get experience before you leap! Look for opportunities to volunteer, go out on a date, or spend a summer month in the city of your dreams to see how it is. Imagining what something will be like is less informative than finding out from others what it is like! And getting personal experience is even better.

Satisficing, Not Maximizing

Another reason people end up unhappy when they think they will fare well is that, unfortunately, they go about the decision-making process in a way that detracts from their overall positive experience. It turns out that deciding between many choices is less desirable than simply selecting one. For example, if you have a desire to visit

Shanghai, and you arrange a trip there, you will be more likely to be satisfied with your vacation than if you chose Shanghai from among several other desirable destinations such as Tokyo and Beijing. As incredible as it sounds, having more choices can actually detract from happiness.

Barry Schwartz, a psychologist at Swarthmore College, has studied how happy people are with their decisions. Schwartz and his colleagues have identified two decision-making styles: satisficing and maximizing. Satisficers are individuals who have a minimum threshold for what is acceptable to them, and maximizers are people who strive to get the very best out of every decision. Being a maximizer sounds appealing until you learn the results of Schwartz's studies. Once maximizers have made a choice – whether it is accepting a job offer, signing a recording contract, or marrying their high school sweetheart – they are likely to second-guess themselves, and wonder whether they could have made a better choice. The funny thing is, although maximizers sometimes achieve better outcomes than satisficers – getting a bit more money for that recording contract, for instance – they also tend to be less happy with their achievements. In fact, they turn out to be less happy in general. Maximizers, according to a series of studies by Schwartz, are lower than satisficers in happiness, optimism, self-esteem, and life satisfaction, and higher in depression and regret!

Take a group of promising undergraduate students who were nearing graduation. Schwartz and his colleagues tracked their lives as they left school and began applying for jobs. The maximizers tried to get the very best jobs possible, whereas their satisficing peers tried to get good jobs with which they were sure to be satisfied. What do you think happened? The maximizers succeeded on average in landing more attractive jobs. In fact, the starting salaries of the maximizers were 20 percent more than that of the other new graduates. Unfortunately, despite the larger paychecks, the maximizers were actually less happy with their jobs! The bottom line is that maximizers may get more and like it less.

If maximizing is an emotionally backward strategy for living, why do so many people do it? Why don't folks simply lower their standards a notch and enjoy the rewards? It may be that maximizers mistakenly believe that finding the very best doctor, buying the very best car, or having the very best kitchen appliances will make them happy. How else to explain the fact that many people spend so much effort on getting their offspring into the "very best" college, when in fact there are so many truly excellent schools? In part, the answer lies in the fact that maximizing can be deeply ingrained, and people are not aware that it is problematic or else don't know how to change it. Understanding the mechanics of maximizing can help you avoid doing it. Maximizers have two characteristic features. First, they rely heavily on external sources for evaluation. Rather than asking themselves if they enjoy their fancy meal or new cell phone, maximizers are more likely to evaluate restaurants and technology based on its reputation, social status, and other external cues.

Second, maximizers typically play out an invisible drama in their heads during the decision-making process, one that is fixated on options. Rather than evaluating a copying machine based on its features, maximizers compare the machine against a wide range of possible office products. In doing so, they may get a better deal, but also open themselves up to regret. Furthermore, they spend so much time making the best choices that they have less time left to enjoy life.

As you think about your own goals and decisions, it is worth considering whether you tend toward satisficing or strive to get the very best from every choice. Bear in mind that selecting the products, relationships, and outcomes that are good enough for you, regardless of what others may think, is a surer route to happiness. It is not that satisficers settle for second-best or third-rate; it is that they want what is "good enough" for them. Satisficers want good doctors and good cars as well, but they understand that there is a personal threshold that will be acceptable to them. They also understand that there is often little difference between the "best" and alternatives, and that there are costs in searching for the very best.

Satisficers also tend to evaluate a single item rather than making comparisons. In choosing a lawyer to draw up a legal contract, for instance, a satisficer might ask herself: "Is this lawyer capable of doing a good job on this contract?" If the answer is yes, there is no reason to look any further. Ultimately, it does not matter if there are four other lawyers who can do a marginally better job; it only matters that this lawyer can do a good job to meet the client's needs. A satisficer asks whether this college is excellent and meets her needs, not whether it is really "the best."

In order to make happy choices, listen to your heart, don't worry about getting the very best all the time, and evaluate each outcome on its own merits rather than against others. Follow this dictum:

Search for a decent parking spot and take it; don't waste your life searching for the best spot in the whole lot.

The Cute Puppy Error: Wanting Versus Liking

There is a difference between wanting something, even wanting it very much, and liking it once you have it. This is wonderfully exemplified in all the children we have ever known. There in the store, or in the television ad, is something that little Jack or Jill wants so, so much. They just beg the adults, and pester them until they get it. Once obtained, the object is given an intense hour of play and then consigned to the toy box forever. Whatever was so attractive about that toy was not so fun in actual play. One of our daughters demonstrated this same phenomenon with her requests for a pet. Her parents resisted her enthusiastic entreaties for a dog for many months, finally relenting and obtaining a cute mutt from the animal shelter. Our daughter was elated, and promised to feed and walk "Jack," as well as play with him and oversee his activities. She had great fun with Jack that lasted exactly one day. After that, no amount of cajoling or threats could get her to remember to take Jack for a walk and feed him, much less clean up Jack's poop. Quite simply, she had played with him, the novelty wore off, and he was no longer fun.

Psychologists describe different brain systems for wanting versus liking. Just because a cute puppy activates the wanting system does not mean that it will later continue to stimulate the liking system. The classic divergence between the two systems is shown in addictions, such as to nicotine. Without cigarettes, the smoker comes to want them very much, even to the point of desperation, but smoking produces mild pleasure at best, not an intense enjoyment that is commensurate with the wanting. The more a person smokes, the less they enjoy each cigarette but the more they want one if none are available. The discrepancy between wanting and liking is yet another reason our decisions can go astray. It is also one reason the economists' model of well-being based on people's market choices is not a perfect guide to happiness.

How might the wanting versus liking distinction apply to us? We can all think of times when we were like the short-term puppy lover. We wanted something shiny and fancy, only to discover that ownership of the item did not produce lasting enjoyment. Perhaps acquiring the item or activity is most of the fun; once obtained, it loses its allure. We may have also experienced the opposite – wanting to avoid something only to discover that the thing was in fact enjoyable. This is one reason that in the section above we so strongly recommend getting experience with the place, object, or job before fully committing ourselves to it.

How can we avoid the cute puppy error in our own lives? Several steps are needed – examining why we want something, considering how our experience will be with it after the initial rush of acquisition passes, and reminding ourselves of that possible wanting-liking dichotomy, at least in the important choices and acquisitions we make. The first step is the hardest-seeing what it is that makes us want a thing, and asking whether that will continue to make us like it for a long time. We might want to show the purchase to others, or proudly tell others about the choice we have made. But what happens when the excitement of show-and-tell wears off?

The second strategy for avoiding the wanting-liking mismatch is to carefully question how the decision will enhance your life in several months, after the novelty has worn off. Will it by then have faded into the background, consigned to the psychological toy box? You are deciding to trade in your trusty-comfortable, reliable, and loving Toyota for a Porsche. An exciting, but costly, choice. After the excitement and the pride of showing the car to friends wears off, will the Porsche enhance your daily experience? Will the car fade into the background as you adapt, or even become a negative due to certain problems that may come with the car? Quite simply, you must take the third step: carefully examine whether you will like the car as much as you want the car. There is a little kid in all of us, and that can be fun. But we have to live for a long time with the choices we make as adults, and so it is most important for us to comprehend the cute puppy error.

Conclusions

Happiness, as it turns out, is not just a feeling in the present. Our future happiness is, in some ways, as important as the joy and satisfaction we experience in the now. Anticipating emotional rewards and punishments is crucial to the choices we make, from the mundane purchasing of a stereo to important life decisions such as occupation and marriage. And anticipation can be half the fun of life. Fortunately, we are pretty good at predicting how we will feel down the road. We know, generally, what will be satisfying and which things will rub us the wrong way. More often than not, we understand what types of movies, meals, and parties we will enjoy, which people we will like and dislike, and which circumstances will make us comfortable or unhappy. We can predict with reasonable certainty that we will bask in a compliment from a spouse and feel embarrassed if we are called up on stage to volunteer at a magic show. We know that donating money to a good cause will feel rewarding, and that getting lost in a foreign city will be worrying. Being able to guess our future feelings, with some degree of accuracy, is important because it helps motivate us to seek out positive, meaningful experiences and avoid unpleasant ones.

Still, we are not perfect. For as good as we are at guessing our future emotions, we make mistakes. There are several predictable thinking errors people commonly make that lead them to incorrectly predict their own future emotions in general, and future happiness in particular:

1 Focusing on a single salient feature or period of time in a choice, rather than looking at the big picture.
2 Overestimating the long-term impact of our choices.
3 Forgetting that happiness is an ongoing process, not a destination.
4 Paying too much attention to external information while overlooking personal preferences and experience.
5 Trying to maximize decisions rather than focusing on personal satisfaction.
6 Confusing wanting something for liking it later, and forgetting to evaluate whether we will enjoy the choice once its novelty wears off.

The good news is that by identifying these errors and learning about why they occur, we can guard against them. We may never be able to overcome them entirely, but we certainly can reduce their impact on our lives. By considering a wide range of information, by remembering our ability to cope and adapt, by tapping personal experience, and by remembering that happiness is an ongoing process, you will be far more likely to make decisions that will make you optimally happy. To make good happiness forecasts, get some experience when you can, and check with others who have had similar experiences to the one you will have. Focus on the entire picture, not just on some salient aspect of it, and think what it will be like after a year, not just during the initial period when things may be either more stressful or more exciting. By becoming a good happiness forecaster, through practice and experience, you will substantially increase your psychological wealth. People who are psychologically impoverished never seem to figure out what makes them happy, and they continue to make bad choices throughout their lives.

One last suggestion about improving your important decisions: eat a healthy breakfast before you make them. Recent research shows that people have better "executive functioning," which includes planning and self-control, when glucose and glycogen in the brain are at high levels. You don't want to be making big decisions when fasting, unless you chug some sweetened lemonade first. Eat a healthy breakfast before making that important decision. And always remember that good decisions are as much about your making them turn out right as they are about which choice you actually make.

11

Take AIM on Happiness: Attention, Interpretation, and Memory

Our friend Randy is employed in the computer industry and has the enviable position of working from home. Randy is a devoted father of two young children, and his home office in Seattle allows him the opportunity to participate more fully in his kids' lives. Randy is thankful for the chance to drive his children to school in the morning and music lessons in the afternoon. Not long ago, he had just dropped his daughter at her violin lesson when he was rear-ended by a furniture truck. Although he wasn't injured, Randy was badly shaken. The trunk of his car was smashed, his taillights were broken, and his rear bumper came loose. The driver of the truck was apologetic and the two men exchanged insurance information. Randy patted the trucker on the back with a huge smile and sense of relief. "At least my daughter wasn't in the car," he said. Randy's optimistic attitude was more than cosmetic. He really was glad that his daughter had avoided a potentially harmful and traumatic experience. Although Randy knew that dealing with the tow truck, insurance company, and auto body shop might be a hassle, he left the scene of the accident feeling that he was a lucky person!

Randy's case is, of course, a perfect example of the power of positive thinking. Positive thinking is not about ignoring negative events or pretending that life is better in the face of adversity. Positive thinking does not magically make things happen. Nor is an upbeat outlook alone enough to overcome hardship. Rather, positive thinking is a mindset in which you recognize your blessings more than you pay attention to daily hassles.

The power of positive thinking can be seen in psychotherapy, where counselors commonly – and to great effect – use a technique called "reframing" to encourage their clients to view their problems in a new, more positive light. Reframing is exactly what Randy did when he shifted his view of the wreck as scary and an annoyance to one of great relief that his daughter was not involved. Everyday language is full of phrases to describe this mode of thinking, such as "When life hands you lemons, make lemonade," and "See the glass as half full." Because positive thinking can be enormously effective, it has made its way into mainstream culture. Many self-help books encourage readers to take up this new way of thinking, and close friends try to get us to "cheer up" by looking at "the bright side," "the silver lining."

The good news is that the research on subjective well-being and other psychological topics confirms that happiness is, to some degree, in your head. While a rosy attitude won't be able to gloss over a painful divorce or cancer diagnosis, positive attitudes can help. When people come to us and ask for advice about how to be happier, we usually point to positive thinking as a fruitful route to increasing well-being. Not only is it easier to change your attitude than it is to change your address, level of education, or income, a shift toward positive thinking can often lead to more gains in happiness than a change of life circumstances. This realization can enhance your psychological wealth!

Unfortunately, most people aren't sure exactly how to apply the advice to think more positively. For folks who are chronically focused on problems and difficulties, this mental shift is challenging. And, for the rest of us, there don't seem to be many clear definitions of what, exactly, positive thinking is, or specific steps to follow to achieve it. Fortunately, results from scientific studies in cognitive psychology suggest that positive thinking is possible, and that the path to it need not be the product of guesswork. Importantly, we need not throw out our connection to reality in order to adopt positive thinking.

In this chapter, we walk you through the nuts and bolts of a happy mindset by encouraging you to "take AIM at happiness." AIM is our acronym representing the basic components of a positive attitude that are necessary for happiness: attention, interpretation, and memory. Because attitudes to life are central to happiness, using the AIM model is essential to your psychological wealth. When most people consider positive thinking, they tend to focus on the interpretation part of AIM. They try to recast negative thoughts in a new, shinier light, but usually overlook how vitally important attention and memory are to the happiness equation. Positive thinking is more than simply looking on the bright side; successful positivity means paying attention to successes and blessings, and being open-minded to positive explanations of events, as well as recalling the good times. Although we doubt that the kind of positive attitudes suggested by self-help gurus are magic cure-alls, we do know that they can increase your happiness.

Attention: Gorillas in Our Midst

What are the chances that you would notice a woman with an umbrella walking through the middle of an exciting play during the Super Bowl or a World Cup soccer match? How about the chances that you would see a person in an alien costume if they walked between the players on the court at your son's high school basketball game? You probably think there is a high likelihood that such an unusual sight would stand out. This would be a reasonable guess, because we often notice things that appear unusual or out of place. But if you are one of thousands of undergraduate students in psychology classes, you probably know better. You know that, even if a person has perfect vision and is very observant, they can often overlook the gorillas in our midst.

The researcher Dan Simons can be credited with one of the most clever and powerful illustrations of attention in the history of psychological experimentation. In his now-classic studies, Simons asks participants to keep track of how many times a basketball is passed by a team wearing white shirts during a video of a basketball exercise. The players, six in all, half wearing white shirts and half wearing black, dart all around one another. As they weave back and forth, the white team passes one ball and the black team passes another, sometimes by bouncing it, sometimes by tossing it through the air. Simons's research participants struggle to keep up, carefully tracking each pass, trying hard not to mix up the two teams or basketballs. As the video ends, Simons asks, "Did you notice anything unusual?" The participants try to think of what might have been out of the ordinary: Was the game played in an office lobby? Maybe there weren't really any teams, just folks passing a ball back and forth? Many participants just shake their heads and say no, nothing stood out as being unusual.

Simons then inquires, "What about the gorilla in the game?" He then plays the same video again and the participants are shocked to see, very clearly, a person in a gorilla suit saunter into the middle of the game, turn toward the camera, pound his chest, and then slowly walk off screen. Many participants protest that the film has been doctored or switched with a new one. It seems astounding, almost impossible, that such a quirky (and now obvious) detail could have been overlooked. Simons insists that it is the same video they just watched, and he is correct. Simons repeated this experiment with a woman walking with an open umbrella, with the same results. In both instances about half the people noticed the unexpected events, and about half overlooked them.

What has happened, amazingly, is that the participants overlooked the gorilla because their attention was so heavily focused on the players in white and attempting to keep track of the number of passes. In their effort to follow one team and accurately tally the passes, most research participants unknowingly block out information about the other team dressed in black. As it happens, they also block out the gorilla.

If you are like most people, you are probably skeptical that you would fall for such tomfoolery. Other people might miss the gorilla, you presume, but not you. Indeed, we would all like to think that we would notice such an outlandish sight. Of course, now that we have told you about the experiment, your chances of seeing the gorilla would be high. We recommend you experience the full joy of this experiment from the experimenter's side by duping your friends by showing them the video clip (available online at www.viscog.beckman. uiuc.edu/djs_lab/demos.html) and watching as they overlook the gorilla! Remember, a few of them will notice the gorilla. But for those friends of yours who miss the hairy creature, the shock and disbelief are priceless.

The take-home message from this powerful experiment is that people are incapable of taking in the whole picture. Our brains are information processors and the world is just too full of stimuli to effectively take it all in. Instead, we have to pick and choose what we pay attention to, and our brains are evolutionarily adapted to do this well. We tend to be on the lookout for potentially harmful things, are adept at reading social cues, and are pretty good at integrating sights, sounds, and smells without even thinking about it. But when the world becomes demanding or complex, we tend to narrow our attention to the things that matter. This is why, when you drive in heavy traffic, you generally see the road, the other cars, and traffic signs rather than the sky, your shoes, or your fingernails. This is why driving while talking on a cell phone is so dangerous – because it draws some of your attention away from the road.

Inattentional blindness is not simply a phenomenon relegated to videos in psychological studies. It occurs in everyday life, and affects how we see the world around us. For example, in the documentary film *Beyond the Call* by Adrian Belic, there is a scene in which a group of Cambodian men are playing soccer. The players ran around kicking the ball toward their opponents' goal. Suddenly, Robert noticed that one of the players had only one leg, an unfortunately common sight in Cambodia. Still, it was inspiring to see the man be able to play soccer despite his amputation. Then, slowly, it dawned on Robert that *all* the players had only one leg! It was a revelation! What at first appeared to be a routine soccer match turned out to be an extraordinary game. Imagine how easy it would have been to overlook this detail with only a cursory glance. You can probably think of similar situations in your own life. Perhaps you went to a crowded party, but once you laid eyes on the woman who was to become your future wife, the gathering seemed thin and she appeared to be everywhere at once.

Simons and his colleagues have conducted other creative experiments on attention as well. For instance, in a series of studies on "change blindness," Simons was curious to see what would happen if he exchanged one person for another mid-conversation. To achieve this, Simons employed a set of tricks in which one person would swap places with another. Imagine, for example, checking into a hotel. The clerk behind the counter drops her pen, reaches down to get it, and another woman pops up to replace her. Would you notice that the hotel employee had been switched with someone new? It is tempting to assume the answer is obvious: of course we would notice such a dramatic change!

Once again, Simons's experiments show that this is often not the case: about half the people in his studies never notice the switch. If the woman behind the counter is exchanged with another person with similar qualities, many people fail to pick up on the swap. For instance, if the clerk is middle-aged and has short hair and glasses, people might not notice the exchange for another short-haired, bespectacled middle-aged woman. If, on the other hand, the hotel clerk is swapped for a young man, or a person of a different ethnicity, people are quick to notice. Change blindness occurs because people have the tendency to encode things by broad category rather than by detail, as a means of simplifying complex information. We seem to notice general information during transactions, but not specific characteristics of the person if they aren't relevant to the transaction.

Consider how you perceive those around you. Like most people, you might start by viewing others in broad categories such as "employee," "Australian," "female," and "young," and then notice more complexity and detail as you get to know them better. This is quite natural. It is also common for folks to pay attention to a single feature that stands out: a person in a wheelchair arrests our attention because we see fewer such people over the course of the day; it is useful to code a conversational partner by gender because it helps us decide what to say and how to say it; we react to children very differently than we do to adults. It often makes sense to define people according to these categories. Of course, we proceed to understand people as individuals the longer we know them, but condensing information to a few descriptive categories can be handy during initial interactions.

Where we focus our attention has been shown to have a direct bearing on happiness. Professor Sonja Lyubomirsky and her colleagues are interested in the thinking habits of happy and unhappy people. They noticed that unhappy people had the tendency to ruminate on their own failings and character flaws. You may have noticed this tendency to dwell on the negative in some of your own friends. Lyubomirsky decided to test the effects of self-reflection by having research participants focus either on themselves or on a distracter, and then record their moods. In the self-focus condition, participants were asked to pay attention to such things as "who you strive to be," "your bodily sensations," and "what your feelings might mean." In the distraction condition, participants were asked to imagine such things as "a boat ride across the Atlantic Ocean." How did looking inward versus outward affect people's moods? Lyubomirsky and her colleagues found that focusing attention on oneself could make even happy people unhappy, and that directing attention away from the self had the power to make even unhappy people happier. Of course, some amount of self-reflection is probably healthy, even if it means small bouts of sadness or worry. But too much attention focused inwardly seems to drag down happiness over the long run.

When analyzing the power of positive thinking, it is helpful to remember that we can have positive interpretations only of what we are attending to. That is, we can only decide if the glass is half empty or half full if we are looking at the glass in the first place! There are people who chronically look at the negative aspects of their lives, and who focus on their failures and setbacks. There are also those who constantly see the faults and shortcomings of others. In contrast, there are those who have cultivated the habit of seeing life's blessings and the beauty and goodness around them. Positive thinking, then, is as much about putting positive information into your head to begin with as it is about interpreting life events as being good or bad.

Noticing – or failing to notice – good things in the social and physical environment is much like the gorillas in our midst. We may tune our attention to problems around us, the little mistakes of others, and fail to notice the good things. For example, we may recognize when a co-worker fails to compliment our new haircut or when our in-laws forget our birthday, but fail to notice when our spouse does us a little favor or when the sunset is magnificent. Because there are always both plentiful good things and bad things a person can notice, a person with the habit of attending mostly to the bad inherits the problems of living in an ugly world. In contrast, a person who develops the habit of attending to beauty, the small good works of others, and what is going right in life will enjoy a pleasant worldview.

Interpretation

A close family member regularly entertains dinner guests with a fantastic story about a time she went on vacation to Cancun, Mexico. On her last day at the beachside resort, she and her husband prepared to check out of their hotel. He took the luggage to the rental car and she took a shower. When she came out of the bathroom, with nothing on but a towel wrapped over her hair, she was shocked to find a local man standing in the bedroom. She screamed, and flicked the man with the wet towel until he managed to scoot by her and fled the hotel room. With a rush of adrenaline, our friend got dressed and stalked off to the lobby to notify the staff and call the police.

When she arrived at the front desk, the woman saw, to her amazement, that the clerk was the very same man who had been in her room! He turned red when he saw her and smiled weakly. What had happened was this: The hotel clerk had seen our friend's husband get into the car with the suitcases and had assumed that it was a guest trying to leave the hotel without paying. Not wanting to jump to conclusions, the clerk rushed up to the room and knocked on the door, but since our friend was in the shower there was of course no answer. The hotel clerk then walked along a narrow ledge from an adjacent balcony, eight floors up, and entered the room through the window just at the unfortunate moment that our friend emerged from the bathroom naked. In the end, the man apologized for the misunderstanding and everyone went away a little embarrassed – and with a terrific story to tell.

Our friend's tale is a modern classic of interpretation. Many situations in life are unclear or ambiguous, and we are forced to fit together the pieces of the puzzle into a picture that makes sense. In this case, our friend assumed the strange man in her hotel room was a would-be rapist rather than a hotel employee. On the other side of the story, the hotel clerk assumed the man leaving with his luggage was absconding back to America without paying. In both cases the interpretation was understandable, but incorrect.

Ed once set out to show Robert and his teenage buddies how important interpretation is for how we experience events. He asked Robert and his friends whether they liked cockroaches, and the group proclaimed loudly that they hated the little creatures. Ed then went out to the garage and "caught" some cockroaches and brought them inside in a salad bowl. (Actually, they were mail-order cockroaches from a laboratory, but the adolescents didn't know this.) Anguished cries arose from the boys as Robert's older sisters, Marissa and Mary Beth, put their hands in the bowl and let the cockroaches climb over them. The teenagers recoiled further when Ed smashed the cockroaches and put them in the microwave.

After minutes of cooking, the cockroaches came out crispy and sizzling hot. Ed and the girls all quickly seized a cockroach and popped it in their mouths. The macho teenage boys were aghast, and sweat was visible. When Ed invited them to have a bite, they all refused. "Look," Ed explained, "it's all in your mind. People all over the world eat bugs; they are just another source of protein. You have learned they are dirty, and you are disgusted by them. But the intense heat has killed all the germs, and they are harmless." Robert ate a cockroach, but his friends still declined. Over the years, the Diener home developed a reputation as a strange place. But notice the valid lesson: whether something is viewed as food or as disgusting offal is in the mind of the beholder. Whether something is good or bad depends on how you interpret it.

Psychological research indicates that interpretation plays an important role in how we go about our days. Take, for instance, the classic study by Albert Hastorf and Hadley Cantril titled "They Saw a Game," based on a football game between Dartmouth and Princeton in 1951. It was an exceptionally rough game, and the All-American Princeton quarterback was taken out in the second quarter with a broken nose and concussion. In the next quarter, Dartmouth's quarterback was taken out after his leg was broken. In the end, Princeton won. One week after the game, the researchers showed participants a film of the match. Hastorf and Cantril asked the participants to judge who started the rough play. Presumably, we live in a physical world where there are objective facts and the number of infractions ought to be easy to tabulate. It should be a simple matter, for instance, to see if a player is off sides, makes a fair catch, unfairly pushes another player, or continues playing after the whistle is blown. But, truth be told, we know things are not always so simple.

Hastorf and Cantril found that the participants who attended Dartmouth viewed the game through a pro-Dartmouth lens, and those who attended Princeton favored their own school. The Princeton students, for instance, "saw" the Dartmouth team make twice as many illegal plays as the Dartmouth students did. How is it that the Dartmouth students could overlook half the penalties? Or is it that Princeton students were overly strict with their criteria for illegal play? When asked which team was at fault for instigating the rough play, the researchers found very discrepant answers. While only 36 percent of the Dartmouth students thought their own side was to blame, a whopping 86 percent of the Princeton students faulted Dartmouth. This classic study highlights a universal truth we have all experienced: people interpret the same objective events around them based on their own personal values, biases, selective attention, and sense of identity.

Positive thinking works in much the same way. How we interpret the world around us plays a large and important role in how happy we are. For folks who have a tendency to interpret events in the world as harsh and threatening, it is likely that their mood will be more negative and distrusting. For people who see the world as full of promise and opportunity, these rose-colored glasses will likely translate to more happiness. We recently came across a wonderful letter to the editor that illustrates the benefits of a positive mindset. Often, air travel is seen as a hassle, with weather and mechanical delays, long lines at security, expensive fares, and overwhelmed clerks. The writer of this letter, which we have paraphrased below, has a refreshingly different take:

Everyone complains about the airlines, but I love air travel. I am 82 years old, and recently had the adventure of my year on an airplane. The flight hit so much air turbulence and stormy weather that we had to be diverted to another airport several hundred miles to the south. The airline could not get us to our destination that night, so they put us up at a local hotel and gave us a meal coupon. I got to see another city for free, got a free room in a nice hotel, and a couple of free meals. Along the way, I met tons of nice people. Life is just great with adventures like these. The following day I arrived home safely, with fond memories. Shoot, some people think flying is a hassle, but it is really a great adventure!

This gentleman takes positive interpretation to an unbelievable extreme, but we are willing to bet that he is happy. What a wonderful way to live life!

Although interpretation colors how we see the world, it is not enough to say that interpreting events positively leads to happiness. If it were that easy, everyone would already be doing it and we would all be a bit happier. It makes sense to dig a little deeper and examine how, exactly, it is possible to think more positively. One way of doing this is by studying the thinking habits of chronically happy and unhappy people. Through a course of several clever studies, Sonja Lyubomirsky identified ways in which dispositionally happy people think in ways that bolster their moods: social comparison and retrospective judgment.

Most people are familiar with the psychological phenomenon of social comparison, which is the idea that you compare yourself to others when evaluating yourself. If your neighbor drives a BMW, for example, then you might be less satisfied with your ten-year-old Toyota than you would be if he drove a rusty 1972 Ford. Many laypersons point to social comparison as a major source of unhappiness. Poor people must be unhappy, for instance, if they live in a wealthy nation where they can compare themselves to millionaires.

The research on social comparison shows that it is not always straightforward. For example, some people are actually inspired by seeing those who are faring better in life. In one set of studies looking at women in a rehabilitation program for patients with heart problems, researchers found that some women were uplifted by other women who had successfully completed the program, while other patients were crestfallen by their peers' recovery of health. Why might some people become inspired while others are dejected by exactly the same thing? What leads a person to think one way or another?

Lyubomirsky and her colleagues analyzed how chronically happy people use social comparisons. In one study, Lyubomirsky had people form teams of four to solve puzzles in a relay competition. After playing a little while, the researchers gave the participants artificial feedback, either telling them that another team had won, or giving them a low ranking within their team. People who, earlier in the study, had scored in the lowest 25 percent on measures of happiness – that is, those folks who were naturally less happy to begin with – tended to take the social comparison feedback hard, and felt depressed or dejected.

The happiest folks were unaffected by the social comparison feedback, enjoying the game and feeling pretty good about themselves regardless of the performance of others. In another study, participants solved anagrams while racing against a research confederate, posing as another subject in the experiment, who solved the word puzzles more quickly than the real participant. Unhappy people became upset more easily by their own inferior performance, while happy folks virtually ignored how other people performed. In short, Lyubomirsky's research suggests that more upbeat people tend to engage less in social comparisons, and that they are less sensitive to information about other people's performance.

In a second set of studies, Lyubomirsky was interested in how people arrive at positive or negative judgments. Common sense tells us that judgments, such as whether or not we like a particular film, are a matter of personal preference. The data suggest that these types of evaluations are the result, at least in part, of positive thinking strategies. In one experiment, participants were asked to rate how appetizing various desserts were. How good does a piece of German chocolate cake look? How about a glazed donut? What about pie? After completing their ratings, the participants were assigned one dessert, but not their favorite, and told they could have it. They were then asked to rate that particular dessert again. Unhappy people, those who fell in the lower quartile on mood measures, tended to be disgruntled with the dessert assigned to them. Happy folks, on the other hand, actually increased their liking for the dessert. That is, they reinterpreted how desirable the confection seemed to be after finding they were stuck with it.

Lyubomirsky and her colleagues also examined how students reacted to being accepted or rejected by colleges to which they had applied. The happiest students tended to like the college that accepted them even better than they had before receiving the letter of acceptance. After all, if the school employed people with the good sense to accept them, it must be good! Not only did the happiest people boost their liking of the accepting institution, but they also liked rejecting schools less than they had before the admission decision was made. This thinking strategy helped protect folks from feeling overly bad about themselves. Unhappy individuals, by contrast, liked the rejecting schools every bit as much as they ever did and consequently felt dejected. In both studies, Lyubomirsky showed that happy people naturally reinterpret events so that they preserve their self-esteem.

For years, psychologists have analyzed the way their clients fall into patterns of thinking that leave them feeling distressed. Some people, for instance, have a tendency to blow small problems or criticisms out of proportion, while others doubt themselves because of low self-esteem. The psychologists Albert Ellis and Aaron Beck cataloged the kinds of irrational thinking that cast people into the heart of unhappiness. But there are positive thinking styles as well. Perhaps the best known of all positive cognitive styles is optimism. Optimists are those who retain a sense of hope for the future and interpret life events in a positive way. Optimism is not simply a matter of inborn temperament, but is also a skill that can be learned by recognizing unhelpful thinking strategies and replacing them with more positive ones. Here is a short list of common thinking pitfalls that leave people feeling bad:

- Awfulizing, in which people exaggerate how negative an event or a person is. For instance, a person might think to herself, "He is totally inconsiderate because he rarely does the dishes."
- Distress intolerance, in which people underestimate their ability to recover from a painful event. People tell themselves, for example, that they wouldn't be able to stand going through a divorce. Although breakups are emotionally difficult, some folks believe that they could never recover from a divorce.

- Learned helplessness, in which folks simply give up because they feel they have no power to change negative circumstances. "Why bother?" is the statement typically associated with this way of thinking.
- Perfectionism, in which people strive to be faultless rather than just successful. Perfectionists often pay more attention to the small details that went wrong than the big picture of everything that went right.
- Negative self-fulfilling expectancies, in which one draws negative responses from others by communicating that one expects a negative reaction.
- Rejection goggles, which cause people to see rejections everywhere, even in normal encounters. Furthermore, even the most minor rejection can be seen as a major slight.

Thinking strategies like these lead people to feel worse about themselves, their relationships, and the world they live in. The good news is that it is possible to get out of these thinking ruts and replace them with more positive styles. By learning to recognize unhelpful thinking in the moment, people can take the first step toward stopping such thoughts and replacing them. The technique most commonly used to swap positive thinking for negative thinking is called "challenging." When clinical psychologists discuss challenging, they are referring to the process of refuting perfectionism and other distressing ways of thinking. You probably have experience doing this with your friends or family members during times when they felt worried or blue. Perhaps you pointed out inconsistencies, exceptions, or possibilities in their logic that they had been overlooking. Many counselors take this same tack with their clients, encouraging them to modify extreme and exaggerated statements such as "he never helps around the house" or "anything less than perfect is failure." By replacing harsh, self-punitive, and extreme language with more realistic messages (for example, "I wish he would help around the house more than he does" or "I want to strive to be very good"), people can mentally set themselves up for success rather than failure. In the face of the fact that some of our happiness is the product of our genetics, the idea of interpretation is refreshing because it is one area over which we have direct control, can make change through effort, and can help ourselves live happier lives.

Memory

Think back to the first date you ever went on with your husband or wife. Chances are that even today, you and your spouse include one of your early encounters as part of your family lore. Perhaps it is a humorous story about awkward moments, things gone wrong, or fumbled lines. Ed and Carol often recount to their kids how they were stopped by the police on their first date, and had a shotgun thrust in their window on their second date. Maybe it is just the opposite: a positive story about instant attraction, a beautiful face, or a smooth pickup line. Regardless of the specifics, there is a high likelihood that now, years later, you walk down memory lane with a smile on your face. Those events from days long ago have taken on a rosy hue and bring you some small amount of happiness. But isn't it interesting to consider whether your current mental picture is really the way things transpired? Isn't it possible that interpretation also colors the way we remember our lives? Indeed, research shows that memory is not an exact match of events, but reconstructs events rather than duplicates them. Furthermore, memory is an important part of a happy attitude.

You may have heard about research that shows there are problems with memory, and that we do not always remember things from the past exactly as they actually happened. While this is true, it turns out that mildly inaccurate memories are not necessarily a bad thing. In fact, there is a growing body of research showing how memory biases can actually work in our favor where happiness is concerned.

Imagine going in for a painful medical procedure, such as a colonoscopy. Most people agree that colonoscopies are invasive and uncomfortable, and medical staff tend to sedate patients to decrease the discomfort. Now imagine two patients, A and B, who both come in for colonoscopies. Patient A has the usual painful procedure that lasts thirty-five minutes. Patient B has the identical procedure, except that five more minutes are added to the end, which are not very painful because the colonoscope is very slowly removed during the extra period. Here's the question: which patient experienced the worse colonoscopy? This is exactly the question asked in a study of more than six hundred medical patients.

The researchers assigned some participants to the longer colonoscopy group and others to the shorter condition. Common sense tells us that the shorter painful procedure is preferable because there is less overall pain. After all, the longer colonoscopy had all the pain of the shorter one, plus five additional mildly unpleasant minutes. This line of reasoning is not, however, what the data showed. According to the researchers, the way we remember events is not necessarily made up of an aggregate of every individual moment. Instead, folks tend to remember and overemphasize the peak (best or worst) moment and the last moment. Patient A, getting the shorter procedure, for instance, would remember the most painful moment and also the last moment (which was also painful) and mentally average these experiences when recalling the colonoscopy. Patient B, by contrast, would remember the most painful moment, and also the end of the procedure, which was less painful, and average these two experiences. Amazingly, Patient B, who experienced a colonoscopy lasting longer than patient A, has a lower overall average of peak and end, and therefore remembers the procedure more positively! Thus, patients who endured the longer, more painful procedure, but who remembered it as less painful, were more likely than others to be willing to come back in for a follow-up colonoscopy.

Speaking of colonoscopies, even this uncomfortable procedure can be a bit of fun if you approach it right. Ed went in for the procedure, and decided to have some fun with the medical staff so as to direct his attention from the discomfort. Beforehand, he put a large press-on tattoo on his rump – one of a wild lizard sporting a party hat and holding a martini. The nurses laughed at the sight and asked Ed where he had received such a tattoo. He responded that the doctor and he had gotten drunk together several weeks earlier and had gone together to be tattooed. The nurses then begged the doctor to show them his tattoo, and were delighted at his embarrassed denials. Making lemonade out of lemons.

This same memory principle found in the colonoscopy study can be applied to other life situations as well. Consider, for example, a vacation to Hawaii. Common sense tells us that a two-week holiday should be about twice as pleasant as a one week trip. However, most folks don't really remember each individual moment, and certainly don't use them all to mentally calculate whether or not they enjoyed themselves. One day on the beach tends to run together with the next. Instead, visitors to the island will remember their best moment – perhaps that day on the whale-watching cruise followed by a beautiful sunset dinner – and the last moments – perhaps the long line at the airport and a delayed flight. The peak-end theory means, then, that a one-week trip will seem, down the road, about as pleasant as a two-week vacation.

Another study focusing on vacations helps illustrate more memory mechanisms that factor into happiness. The psychologists were interested in how much fun university students have while on spring break. This particular week has the reputation for being seven days of unadulterated partying, and students look forward to it as eagerly as their parents dread it. The researchers gave palmtop computers set with preprogrammed random alarms to participants before they left for their vacation destinations. Several times a day, the computers signaled the students to complete a mood and activity questionnaire, and recorded the time and date they did so. The students filled out the brief surveys in the mornings, during the afternoons, and in the evenings, so that the researchers were able to calculate an average mood across the day, as well as chart an average across the week.

Two weeks after the participants returned from break, they came to the research lab and filled out a questionnaire asking them how much they remembered enjoying their vacation, and whether they were likely to take a similar one in the future. Although common sense tells us that the actual experience of the vacation – whether the individual moments were fun or not – should be vitally important, two interesting findings altered this notion. First, the students' moment-to-moment experiences were similar to, but did not perfectly match, their memories of the vacation. They tended to slightly enhance or downplay the break, recalling it as somewhat better or worse than the sum of the actual experiences would suggest. Second, it was this inaccurate memory that best predicted whether they would take a similar trip in the future, not their actual experience.

Earlier we asked you to walk down memory lane, thinking about an early date or encounter with your current romantic partner. The quality of that memory can be a powerful indicator of your satisfaction with your relationship. In a study conducted by the psychologist Shigehiro Oishi and his colleagues, the memories of dating couples were examined. He asked participants to recall how much happiness they had experienced with their partner in the past. He found that people who recalled having fun with their mate were more likely to be together six months later than those who did not. No surprise there! Oishi also found, however, that these positive memories were better predictors than the couples' actual feelings!

Think about it: much of the time you spend with your partner is somewhat mundane, coordinating car pools, washing dishes, making grocery lists, sitting together and reading, or brushing teeth. These are, emotionally speaking, neutral activities. And then there are the good and bad times, such as a pleasant hike in the woods or an argument over finances. A realistic tally of individual events in a marriage might seem like nothing to brag about, even if it tips the balance toward the positive side. But add a healthy sprinkling of positive memory bias, and the relationship starts seeming very rosy. Instead of recalling the forty-five minutes of silence while reading in bed, you might be likely to remember that five-minute conversation where your husband shared an interesting point from his book. It is not surprising, then, that Oishi found that dating couples who mis-remembered their times together as being more positive than they actually were turned out to be more likely to remain together than those who were dead-on in their memories.

How is it possible to tend toward positive rather than negative recall? One helpful guide is to look at the actual memory habits of happy people. Sonja Lyubomirsky analyzed the recall of chronically happy people. In her study of undergraduate students, Lyubomirsky found that happy folks were no different from others in the amount of positive and negative events they experienced. We all receive parking tickets, get stuck in rush-hour traffic, and have children who come down with the flu, just as we all receive compliments, experience occasional success at work, or have a favorite sports team that wins a game. Where the upbeat participants differed was in how they recalled events weeks later. According to Lyubomirsky, dispositionally happy folks had the tendency to err on the positive side, even treating adversity with humor or mentally emphasizing personal recent progress rather than focusing on problems.

A promising body of new research shows that, with a little mental effort, recalling good events from the past can boost well-being. Psychologists have begun studying "savoring," the process of active enjoyment of the present, and of using active appreciation to enjoy a past success. They ask subjects to spend some minutes reminiscing about a specific past event in a positive way. The savoring subjects report feeling happier than those in a control group. The key component to effective savoring is focused attention. By taking the time and spending the effort to appreciate the positive, people are able to experience more well-being. This research suggests that positive people have developed the habit of taking a mental snapshot of successes as they happen, paying attention to their details and memorizing vivid images, which makes them easier to recall and enjoy later on.

Conclusions

Our happiness is only partially related to actual life events. Sure, sometimes we are involved in tragic events, such as the death of a spouse, a chronic illness, or a traffic accident. By and large, though, most of us experience a mix of positive and negative events. Even good-looking, successful, well-liked people are vulnerable to financial crises, illness, divorce, and disappointment. The reverse is just as true: star-crossed folks in tough circumstances are likely to receive some meaningful social support, can have purpose in life, and often catch a "lucky break." Life is a roller coaster, full of ups and downs for all of us.

An important difference is in how each of us, individually, takes the events of our lives. Some people get extremely upset if the newspaper arrives later than its usual time, while other folks seem able to shrug off a burst water pipe in their attic, which floods and damages their entire house, by saying, "These things happen." We know, because this happened to Ed. It may be too much to ask you to change the way the world works, but it is probably not absurd to suggest that you can control your attitude toward the world. In fact, exercising some mental control where attitudes are concerned appears to be a good investment, as happiness is, at least in part, in your head.

Happy people, as it turns out, are different when it comes to attitudes. Chronically happy people, through birth and effort, are more likely to have developed positive thinking strategies. Upbeat folks tend to look for positives (attention), often think of neutral events as being positive and find growth in adversity (interpretation), and recall more rewarding memories (memory). Attention is a crucial element in the AIM approach to happiness because a positive focus determines the information that is interpreted and recalled later. The more positives that make it into your head, the easier it will be to experience psychological well-being. Getting into the habit of looking for successes and seeking out the good in others rather than nitpicking and fault-finding will go a long way toward making the world seem like a friendly, hospitable place. Each day, noticing people you should be grateful to, even for little things like holding the door for you, can focus you on the positive in others. Look around and see the good, beautiful, and amazing things that are going on all around you.

Similarly, interpretation is important for happiness. While terrible events have the power to bring even the most resilient people down, most of life is milder. By avoiding a pessimistic cognitive style, such as perfectionism, and by instead using more positive interpretive strategies, such as appreciating what you have, you will have a more enjoyable life.

Finally, memory also plays an important role in the happiness process. Folks who make the effort to notice and appreciate positives as they happen, so that they are easier to recall, and those who spend time reminiscing about past successes instead of failures tend to be happier. In fact, the memory part of the AIM approach to happiness is so important that it is a good predictor of whether couples stay together, and how people go about making important decisions for the future, such as their choice of vacations or receiving preventative healthcare. Taken together, attention, interpretation, and memory account for a large portion of the happiness over which you have direct control.

Some self-help gurus and self-growth organizations suggest silly interventions for positive thinking that want us to be cheerful all of the time. This approach is, of course, unrealistic and doomed to failure. We need to attend to serious problems in our lives and react to them, even if it means bouts of anxiety, guilt, or sadness. It is in your interest to worry a bit about whether that spot on your skin is cancerous, and it is desirable to feel bad about snapping at your wife unnecessarily. If your spouse is having an affair, it might be best to worry about that a bit. Thus, we are not advocating psychological bubbliness or positivity that is devoid of reality. Instead, we ask that you begin thinking more intentionally:

- Direct your focus, where possible, to the positive aspects of life.
- Pay attention to how you interpret daily events and actively challenge and alter unhelpful thinking patterns.
- Savor happy moments, concentrate on recognizing them, and take the time to remember and bask in them later.
- Notice the good things that others do, and express your gratitude to them.

In the end, many people think that they are happy or unhappy because of what is happening to them, and this is partly true – because what happens to us does influence how we see the world. But most people underestimate the degree to which attention, interpretation, and memory also affect happiness. Often, these mental factors are far more controllable than circumstances and are, therefore, where our mental energies are best placed. So take AIM on happiness and you will increase your psychological wealth.

Measuring Your AIM

Check each of the statements that might apply to you, and then add up the number of checks for each of the two sections:

Negative thinking
_____ I quickly notice the mistakes made by others.

_____ I often see the faults in other people.

_____ I see my community as a place full of problems.

_____ When I think of myself, I think of many shortcomings.

_____ When somebody does something for me, I usually wonder if they have an ulterior motive.

_____ When good things happen, I wonder if they will soon turn sour.

_____ When good things happen, I wonder if they might have been even better.

_____ When I see others prosper, it makes me feel bad about myself.

_____ I frequently compare myself to others.

_____ I think frequently about opportunities that I missed.

_____ I regret many things from my past.

_____ When I think of the past, for some reason bad things stand out.

_____ When something bad happens, I ruminate on it for a long time.

_____ Most people will take advantage of you if you give them the slightest chance.

Positive thinking

_____ I see much beauty around me.

_____ I see the good in most people.

_____ I believe in the good qualities of other people.

_____ I think of myself as a person with many strengths.

_____ When something bad happens, I often see a "silver lining," something good in the bad event.

_____ I sometimes think about how fortunate I have been in life.

_____ When I think of the past, the happy times are most salient to me.

_____ I savor memories of pleasant past times.

_____ When I see others prosper, even strangers, I am happy for them.

_____ I notice the little good things others do.

_____ I know the world has problems, but it seems like a wonderful place anyway.

_____ I see many opportunities in the world.

_____ I am optimistic about the future.

Interpretation

Here are some guidelines for interpreting your answers:

Negative thinking

Low	1–4
Medium	5–9
High	10–14

Positive thinking

Low	1–4
Medium	5–8
High	9–13

If you find yourself agreeing with many of the negative thinking statements and disagreeing with many of the positive thinking statements, it is time to change. Remember, thinking is like any other habit – it can be changed with effort. And remember that if you are a negative thinker, this is not because this is the way the world truly is, but is in the way you choose to see that world. If you scored high on positive thinking and low on negative thinking, you are in the long run very likely to be a basically happy person. If your negative score is higher than your positive score, you have developed a negative way of thinking about yourself, the world, and others. You should evaluate whether this approach actually works for you, or whether you might function more effectively with more positivity.

Part IV
Putting It All Together

12

Yes, You Can Be Too Happy

A crowd of people out there wants you to be happier. Self-help authors and inspirational speakers seek to make you joyous: possibly because they want you to buy their products, perhaps because they have faith in their mission. Authors want to sell you their "secret" or list of happiness-producing habits. Positive psychologists and psychotherapists, often motivated by empathy, want you to be happier. Your elected officials want you to be happy because if you are, you most likely will elect them again. Your mother wants you to be happy, because she loves you, and she might feel that she is a failure if you are unhappy. Somewhere, at this very moment, a technician in the lab of a major pharmaceutical company is working on a new drug to make you happier. There are even people that would like to give you special ozone enemas to make you happier. A large happiness industry has blossomed, and it has developed so many ways to help you – including self-improvement, meditation, positive thinking, natural herbs, the enemas we mentioned, medications, and many other personal and spiritual techniques. As surprising as it may seem, the authors of this book touting the benefits of happiness might not want you to be happier, because we think many of you may be happy enough already!

The attempts to make you happier are usually meant sincerely, and may be a good thing if you are chronically unhappy. As we have seen, happiness conveys benefits to those who experience it, and for those unfortunate individuals who are perpetually sad or angry, a dose of increased well-being may be just what Doctor Happiness ordered. But what about the rest of us, the majority who are already happy? Do we need to be happier? Do you really want to be happier? You might feel that even if you are happy, you are not happy enough.

Might all the well-intentioned meddlers be making you unhappier by insisting that you need more happiness? And might they be selling you something that you don't really need?

Too Nice in the Big Apple

For those people who think that limitless happiness is a desirable emotional trophy, consider an interesting and ill-fated experiment conducted by a group of well-meaning New Yorkers. This group decided that they could improve their lives and generate more positivity to the world by saying "yes" to everything – absolutely everything – that was asked of them. At first glance, this sounds like a fun social experiment, and a refreshing remedy to all the turnoffs, rejection, and negativity we encounter in our daily lives. Just imagine: a world in which people feel safe to pick up hitchhikers, give money to beggars, allow you to pass them in line, consent to overtures in the bedroom, and allow you to try out new, creative ideas at work. Sounds pretty good, doesn't it? Unless, of course, you are the one who must say yes to everything.

The sweet New Yorkers began the month of their experiment feeling very positive. They were extraordinarily generous to people, and put their friends and co-workers in a good mood with their unexpected acquiescence and happiness. They were taking on extra tasks at work, fetching cups of coffee, volunteering to pick up kids from school, and allowing strangers to steal the taxis right out from under them. But, as the month wore on, they began to feel spent. Their time, energy, and other resources were stretched thin, and they were having a difficult time functioning effectively. Toward the end of the month, they were absolutely depleted, had put themselves in compromising situations, and were, ironically, feeling negative toward others and harboring feelings of being taken advantage of. Clearly, happiness and positivity with no checks whatsoever can be downright problematic. Especially in New York City.

Problems of Being a "Happiness Ten"

Many of us harbor doubts about whether it is good to score a ten on the happiness scale. Might a little unhappiness or complaining be okay? Keep in mind that on a one to ten scale, the majority of people in economically developed nations fall in the six to nine range; few score in the unhappy zone and very few score a ten, the top of the scale – extreme happiness. It seems that some people enjoy complaining a little, and the moral imperative to be constantly cheerful can feel oppressive. At times, extremely happy people seem a bit naïve and we wonder whether the superhappy will worry when it is needed. These concerns make sense: in great novels and engaging movies, we want to see conflict, not simply people having a very pleasant and very boring life. Imagine *Crime and Punishment* without the murder and guilt, or *Jaws* without the shark attacks. The story of Cinderella would lose its narrative power if the beloved protagonist had been a young girl living with her wealthy, loving, intact family. We are often drawn to stories in which people overcome adversity, rather than those where everything seems to be fine.

Critics wonder whether our energies might be better placed in focusing on the welfare of others rather than our own personal enjoyment. For that matter, might trying to achieve a complete sense of satisfaction hobble our motivation to improve the quality of our own lives? Despite the clear benefits of happiness, nagging questions remain. Even if we accept happiness as a worthwhile pursuit, might we already be happy enough? Is there, in fact, an optimal level of happiness?

Many people across the globe find the American idea of being ever-cheerful to be silly. Always smiling, always saying "Great!" and "Super!" and always looking on the bright side seem distasteful to many. To many, constant cheerfulness seems phony and shallow, if not downright stupid. What about duty, hard work, critical thinking, and responsibility? What about facing the difficult problems that plague the world? When one of the authors of this book, Ed, spoke at a roundtable meeting with VIPs in Scotland, many expressed skepticism at the idea that happiness is a good thing. They said that many Scots are dour, and like it that way, and they did not want an American telling them that they should be happy.

The idea that there may be an optimal level of happiness, a point at which we say "enough," is provided by examples of extreme individuals – those who, for one reason or another, appear too happy. Take, for instance, the case of bipolar (manic depressive) individuals, who are flooded with expansive, joyful feelings when they are in their "up phase." Rather than conferring the usual benefits of health, productivity, and sociability, mania is often detrimental to an individual's life. Consider the case of Peter.

Peter was a student at a university where one of the authors taught. He attended classes on a disability scholarship – his disability was a mental problem rather than a physical one. Peter was a bright mathematics major, and as long as he stayed on his lithium, which controlled his moods, he could function appropriately as a college student. But he felt that the medications "kept him down"; that is, interfered with his creativity and high moods, and so he quit taking the pills. Very quickly, his energy levels skyrocketed. He met with his professor and confided that he had started writing three new books that very morning, and was very excited about each of them. He had so many good ideas, it was impossible to keep track of them.

Because Peter was so enthusiastic about the topics of his classes, he attended them regularly, but was too excited to take notes. One day, from the front row of a classroom of two hundred students, he stood up in the middle of the lecture, turned to the class, and shouted out, "I love you all." He attended advanced seminars and sat on the floor, appearing enraptured by complex statistical tables that were far beyond his level of understanding. His grades plummeted from B's to F's, and soon he was expelled from the university.

But Peter's story does not end there. Even after being ejected from the university, he continued to attend classes and hang around the campus. A professor picked up Peter hitchhiking in the snow barefoot. Although his parents lived over a thousand miles away, Peter would hitchhike to see them. Peter claimed the cold didn't bother him and, besides, he was interested in the experience of traveling through the snow barefoot. Peter told the professor that he was working on a book of poetry and had secured a job doing menial labor. Unfortunately, his employers demanded that he wear shoes, and so he was not sure the job would work out. His employers also demanded that he come to work on a regular basis, and frequently Peter would get so excited by something else that he just could not pull himself away to attend work. Nonetheless, he told his former professor that his life was wonderful because it was filled with exciting activities every second of the day.

Although the things Peter did might seem amusing because they fly in the face of social norms, his story is a tragic one. Peter experienced a constant flood of energy and enthusiasm, but was unable to function effectively. He was more intelligent and far more creative than many of his peers at the university, but when he quit taking his medication, Peter lacked the ability to maintain his focus on projects, and tended to behave in strange ways that alienated him from others. Of course, mania is not the same thing as happiness, but Peter's story illustrates the potential downsides of having too much exuberance.

Sociopaths or psychopaths provide another example of the dangers associated with an inability to experience negative feelings. We are not talking about the Hannibal Lecter evil geniuses of the world, but those more common individuals who, for some reason, tend not to experience the negative emotions of worry, anxiety, guilt, and shame. Sociopaths can be both fearless and guiltless and, as a result, often lie effectively. The experience of negative emotions, such as guilt and anxiety, make the rest of us reluctant to lie, and if we do so, these emotions often make it hard for us to be convincing. Sociopaths single-mindedly pursue pleasure and can therefore easily rationalize hurtful, immoral behaviors. At their worst, they are capable of committing heinous crimes without guilt or shame. In the case of sociopaths, we see that negative emotions such as guilt are tied to our moral sensibilities, and that a lack of negative feelings is just as problematic as experiencing mania. Thus, extreme mania as well as the complete absence of negative emotions can both be extremely detrimental to effective functioning.

Scientific studies on emotion have pointed to similar conclusions. Take, for example, the case of the "Termites." In the 1920s, Lewis Terman assessed a large group of exceptionally gifted children, little geniuses who were later dubbed "Termites" because of the man who devoted his life to studying them. Many years later, researchers located the Termites, curious to see how they were faring, at a time when many were dead. What they found was surprising – the happiest Termites died at a younger age than the less happy savants.

When we examined the Termite data, it was clear that all of the gifted individuals were quite happy, and therefore the researchers were not comparing unhappy individuals to happy ones, as is often the case in such research. Instead, the comparison was between the very happy and the extremely happy, with the very happy living longer than their extremely happy peers. Perhaps the happiest Termites did not pay close attention to their physical symptoms, leading to poorer health strategies, or were more likely to take more risks, such as driving fast or drinking too much. Regardless of the reason, the Termites provide a test case from research that suggests that, at the extreme levels, happiness might be associated with some drawbacks.

Another informative example comes from research conducted by the Swiss psychologist Norbert Semmer on how job dissatisfaction can sometimes be beneficial. He studied people dissatisfied with their work by following them over a period of time and assessing various outcomes, such as length of employment. It will come as no surprise that Semmer found that dissatisfied workers were more likely to quit their jobs and find a new work-place. What is interesting is that his findings showed that many of these dissatisfied workers were happier in their new workplace, suggesting that they were not simply dyspeptic people who would be unhappy wherever they worked. Apparently, for many of the participants in Semmer's study, their original workplace was a poor fit for them or it was simply a bad place to work, and they were more satisfied once they found a new job. In other words, their job dissatisfaction in their first job was not bad if it led them to find a more appropriate job.

The moral of Semmer's research story is that dissatisfaction and the emotions that accompany it, such as anxiety and frustration, can be useful signals that things are not going well, and can therefore provide the appropriate motivation to make positive changes. In some research studies, people who are put in a sad mood outperform those who are put in a happy mood, in tasks ranging from moral reasoning to logical thinking, indicating that in some situations, a negative mood can sometimes actually facilitate performance. Although people in a happy mood may outperform others in many tasks, in some cases they are careless and rely on habits that don't work in that situation. A negative mood may motivate the person to work harder to change the situation, or be more careful and cautious. In some situations, these responses are exactly what is needed. Thus, occasionally feeling sad or dissatisfied, but not chronically so, can enhance effective functioning.

Remember the wit of Flaubert, who said that stupidity was necessary for happiness. Too much happiness and zero unhappiness might be a bad thing. Does this mean, then, that Flaubert was right? Of course, it does not. Flaubert made the mistake of dismissing happiness as a fool's errand when it is, in fact, widely beneficial. But studies of subjective well-being suggest that there is an optimal level of happiness – that we should feel some, but not excessive, positive emotions. Here we break ranks from those who encourage the pursuit of limitless happiness because, although happiness is beneficial, not all forms of happiness are, and not in all cases.

How much happiness is enough? Research shows that the optimal level of happiness depends on the aspect of happiness we are talking about, our resources, and the type of outcome and activity in which we are interested. It makes a difference, for example, whether we consider how frequently a person experiences happiness versus how intensely they experience it. In determining the optimal level of happiness, it also matters which measures we look at: for example, whether we pay attention to a person's work achievements or their social life. Finally, the optimal level of happiness depends on the other resources a person has available for achieving goals.

Life Outcomes of Extremely Happy People

Earlier, we reviewed outcomes where happiness is clearly beneficial. In study after study, for example, the happiest people reap the most benefits where friendship is concerned. In research from many countries employing longitudinal designs (in which people are measured over time), those who are "extremely happy" are more likely to be in long-term relationships and involved in volunteer activities. Happy people like and trust others more, and are liked more in return.

To determine the optimal happiness for social relationships, we intensively studied over two hundred college students. It was clear that the extremely happy were doing better, socially speaking, than were any of the other groups. Self-confidence, energy, confidence, and sociability were highest among the extremely happy. The extremely happy group dated more and had more friends than even the very happy group, and their margin over the unhappy group was very large in the case of social relationships and feelings of energy. Thus, in the realm of sociability, more happiness is better. Unhappy people had the least energy and self-confidence, and the fewest close friends.

The case of health provides another interesting example of the tangible benefits of happiness. Happiness, as we learned earlier, often translates to healthier behaviors and a more robust physiology. But remember also the possible dark side to the health-happiness connection. In a review of dozens of studies relating health and happiness, researchers found that the happiest people who had late-stage or terminal illnesses were more likely to die than those who were less happy, possibly because they did not take the threat seriously. Another finding was that highly aroused positive emotions, such as elation, might raise blood pressure and heart rate. The research findings on health indicate that there might be an optimal level of happiness, wherein too little subjective well-being fails to convey the potential health benefits of happiness, and too much might also be detrimental. With this cautionary note in mind, it makes sense to ask: Might there be other domains of life where extreme happiness is not desirable, and where emotional balance is needed?

Magic Eights

Take achievement, for instance. Achievement means working toward important long-term goals, such as getting good grades and earning a high income at work. What we know about the benefits of happiness tells us that the happier people are, the more likely they are to pursue, persevere, and obtain these favorable outcomes. In fact, this is true when comparing happy people with their unhappy counterparts. But what about differences between people on the positive side of the spectrum? Do the extremely happy achieve more than the very happy? Surprisingly, the answer is no. When individuals complete happiness surveys that use a one to ten scale, those scoring around an eight often tend to fare the best in achievement. Why might the eights of the world outperform their friends and neighbors who are nines or tens? It could be that eights benefit from the creativity and energy of happiness, but also maintain a touch of worry that helps to motivate them.

Let's analyze this "number 8 phenomenon" in more depth. We found an interesting and surprising result when we examined data from college students. In 1976, thousands of students from elite colleges, small liberal arts schools, large state universities, and traditional black colleges completed a large survey, which included a single question about their levels of cheerfulness. Twenty years later, when the students were about 37 years old, they were contacted again and asked to report their incomes. It may seem incredible that a single item filled out on a particular date two decades earlier could be used to predict income years later, but it did. The happy folks seemed to be outearning the unhappy people, but the next-to-happiest group was earning the most!

Similar results can be found in an analysis of a huge sample by Shigehiro Oishi, who analyzed the satisfaction scores of over 100,000 respondents from all over the world. Those who scored well on happiness – the sevens, eights, and nines on a ten-point scale – had higher incomes and more advanced educations than both the tens and those who were unhappy.

How is it possible that a person can achieve more happiness, or put on the emotional brakes if they seem to be getting too much joy in the wrong places? For that matter, how is it possible to even know if we have too little, too much, or just the right amount of happiness? As we shall explain below, it all depends on which aspects of happiness one is considering. Because happiness is complex and multifaceted, most people are quick to make one-sided and sweeping pronouncements about whether or not it is a worthwhile pursuit. But in the extraordinarily important issue of the optimal levels of happiness, it is necessary to take a deeper, more intricate view of subjective well-being and its role in people's lives.

What Do You Mean By Being Happy?

There are many types of happiness. Happiness can include optimism and joy, but it also includes feelings of calm and harmony. This is why subjective well-being researchers try to take a broad view. We are interested not only in the specific emotions that make up happiness, but also in how these emotions work together as a constellation. We are interested, for example, in the way that positive and negative emotions balance one another, and in how strongly each of these emotions is felt. Although happiness is beneficial, some forms of happiness may be less so, and some forms of negative emotions may be more helpful than others.

Take the case of feeling positive emotions very intensely. Although extreme emotional highs feel good, they are generally not where the action is in terms of the optimal level of happiness. Some studies show, for instance, that people who are prone to intensely positive feelings are also more likely to experience intensely negative feelings. These folks are just intense people, and the price they pay for their joyful exuberance when things are going well is the intense anger or depression when things go poorly. Of course, we all experience the occasional highs that come when we get married or receive an unexpectedly large end-of-the-year bonus, but this sense of euphoria rarely lasts. Those individuals who chase emotional highs, and view excited, euphoric emotions as synonymous with happiness, endanger themselves. These folks set themselves up for failure because it is difficult, if not impossible, to stay intensely happy.

Our physiology and psychology are not built to produce or handle constant euphoria. People who chase continual emotional highs will usually fall short because the biological cards are stacked against their being able to sustain this emotional intensity. In the quest for continuing intense positive emotions, some individuals turn to drugs such as methamphetamines and cocaine. In addition, euphoria-chasers may run some health risks as well. Just as the physiological arousal associated with chronic stress takes a toll on health, so too can the sustained arousal of intense positive emotions.

We recommend that people think of happiness in terms of mildly pleasant emotions that are felt most of the time, with intense positive emotions being felt occasionally. If you feel fairly energetic and upbeat most of the time on most days, and are generally satisfied with your life with only the occasional complaint, you are, by our definition, happy. Some of us will feel more intense emotions and some of us less intense emotions due to our different temperaments, but frequent positive emotions should be the goal, rather than continuing intense highs.

Do Worry, Be Happy

When one of the authors, Ed, had a dialogue with His Holiness the Dalai Lama in front of an audience of thousands, he showed the esteemed monk the quote from Flaubert that says that to be happy, one must be stupid. The Dalai Lama laughed aloud, and said that some happiness is definitely stupid happiness. It is silly to be happy when a bear is chasing you, and some people are indeed happy in a shallow, unthinking way. Thus, although His Holiness counsels happiness, he does not counsel blind, thoughtless pleasure. Although he recognizes that negative emotions are very often harmful, he does not recommend constant exuberance for no reason whatsoever. Although the first enemy is stress and depression, we must also be wary of "stupid happiness."

Even when things are going well, there can be a negative emotional snake hiding in the grass. Research on goals and emotions conducted by Eva Pomerantz shows that there may be some hidden psychological trade-offs associated with the pursuit of achievement and success. Working toward goals is good for happiness, and happiness in turn is beneficial to our personal strivings. However, Pomerantz's work suggests there is more to the story. In her study, Pomerantz noticed that the more heavily individuals invested in personally important goals, the more people worried about achieving them.

Consider some goals that are personally important to you. Perhaps you want to start a home business, or write a meaningful toast for your parents' anniversary celebration, or catch a plane with a tight connecting time. Chances are, in each case, you will experience a degree of stress related to performing well and achieving your goal. The more heavily you invest in success, the more stress you are likely to feel, although the amount of worry will also depend on your temperament. This is another case where some amount of negative emotion can motivate us to do a good job. If you take the view that everything will always turn out all right regardless of what you do, you may not prepare enough.

People have successful home businesses because they *do* sweat the small stuff, give memorable toasts because they take the time to prepare, and make their connecting flights because they scurry, not amble, across the airport. The upside to all this is that the more heavily people invest in their goals, tolerating some stress along the way, the more happiness they experience when they are successful. This might be why there is such a thing as "eustress," positive stress, in which people feel stress in combination with positive emotions. Indeed, we have found that in nations that are relatively higher in both stress and pleasant emotions, there also tends to be high life satisfaction.

The research presents an interesting quandary. If the pleasant feelings of happiness serve as motivators, why are people willing to tolerate the stress involved with challenging goals? Why don't we just throw our hands in the air and choose easier, less anxiety-provoking aspirations? The answer lies in the fact that, for most people, happiness is not their only goal. Giving a touching, humorous, and well-received toast can be a worthwhile pursuit, regardless of whether some anxiety is involved. In one study, it was shown that kids who are working toward important goals achieve more joy when they achieve those goals, but they also experience more worry about those goals. The psychologist Maya Tamir has investigated this same phenomenon and found that people are often willing to experience a wide range of affect – both good feelings and bad feelings – if those moods will likely lead to final success. That is, most folks are generally willing to accept a little worry and guilt in pursuit of other worthy goals. Furthermore, it might be that our creativity is higher when we experience both positive and negative moods, not just positive ones. In one study on the workplace, positive emotions predicted creativity. But employees who had positive emotions and some negative emotions, in a supportive work environment, were the most creative.

We acknowledge that stress keeps us alert and helps us navigate safely through rush-hour traffic. We understand that a bit of performance anxiety can be just the motivator we need to prepare a terrific presentation at work. The mild stress that motivates us to take on challenges has been called "eustress." Thus, the pursuit of happiness is much more than hectic grasping at a feel-good emotion. Instead, most folks want to pursue just the right amounts of happiness, and at the appropriate times and places. However, not all negative emotions are the same. Both Australian and Canadian researchers have found that depression lowers life satisfaction more than worry does. Stress that is accompanied by uncontrollable events, such as the fatal illness of a child, is not so likely to be beneficial.

Conclusions

Some people are sick and tired of positive psychologists trying to make them happier. One woman with cancer objected loudly when overly positive friends told her that her cancer would be a "great learning experience." Kind of like when your sewer line gets plugged and your toilet flushes back into your bathtub during a party, and this is just one more growth experience. There are better and worse ways to cope with these misfortunes, but some people object when every misfortune is labeled as a happy opportunity. Some things are good and some things are bad, and it makes happiness into silliness to deny this.

Psychologists have rarely discussed optimal levels of happiness, or whether it is possible to be too happy. For the most part, people in the psychology profession have been focused on helping those unfortunate souls who suffer from depression, chronic anxiety, or frequent anger. But psychologists have, on a few occasions, argued against putting undue emphasis on simply being happy.

Martin E. P. Seligman, the founder of the positive psychology movement, is a notable exception. According to Seligman, happiness is more than just living a pleasurable life full of titillating conversation, delicious food, and soothing massages. He encourages people to look at other aspects of happiness, including living a meaningful and engaged life, that do not always feel good in the short term but that ultimately deliver lasting satisfaction. He suggests that sometimes to achieve life satisfaction and meaning, we must sacrifice some pleasant feelings and even experience some negative feelings. The trade-off is worth it, however, because long-term satisfaction, engagement, and meaning are worth the price of occasional negative feelings along the way. Although high life satisfaction is considered to be a good thing, chronic euphoria is not a desirable goal.

The psychologist Robert Schwartz maintains that there is an optimal balance between positive and negative thinking, with some negative thinking being necessary for effective functioning. Emotions are like a gas gauge, giving us important feedback about what is happening on the road of life – many miles of smooth driving or a sputtering loss of power. But for those people who strive only for positive emotions or those individuals who encourage you to be ever happier, it is like having the gas gauge stuck on full. Anyone who has driven a car with a broken gauge knows that it is missing vital feedback. It is good to not have an empty tank, but it is also good to have a gauge that accurately shows us how much gas we have.

The Mona Lisa gives us a hint about the desirable level of happiness. Scientists recently computer-analyzed the emotions expressed in this famous lady's face, and concluded that she is 83 percent happy, with about 17 percent negative emotions such as fear and anger mixed in. Interestingly, we find that people who are happy, but not perfectly so, do well in many domains of life. Perhaps Leonardo da Vinci was onto something, and the widespread appeal of his famous painting may be due to the fact that his lady projects the look of success. Think about a frowning Mona Lisa who looks distraught; probably not someone you would want to date. But a superhappy smiling-face Mona Lisa might look like a cheerleader – fun, but possibly superficial. A happy Mona Lisa might look like she would be fun at the beach, but maybe not wise enough to run a country. Positive emotions are beneficial, but a few negative emotions can help us to be more fully functioning individuals. Thus, our admonition: Be like Mona Lisa! We don't mean feel negative emotions 17 percent of the time – that is probably a bit too much in most circumstances – but allow yourself to feel them sometimes, against a backdrop of mostly positive feelings.

Do not let others, including the authors of this book, dictate your level of positivity. Happiness, like spirituality, is partially a private pursuit, defined by individuals based on their personal values. Be wary when people tell you to live for the moment, to strive for an exciting life, or that you ought to be happier. Maximize your psychological wealth, and this will mean occasionally experiencing a few negative emotions. Decide for yourself what your optimum level of happiness is, keeping in mind that being in a frequent mild good mood is functional, and negative emotions, so long as they are felt only occasionally, can be helpful too. Then enjoy pursuing the goals and values that are important to you.

13
Living Happily Ever After

A major theme of this book is that happiness does not just feel good, but that it also is beneficial to success. We can function well when we are happy, and chronically unhappy people tend to fail at the important tasks of life. When we are in a positive mood, we tend to interact better with others, think more creatively, and have more energy. We are not talking about acting cheerful or giddy – we are talking about being in at least a mildly positive state. Happiness is good for you, and those around you:

- Those who are engaged and happy at work on average are better workers.
- Happy people tend to have more and closer friends.
- Happy people seem to have better health on average, and live longer.
- Happy people are more pro-social in trusting and helping others.
- Happy people have more peaceful and cooperative attitudes.

Thus, the take-home message of this book – the point we very much hope sticks with you – is that happiness is worthwhile because it can be very beneficial! It will not only help you feel good, but will make you more likely to succeed in social relationships, spirituality, work, and health. In short, happiness is a vital, useful life resource that you need to cultivate. It will add greatly to your overall psychological wealth. And the good news is that happiness is something you have control over. Of course, there are some things that affect your well-being over which you have only slight control: for example, your genes and the society around you. Many things, however, you have direct control over – your attitudes, choices, and activities – and these have a substantial impact on your happiness. For example, spiritual emotions, such as gratitude and compassion, can be developed with practice; they are under your control. Although you may not be able to simply will yourself to be happy, you can with practice learn to stand tall in terms of well-being. In tough times, of course, we need the help of others – our family and friends, and perhaps even a therapist or coach. Happiness need not be a lonely endeavor; others are there to help and to be helped by us.

Psychological wealth is like a multivitamin: it helps us in several ways. It is not magic and won't cure all our problems, but it has tonic effects. Just as a multivitamin can promote health and prevent illness, psychological wealth can help with success in many different areas of life. Psychological wealth won't automatically give you everything you want, but it is your best shot at the life you value. And without it, other aspects of your life won't mean much. When people raise their children, it is typically their aim to give them the ability to be psychologically wealthy. Most folks try to instill a sense of value, advocate a spiritual approach to life, attempt to inculcate a positive attitude, and emphasize the importance of social relationships. Schools, youth television programming, and children's literature all share clear messages that speak to the importance of the various aspects of psychological wealth. When we plot our own lives, psychological wealth should similarly be our overarching goal.

Happiness is good for you, but you don't necessarily need more of it, any more than you necessarily need more vitamins. Are you happy enough? If you were happier, could you function better, or as well? Just because people write books about happiness and tell you to be happier doesn't mean that many of you are not already happy enough. And it is important to consider the different types of subjective well-being when you consider whether more happiness is better. For example, you might want more satisfaction with life, but feel good about the amount of positive emotions you experience. Or you might want more work satisfaction, but feel very good about your marital satisfaction. Thus, wanting to be happier requires you to carefully consider what type of happiness it is that you desire to increase.

Toward the Happy Society: National Well-Being Accounts

Most programs, books, and workshops about happiness focus on individual well-being. They make promises about and provide steps for achieving more happiness on an individual level. But if happiness is so beneficial, shouldn't there be some discussion about widespread happiness? Shouldn't we be having a collective conversation about raising the well-being of whole societies? Just as antismoking campaigns are not simply about getting individuals to quit smoking, but are also about promoting community and environmental health, we can also talk about whole societies flourishing emotionally. We need national accounts of well-being to parallel national economic accounts, because societies take notice of things that are measured. When measures are available, societies try to take steps toward improving numbers that are too low. If we have a measure of poverty, for example, as a nation, we tend to pay attention to it. If we assess the number of divorces in our society, we can discuss whether or not it is a matter of concern. When figures are published measuring our schoolchildren's success in different subjects, the attention of politicians is grabbed when the figures are disappointing.

What might we monitor in national accounts of well-being? There are many policy-relevant target groups that we could examine if we had national accounts of well-being. We would be able to track, for example, whether kids are happier or less happy than they were in the past, and which kids are having problems. Are our children becoming more stressed or depressed? Are there segments of the child population who are flourishing? People harbor opinions about the quality of life of contemporary children, but without national data it is difficult to arrive at useful, firm conclusions. We could also track which workers are engaged, and which ones hate their work, and why. Another question is whether there are pockets of misery, for example certain ethnic groups, that require societal concern. Are there groups related to policy discussions, such as caregivers of the elderly, who are miserable, and could profit from organized services, such as adult day care for their patient? Are there activities, such as commuting, that are causing increased stress and lower life satisfaction in modern societies?

Most people in industrialized nations score above neutral on measures of happiness; however, high stress and burnout also characterize many people in modern societies. Many are not engaged at work, or are often bored and stressed. Thus, even though the majority of people are above the neutral point of overall happiness, and in at least the slightly positive zone, for many people there is still much room for improvement. Many people can be happier and more engaged at work; many children can enjoy school more, and depression among kids is a major societal concern.

Building a society that maximizes well-being, not just economic growth, should be an aim of the nations of the world. We believe that the science of happiness has begun to provide a framework that can extend policy discussions beyond an almost exclusive reliance on income and material growth, to ask what will now create a truly better, happier society. We can't ignore money and economic prosperity, but as a society we don't want to focus on it as our only criterion of success. National accounts of well-being can provide a broader framework for evaluating improvement, and help us weigh our progress with factors in addition to money, such as societal trust, engaging work, happy children, and rewarding leisure.

The Happiness Recipe

As we mentioned at the beginning of this book, Cinderella was said to have lived happily ever after in the tradition of all fairy-tale endings. How can we be sure that she, and you, will "live happily ever after"? Many books about happiness give you some secret about how to get it, or a simple magic ingredient that will make you happier. Some even propose that if you just think in a positive way about things you want, they will automatically come to you. But we have seen in this book that many things lead to happiness and psychological wealth, and that you need more than one simple ingredient to live the fullest life. No single secret is likely to make you or Cinderella happy forever; no Prince Charming can ensure eternal bliss. Instead, it takes a recipe to do the trick, and happiness is an ongoing process. Here is our list of fundamental ingredients that make up the delicious dish of happiness.

Have Direction: Important Goals and Values

Humans are unique among animals in many respects; perhaps chief among them is the ability to live virtuously and find purpose in life. As humans, we actually require a sense of meaning to thrive. Lives that seem pointless leave us despondent and listless. We do not operate simply on instinct. We need to have values that we care about

224

and outcomes that are worth working for. If we have goals that spring from our values, and aims we care about beyond our own momentary happiness, we are able to gain satisfaction from working for the things about which we care deeply. Recently, we taught a class in which we assigned the participants two activities. The first was a hedonistic activity. We instructed them to go out and do something fun (but legal!). Go dancing, enjoy a nice meal, that kind of thing. Next, we asked that they go out and engage in a meaningful experience, one that they themselves could find purpose in. This could include volunteering, cleaning up litter, helping a niece with homework, or any other activity that might sound rewarding, but not necessarily fun. A week later, the participants came back to us to report on their experiences. Without exception, they thought the hedonistic activities were fun. Test driving a new car and eating a fancy dessert felt good in the moment. But the positive effect seemed to wear off quickly. The vast majority of the class participants told us that if they had to recommend one of the two types of activities to a friend, they would suggest the meaningful activity. Even though the meaningful activities weren't always fun, they tended to feel good later because they resonated with deeply held personal values. Taking stock of your values, and making sure you live a life that is consistent with them, is a vital part of psychological wealth.

Strong and Supportive Relationships

To put it simply, other people are crucial for our happiness, as we described in chapter 4. We find meaning, comfort, and entertainment in our relationships. Some folks need lots of family and friends around; others need only a handful of strong relationships. But we all need people to love and to love us. One key to close relationships is the positive (also called Gottman) ratio – many more positive than negative interactions. So remember to be positive most of the time with others. Remember that criticism and correction are permissible if they are not too frequent, but they need to occur within an overall context of a positive relationship built on praise, support, and favors. A world without others who care about us and about whom we care would be a cold, lifeless place. As adults we need to have others and do things for them to experience psychological wealth.

Material Sufficiency

As much as we would like to recommend positive attitudes and spiritual growth alone, the truth is that we live in a physical world. We are shackled to this life by our bodies, and material goods therefore play a part in our well-being. Our bodies have many physical needs, and when these are not met it can detract from our happiness. In order to be at our happiest, we need good health; sufficient resources, such as food, to meet our basic needs; and adequate money to experience some of life's pleasures. In chapter 6, we showed that to be happy we don't need to be rich, but material sufficiency beyond poverty is clearly helpful to happiness. Although wealthy people tend on average to be happy, and it is a myth to believe they are not, we must be careful of materialism – valuing money and things more than we value people, love, and our society. We also must be careful that our material desires don't rise forever, or we can feel poor no matter how rich we become. Health and material sufficiency are helpful to happiness because they free the mind for other things, but they are not sufficient for happiness. And if the pursuit of wealth interferes with our relationships and other aspects of psychological wealth, our well-being and that of those around us will suffer.

Cultivating the Spiritual Emotions

Positive emotions make us feel good, and feeling positive most of the time is a key ingredient of a happy life. We want to feel proud of our accomplishments and loved by others. We want to enjoy our work, friends, and leisure. However, in chapter 7, we discussed how the spiritual emotions that connect us to others are particularly important because they increase the well-being of others. Furthermore, these are emotions that we can cultivate. We can develop our gratitude toward others and our love for them. We can nurture feelings of compassion for those less fortunate than ourselves, rather than developing a superiority complex. And we can develop a sense of awe at the beauty and the order of the universe. Emotions that connect us to others and things larger than ourselves are a helpful route to happiness because they are under our control – we can generate these emotions with our thoughts. The spiritual emotions are essential to psychological wealth because they help us transcend our own individual worldview and connect us to something larger than ourselves. Importantly, they are also likely to make those around us happy.

Inborn Temperament

Happiness, like height and depression, has a genetic component. As described in chapter 9, it helps to possess a biological predisposition to be happy. Some folks are lucky and are born with "happy genes" – that is, they tend to be extroverted and not to worry overmuch. Although happiness comes naturally for these people, they must still be careful to take the other steps to happiness – genes don't guarantee happiness, but only help it. Just as a person born with high intellectual ability does not necessarily know a lot unless she makes an effort to learn, or a child with promising talent must develop it to achieve artistic mastery, a person with a happy temperament must work to fulfill his or her happiness potential. A person born with an unhappy temperament will necessarily need to exert more effort to be happy, and sometimes even need help from others to overcome stress or depression. Remember that genes are part of the story, but not the whole story. For instance, gene expression can be changed by our environment. Although temperament can aid happiness, just as athletic ability can help us succeed in sports, it must be cultivated by the habits of mind and behavior we develop. Our happiness set point can be changed!

Intelligent Forecasting and Wise Choices

There is no substitute for good old-fashioned wisdom. We all know people who seem hell-bent on messing up their lives. Despite being smart, kind, good-looking, or well-to-do, these folks seem almost incapable of making good choices with regards to dating partners, saving and spending, or career choices. You probably know someone who is stuck in a job that is a bad fit for her, or someone who gravitates toward problematic romance. By contrast, most of us also know others who seem to almost always make smart decisions. They have a strong sense of identity and personal boundaries, and they have a grasp of what long-term happiness requires. In order to be happy, we don't have to be prescient and fully understand the future. What we need is to understand some of the fundamentals of happiness forecasting, such as those reviewed in chapter 10, and then make important choices with long-term goals in mind.

Many of the errors we make are a natural by-product of how we think. There is too much information in the world for our brains to easily digest, so our subconscious minds take little short cuts. Because of this, people consistently make forecasting errors that lead them away from rather than toward happiness. The focusing illusion, for example, causes folks to focus on a single obvious feature of a choice and overlook other important features. For instance, when you go house hunting, you might be easily taken in by a large yard or particularly cute attic room while overlooking the quality of the electrical wiring or the noise late at night from a nearby street. Another forecasting problem comes from not getting firsthand experience with the choice, but relying on your imagination. It is easy for most folks to picture themselves sunning on a tropical beach, but most people overlook the less-than-pleasant flight to their vacation island. Similarly, nobody should choose a career, such as physician, lawyer, farmer, or teacher, without obtaining relevant experience, through volunteer work, summer jobs, or talking with someone in the given profession. Finally, people need to remember the importance of ongoing activities, goals, and attitudes to happiness, understanding that no set of life circumstances guarantees long-term happiness. The use of intelligent forecasting allows each of us to make better choices to maximize our psychological wealth.

AIM Your Mind

Have you ever taken a long road trip on a sunny day? Perhaps you wore sunglasses for so long that you were surprised at the color of the sky when you finally took them off! Our minds work in much the same way, filtering the world around us. In chapter 11, we described how the attitudes you develop toward the world, and the accompanying mental habits, have a lot to do with how happy you are. Some folks develop the habit of noticing what could go wrong, dwelling on failures, or complaining about problems. This kind of negative interpretation of the world is a sure way to make yourself unhappy. Happy people, on the other hand, see possibilities, opportunities, and successes, and interpret most of what goes on in a positive light. When they think of the future, they are optimistic, and when they review the past, they tend to savor the high points. Positive interpretation is one of the most exciting elements of psychological wealth because it is one that you have the power to change. But, for individuals in the habit of negative thinking, reading this book alone won't be enough for a turnaround – more active work is required to become a positive thinker. New habits of thinking and responding to others must be planned, rehearsed, and practiced. Just as with a diet, or breaking a bad habit, there will be backsliding into the old ways. Pride will over-shadow gratitude, and practice and effort will be needed over a period of months to break out of chronic negative thinking. With work and motivation, however, you can move upward in happiness, and become a more pleasant person for your family and friends to be around.

We don't pretend that developing positive AIM will be easy for all of you. Some of you grew up in places where griping seems endemic and people demonstrate their intelligence by criticizing others. Some of you have spent decades of your life finely honing your skills of seeing the faults of others and complaining about them. So remember the three steps of the AIM model. Attention – attend to the beautiful, the good in others, and the things that are going right. Interpretation – sure, people are imperfect and make mistakes. But most people are doing their best to lead a good life, and people with serious problems usually deserve your compassion. Memory-take time to savor the good things in your past. Sure, there were some bad things, but isn't it time to put those behind you and move on to creating a happy life in the present? Happiness is partly under your own mental control, based on attention, interpretation, and memory.

Living as Though Happiness is a Process, Not a Place

Journalists often ask us whether there is anything we have learned in our studies that we apply to our own lives. The answer is yes. We integrate many things from our research into our own lives, but learning that happiness is a process, not just a set of good circum-stances, has been especially helpful. Like most people, we had come to think if we could get all of our ducks in a row – a good income, success at work, a good mate, and so forth – then our happiness would be guaranteed. Like Cinderella, we got these things. And then the question became: What now? One answer is more ducks – striving for more things. But we came to realize that it is enjoying the activities and the striving that create happiness, and that getting the ducks provides only short-term boosts to happiness. If a person hopes to win a certain award, working for the award had better be enjoyable, because the award itself will produce only a short burst of happiness. In contrast, activities and striving for our goals is a lifetime endeavor.

Think for a moment about the father and son writing this book. Think about how we might approach this long process. We might think that writing the book is a drag – we have to research, read, write and rewrite, and endlessly go over our grammar and spelling. But we might predict that the outcome is worth the toil because our book might be very successful, it might make a difference in someone's life, it might educate people, it might lead to other professional opportunities for us. Of course, none of these things might happen, but the issue is whether writing the book is worth a lot of unpleasantness because it might lead to success. Our point here is that happiness requires exactly the opposite frame of mind – we must enjoy writing the book and promoting the book. Then, regardless of whether it is successful or not, we will have had a very enjoyable time. Of course, it would be nice if the book did well in the marketplace, but the more important thing for our own happiness is that we enjoyed working together and got joy from thinking about the content of a book that might help people. In fact, we can say that this has been our experience. We haven't argued, have had many stimulating discussions about the content in this volume, and have learned new things in authoring the book. We have enjoyed talking to others to get ideas for the book, and trying out different ideas on ourselves. With happiness as a process, not a place, the book has already been a great success for us – and any sales of the book will be a bonus. Of course, occasionally we must endure unpleasant activities and hardship to obtain certain goals. But we are saying that this should be the exception rather than the rule. If most of your goals are unpleasant to work for, you better change either your goals or your attitudes.

Whether you are a famous movie star, the president of the United States, a Forbes list billionaire, or a Nobel Prize winner, you can be unhappy or happy. Whether you have everything you ever wanted or live a simple life, you can be happy or unhappy, because process is the key. We have asked people who have won large awards, such as the Nobel Prize, whether the award made their lives happy – they say it did for a day, a month, maybe even a year, but life continues and they must find new activities to enjoy.

There is a temptation when envisioning a happy life to think only of desirable life circumstances – money, health, and friends – and certainly these things can help. But we hope that we have also shown you that happiness requires more – positive attitudes and working toward meaningful goals and values. Perhaps most important, you need to understand that, as we have said repeatedly, happiness is a process, not a place; a way of traveling, not a destination. Happiness requires positive attitudes about life and the world, and continuing fresh involvement with activities. A life full of meaning and values, supportive social relationships, and rewarding work is the framework for a happy life. The processes of happiness within that framework require positive attitudes, spiritual emotions such as love and gratitude, and material sufficiency.

Changing Your Set Point

Many things that we look to for happiness make us happy for only a short time because we grow accustomed to them. In psychology jargon, we adapt. A raise or promotion at work, a daughter marrying a great guy, winning an award – these can be real boosts, but usually don't change our long-term level of happiness. They make us happy for a month or two, and then we drop back to our old baseline. So the search is on for things that can raise our baseline, which can lead to long-term increases in our happiness. Some really good and bad things can do this – finding a wonderful marriage partner on the positive side, or losing that partner on the negative side. But even with these large good and bad events, we adapt to some extent over time.

As we describe above, how you travel and react, your positive AIM, is the most important aspect of raising your set point. Changing your set point for happiness also requires that you understand the types of happiness, and what is possible in terms of changing them. Happiness includes life satisfaction, feelings of meaning and purpose, and positive emotions and interest. It also includes the spiritual emotions, such as love and gratitude. However, happiness is not a continual high of elation or ecstasy, and it is not an absence of all unpleasant emotions, such as worry and sadness; occasionally these are appropriate and beneficial. The search for intense highs and avoiding all negative emotions can even be harmful. You don't want to be continually elated or ecstatic, because then you could not react to new good events and activities. This is why heaven must wait; we can't experience heaven on this earth, as some try doing with drugs, because if we do, it creates a hell in which we can no longer function as healthy adult humans who can respond to the wonderful things that occur in life. Raising your set point means feeling positive most of the time, but not continual bliss.

Conclusions

Our book has the ambitious goal of describing how you, and the next generations, should live your life. We do not describe the concrete details or the differing paths people might take. We do describe the components of psychological wealth that are essential for a good life. To have the highest quality of life, you must live a life full of meaning, values, purpose, and strong social connections: a life filled primarily with positive emotions, including the spiritual emotions, such as love and gratitude, with occasional negative emotions in situations where they are helpful; a life built around activities in which you enjoy working toward your values.

People have values besides their own happiness, and therefore we must sometimes sacrifice our own short-term enjoyment to obtain those other valued goals. We might, for example, visit people in the hospital because we value their friendship and want to cheer them up, even though we find a hospital visit unpleasant. We do activities that we think are required or the right thing to do, even when we don't enjoy them, in order to act morally. Here it is important to keep the different types of happiness in mind, and the difference between enjoyment and life satisfaction. Many valued activities, even when unpleasant, can increase our long-term life satisfaction because they make our overall lives better, even if they lead to less pleasure at the moment. And they may even bring greater pleasures in the future, because they improve our circumstances, or strengthen our relations with others. Regardless, we often do the right thing without considering whether it will increase our own happiness, and that should increase our psychological wealth.

Money will do us no good if it does not increase our psychological wealth, and at times the pursuit of money can detract from psychological wealth by distracting us from other important values. To flourish, we need to feel competent, have the ability to make important decisions about our lives, and help others. We need meaning and purpose that take us beyond immediate hedonism. In the end, our psychological wealth includes not only our happiness and life satisfaction, but also the degree to which we are flourishing. When we are psychologically wealthy, we have the "good life," as it has been described by wise people throughout history. Rather than making income our major goal in life, we need to design our lives, including how we pursue money, around the goal of being psychologically wealthy.

As authors, we have the extremely lofty goal of changing both you, the reader, and the society in which you live. We hope to ensure that you are a happy person, and that should be beneficial to you, your family and friends, and your society. Our vision of the future is one in which relationships are supportive, work is interesting and engaging, you feel competent in the tasks required of you, people seek happiness in working for their long-term values, and stress is rare. We have shown in this book what we think is a revolutionary idea – that happy societies are more likely to be successful ones, and happy individuals are more likely to be successful as well. Achieving psychological wealth is, ultimately, the most important goal in life. Now it is up to you.

14

Measuring Psychological Wealth: Your Well-Being Balance Sheet

Measuring Your Satisfaction With Life

Below are five statements with which you may agree or disagree. Using the scale below, indicate your agreement with each item by placing the appropriate number on the line preceding that item. Please be open and honest in your response.

7 Strongly agree
6 Agree
5 Slightly agree
4 Neither agree nor disagree
3 Slightly disagree
2 Disagree
1 Strongly disagree

_____ In most ways, my life is close to my ideal.
_____ The conditions of my life are excellent.
_____ I am satisfied with my life.
_____ So far, I have gotten the important things I want in life.
_____ If I could live my life over, I would change almost nothing.

Now simply add up your total score for the five items: _____

Interpretation

31–35 Extremely satisfied
26–30 Satisfied

21–25   Slightly satisfied
20   Neutral; an equal mix of satisfaction and dissatisfaction
15–19   Slightly dissatisfied
10–14   Dissatisfied
 5–9   Extremely dissatisfied

Extremely satisfied
You feel that your life has gone very well, and the circumstances of your life are excellent. Most people who score in this range feel that the major areas of their lives are positive – work, leisure, relationships, and health. They don't feel that their lives are perfect, but that their lives are very rewarding.

Satisfied
Your life is rewarding, but you would like to see improvement in some areas. People in this range are happy and feel very good about their lives.

Slightly satisfied
You feel that generally your life is going well, although you would like to see improvement in some domains. Some areas of your life need improvement, or most areas are going modestly well, but you have not yet achieved the level you would like to attain in many areas.

Neutral
There is a mix of good and bad in your life. There are about as many things going well as things you would like to improve. Things are not terrible, but neither are they as rewarding as you would like.

Slightly dissatisfied
If your score on life satisfaction has dropped recently due to specific bad events, then a score in this range is not of concern. However, if your score is chronically in this somewhat low range, you might want to ask why, and what you can do to increase your satisfaction. Perhaps there are things in your life that cannot be changed at this point, but in this case, should you change your expectations? Perhaps there are conditions that you can change? If your life is on an upward

trajectory and you are optimistic about the future, there is probably no concern.

Dissatisfied
Life satisfaction scores in this low range can be a matter of concern, and you should think about how to improve things. Would seeing a clergyperson or mental health professional help? Perhaps you are just going through a temporary bad time or have not achieved many of the things you hope to, in which case your score might not be of concern. However, in other cases, scores in this range point to some areas of your life needing strong improvement.

Extremely dissatisfied
Perhaps some recent extremely bad event has influenced your current life satisfaction. However, if your life satisfaction has been in this low range for some time, some things in your life are in need of change, and you might need the help of others, including professionals, to improve your situation. A number of things may be drastically wrong, and it is time to make very serious efforts to turn your life around.

The Causes of Life Satisfaction

For most people, life satisfaction depends on doing well in major areas of life, such as relationships, health, work, income, spirituality, and leisure. When a person is doing badly in one of these areas, it can color his or her overall life satisfaction. People who score high on life satisfaction usually have close and supportive family and friends, often have a close romantic partner (although this is not absolutely necessary), have rewarding work or retirement activities, enjoy their leisure, and have good health. They feel that life is meaningful, and have goals and values that are important to them. People who score high in life satisfaction usually do not have problems with addictions, such as gambling, drugs, or alcoholism.

The first three items of the SWLS focus primarily on a person's current life, whereas the last two items ask how one's life has been previously, up until the present. Some people score high on the first three items of the life satisfaction scale, but score lower on the last two items. This suggests that their lives are going well now, but that they are not entirely satisfied with their pasts. Other individuals might score low on the first three items, but higher on the last two items. This pattern suggests the respondent sees his or her past as more desirable than the present. Thus, a discrepancy in the scores between the first three items and the last two items can reveal whether people view their lives as improving or declining.

Measuring Your Emotional Well-Being

Please think about what you have been doing and experiencing during the past four weeks. Then report how much you experienced each of the following feelings, using the scale below. For each item, select a number from 1 to 5, and write that number on the line next to the feeling:

1 Very rarely or never
2 Rarely
3 Sometimes
4 Often
5 Very often or always

_____ Positive (1)
_____ Negative (2)
_____ Good (3)
_____ Bad (4)
_____ Pleasant (5)
_____ Contented (6)
_____ Interested (7)
_____ Stressed (8)
_____ Unpleasant (9)
_____ Happy (10)
_____ Sad (11)
_____ Angry (12)
_____ Afraid (13)
_____ Loving (14)
_____ Depressed (15)
_____ Joyful (16)

A Pleasant feelings: Add up your scores on items 1, 3, 5, 6, 7, 10, 14, and 16 (8 items), and place your score here: _____

B Unpleasant feelings: Add up your scores on items 2, 4, 8, 9, 11, 12, 13, and 15 (8 items), and place your score here: _____

Pleasant feelings

  8–13 Extremely low pleasant feelings
14–18 Very low
19–23 Low
24–27 Moderate
28–30 High
31–35 Very high
36–40 Extremely high pleasant feelings

Unpleasant feelings

  8–11 Extremely low unpleasant feelings
12–16 Very low
17–20 Low
21–25 Moderate
26–28 High
29–31 Very high
32–40 Extremely high unpleasant feelings

Your happiness balance

Besides your overall pleasant and unpleasant scores, we can also examine the relation between the two, in what we call "hedonic balance," or the amount of pleasant feelings you experience minus the frequency of your unpleasant feelings.

Subtract your Unpleasant Feelings Score from your Pleasant Feelings Score and put your answer here:

Balance scores

24 to 32 Very happy
16 to 23 Happy
  5 to 15 Slightly happy
  4 to –3 Neutral, mixed
–4 to –12 Somewhat unhappy
–13 to –23 Very unhappy
–24 to –32 Extremely unhappy

Individual emotion items

Besides the summed scores and their balance score, you can also examine individual items.

You ought to be feeling general positive feelings, such as "good" or "positive," the majority of the time, unless some bad event has just occurred in your life. If you are not feeling positive, good, or pleasant most of the time, and only experience these feelings rarely, you should examine why.

You should be feeling negative feelings only rarely. If you feel stressed sometimes, but not often, you may feel that this is not too much. But for some feelings, such as "depressed" and "angry," feeling these emotions only rarely or very rarely is usually most beneficial.

Do any of your individual emotions stand out? That is, which of the positive feelings do you have less often? If you are interested and positive most of the time, this is a very good sign. When you examine your negative feelings, are there any that you feel substantially more often? If you are frequently afraid, angry, sad, depressed, or stressed, are there steps you can take to reduce these emotions, which can interfere with your happiness and with your effective functioning?

The Causes of Emotional Well-Being

To some degree our levels of pleasant and unpleasant feelings are due to our inborn temperaments. Some people don't feel that positive simply because they are "low-key" individuals. This might not be a matter of concern as long as the amount of positive emotions you are feeling does not bother you. But remember that there are ways of thinking and living that can also influence our emotional lives, and that we can probably increase our pleasant feelings if we take efforts to do so. Low levels of pleasant feelings are of most concern when levels of unpleasant feelings are equal to or exceed the pleasant feelings. When a person is low in pleasant feelings and high in unpleasant feelings, this is a true matter of concern. However, if a person scores only in the middle on pleasant feelings, but is extremely low in unpleasant feelings, this might mean that she or he is just not an emotional individual, but might still be very happy. When a person scores high on both pleasant feelings and unpleasant feelings, this means he or she is intense-but hopefully still higher on the pleasant feelings than the unpleasant ones.

Psychological Flourishing Scale

Below are twelve statements with which you may agree or disagree. Using the scale below, indicate your agreement with each item by placing the appropriate number on the line preceding that item.

7   Strongly agree
6   Agree
5   Slightly agree
4   Mixed, or neither agree nor disagree
3   Slightly disagree
2   Disagree
1   Strongly disagree

_____ I lead a purposeful and meaningful life.
_____ My social relationships are supportive and rewarding.
_____ I am engaged and interested in my daily activities.
_____ I actively contribute to the happiness and well-being of others.
_____ I am competent and capable in the activities that are important to me.
_____ I am a good person and live a good life.
_____ My material life (income, housing, etc.) is sufficient for my needs.
_____ I generally trust others and feel part of my community.
_____ I am satisfied with my religious or spiritual life.
_____ I am optimistic about the future.
_____ I have no addictions, such as to alcohol, illicit drugs, or gambling.
_____ People respect me.

Add up your scores on the twelve items of the psychological flourishing scale and place your answer here: _____

Possible scores range from 12 to 84:

80–84   Extremely high flourishing
74–79   Very high flourishing
68–73   High flourishing
60–67   Flourishing
48–59   Slight lack of flourishing
32–47   Lack of flourishing
12–31   Extremely low flourishing

In this flourishing scale, we assess aspects of psychological wealth that go beyond positive emotions and life satisfaction to also measure how you are doing in other essential areas of your life. This scale measures not only that you generally feel good about your life, but also whether key aspects of psychological wealth, such as strong social relationships, self-respect, competence, engaging work, and spirituality, are in place, and whether your life has purpose and meaning. Flourishing indicates aspects of your life that psychologists such as Carol Ryff, Corey Keyes, Ed Deci, and Richard Ryan believe are missing from pleasure and simple emotional feelings of happiness. Flourishing goes beyond an individual's pursuit of her own happiness to include her contributions to society and the happiness of others. At times you might be flourishing despite having emotional troubles, and at other times you might be having a fun time without truly flourishing. It is, of course, best when the various elements of psychological wealth all come together.

Your Happiness Profile

Place an "X" in each row to denote the box where your scores fall on each of the four scales.

Although psychological wealth requires all four elements above, a degree of it can often be experienced by those who score well in only two or three of them. A very low positive feelings score or a very high negative feelings score is likely to make life less rewarding even if the person has a high degree of flourishing. Indeed, it will be difficult to be high on flourishing or life satisfaction if you are depressed. You need not aim for ecstasy to be happy, but achieving some success in each type of well-being is an eminently reasonable goal.

Table 14.1 Your happiness profile

Components of psychological wealth	Extremely unhappy	Very low	Low	Average	High	Very high	Extremely high
Life satisfaction	(5–9)	(10–14)	(15–19)	(20)	(21–25)	(26–30)	(31–35)
Positive feelings	(8–13)	(14–18)	(19–23)	(24–27)	(28–30)	(31–35)	(36–40)
Low negative feelings	(32–40)	(29–32)	(26–28)	(21–25)	(17–20)	(12–16)	(8–11)
Flourishing	(12–31)	(32–47)	(48–59)	(60–67)	(68–73)	(74–79)	(80–84)

Your Overall True Wealth

You probably did not make the Forbes list of billionaires, but are you a billionaire when it comes to psychological wealth? Here is how to interpret your score:

All Extremely High	A billionaire – Psychological Wealth Top 400 List
All Very High and Extremely High	You are rich
High to Very High	Upper middle class
Average or Mix of High and Low	Middle class
Low and Average	Working class
Low and Very Low	Poor
Low to Extremely Unhappy	Abject poverty

If you are high in psychological wealth, congratulations on a life that is well-lived. If you are impoverished, or poorer than you would like to be, now is the time to increase your wealth, and hopefully this book has given you knowledge to help you get started.

Epilogue
About the Science of Happiness

Why do we rely on science rather than on great philosophers, self-help books, or our mothers for our understanding of happiness?

Opinions and the People Who Belong to Them

Recently, a man who claimed to be a vampire announced plans to picket the White Castle fast food chain. Presumably, the protest would be staged at night. What would prompt such an unusual political action? The man told local news reporters that he was incensed by a new menu item: a garlic hamburger. Clearly, the restaurant had neglected to consider the obvious problems the new sandwich could cause for Cincinnati's nocturnal blood-sucking population. The garlic burger, according to the picketer, "angered the undead." As amusing as this true story is, it highlights the fact that the modern world is a place where it is easy to form strong opinions on just about any topic. In a world as full, complex, and ever-changing as ours, it seems that there is little that escapes controversy, whether it is fast food or happiness.

Happiness has been a human concern for the length of our recorded collective memory. Aristotle, perhaps the greatest philosopher of all time, wrote a book on the topic, in which he equated happiness with the desirable state that comes with virtuous action and positive life circumstances. In contrast, the hedonists believed that happiness was the result of satisfying passions in pleasurable pursuits. The Greek Stoics, the hedonists' intellectual rivals, believed that it was best to avoid unhappiness through self-control and mastery. In the Christian tradition, Jesus of Nazareth spoke of well-being in his famous Sermon

244

on the Mount, in which he suggested that people with good character would be specially blessed.

European history is packed full of philosophical luminaries, such as St. Augustine and Immanuel Kant, who offered opinions about happiness. In modern times, respected thinkers, such as the Dalai Lama, have turned their attention toward happiness. The Dalai Lama's book *The Art of Happiness* was a worldwide bestseller, proof that this emotion is of mainstream interest and speculation. Although these iconic cultural figures might disagree about the best way to achieve happiness, they all believed that happiness was worth the pursuit. The Diener family also agrees.

Science offers a new way to examine happiness. In the past, this much-sought-after emotion was the domain only of philosophers, religious scholars, and armchair thinkers. Throughout the ages, people have applied common sense, logic, folk wisdom, and personal experience to questions of happiness and have come up with contradictory conclusions. Some folks have argued that money creates misery (not true, according to the data) while others, such as Flaubert, have looked down their noses at happiness as a fool's errand (again, the data tell a different story). While many valuable insights have been offered up over the centuries, science brings new ideas to its pursuit. It is one thing to come to the conclusion that divorce leads to misery based on the single instance of your best friend, and quite another to assess the impact of thousands of divorces.

By using the scientific method, we have been able to debunk many myths attached to happiness. We know, for example, that the elderly are about as happy as people in their twenties and thirties. We know that money adds to happiness, but often only a modest amount. We know that in many nations religious people are happier on average than their nonreligious peers, but not in all societies. We know that long commutes to work drag down a person's happiness, even when people are traveling to a better, higher paying job. Just as science once helped humanity understand that the world is not flat, and later produced vaccines, electricity, and hurricane-warning systems, it is now expanding our understanding and control of the subjective world. Scientific inquiry is not a replacement for religious understanding or philosophical insights, but causality and generalization add helpful new dimensions to these age-old sources of wisdom.

To understand happiness in a scientific way, we first need valid measures. Second, we need broad and large representative samples of people so that our conclusions are not based only on our acquaintances or people who stand out in our memories. Third, we can't rely solely on surveys; we need to use experiments and studies over time to truly understand what leads to happiness, and what happiness in turn causes. There is nothing mysterious about science – it is using rigorous methods to obtain the best information that is available. We have been building the science of happiness for several decades, and the reader will see that we have learned some important things that were hitherto unknown.

The science of happiness is new, and there is much we don't yet know. We have one important warning for readers of this book: the findings we describe are based on group averages, and don't necessarily apply to all individuals. For instance, even if we find that marriage leads people to be happier, this is the average reaction, and some individuals will nevertheless be made unhappy by marriage. The science of happiness is not at the stage where we can tell to which individuals our generalizations will apply. Thus, when you read that rich, religious, and sociable people tend to be happier, remember that this is based on averages, and may or may not apply to you. Therefore, although a science of happiness is rapidly developing, the ability to apply these findings to individual lives is still largely an art.

Some findings from the field based on early studies (for example, that lottery winners are not significantly happier than others) have been overturned by later research (two studies have found that lottery winners are happier). Our own views have changed over time. A hallmark of science is that answers are provisional until better studies are conducted, and we realize that some of our conclusions are likely to be overturned. At the same time, we believe that the findings in this book represent the best understanding of happiness that currently exists. We are optimistic that just as science transformed our material world in the twentieth century, it can revolutionize our understanding of happiness in the twenty-first century.

The Components of Complete Happiness

Take a moment and consider happiness in your own life. Think of a time, perhaps recently or perhaps long ago, that you felt very happy. Maybe it was the day you received the job offer from your first employer. Maybe it was the first day of warm weather after a long cold winter. Perhaps it was last weekend, when you took your daughter to the park and napped on the sofa afterward. Without question, a variety of circumstances and events can make you happy. And even the experience of happiness itself can vary from time to time. That job offer was probably exciting, while the warm weather might have been emotionally refreshing, and the quiet Saturday probably left you feeling content. Each of these states suggests a different facet of happiness.

When it comes to the sticky definition of happiness, we realized early on that people have all sorts of idiosyncratic ideas about happiness, and that they could argue forever about which definition of happiness is the real one. We solved the issue by thinking about happiness as "subjective well-being." That is, we view happiness as a subjective state, defined by the individual. In happy states, we believe that our lives and current events are going well. Happiness includes all of the pleasant emotions – ranging from joy, to affection, to gratitude – that we experience as positive and pleasant. Therefore, when we investigate happiness, we are interested in the full range of people's pleasant moods and emotions. We ask about harmony and peace, enthusiasm and joy, pride and contentment, and don't try to argue that one of them is "not happiness." By taking a wide view of happiness, we stay flexible enough to account for individual variation in the experience of happiness and how individuals define it.

Where do negative or unpleasant emotions fit in our definition of happiness? Let's be realistic. The emotional part of happiness is not about a permanent, intense emotional glow that never fades. Even the most upbeat people have down days and experience problems. In fact, most of us would treat a person who claimed to be perfectly happy all the time with suspicion. Negative emotions, such as guilt and worry, can be useful at times. We need to feel them in order to function effectively. Imagine a society in which we did not feel guilt when we behaved poorly or disappointment when we failed to achieve a goal. It would be terrible. Indeed, unpleasant feelings provide us useful feedback about the quality of our lives, as well as motivating us to make changes. Happiness, then, allows for a small dose of negative feelings while we are frequently experiencing positive ones. The balance, however, should heavily tilt in favor of the pleasant emotions.

Happiness is more than simply an emotion; it is a broad psychological state of which emotions are only one part. There is also a "cognitive," or thinking, component to well-being. People tend to stand back and evaluate their lives – judging how they are doing – and we call this type of happiness "life satisfaction." This component of well-being consists of people evaluating how well they are doing in life and the domains that are important to them. In measuring life satisfaction, we leave the exact standards for happiness up to the individual. One person, for example, might be overjoyed with an income of $40,000 a year, while another would be panicked by that same amount. Allowing each individual to gauge the quality of her own life paves the way for tapping people's unique experiences and values.

In addition to being satisfied with life in general, a person's satisfaction with important domains is also needed for consummate happiness. A person should not only be satisfied with life, but positive about important areas, such as health, work, relationships, and leisure. In addition, a person should feel good about himself or herself, as well as feeling competent and respected. These positive evaluations of important aspects of life have been called "flourishing" because they suggest that the person is doing well across the core aspects of human functioning.

Feeling Good, but for the Right Reasons

Would you accept permanent happiness if it meant giving up actual work, relationships, and even pain? What would you choose? Would you sacrifice the ups and downs of life and give up your job, friends, and family, if it meant guaranteed happiness? These questions were asked in a thought experiment by the late philosopher Robert Nozick. He proposed the idea of an "experiencing machine," in which your brain could be hooked to a computer. Imagine that the experience machine would inject your thinking and feeling organ with just the right combination of dopamine, opiates, and serotonin so that you would feel permanently blissful, and the computer would project images into your brain so that you believed you were winning awards, going to your child's choir concert, and making love to your spouse. But there is a catch. As a brain hooked up to a computer, you would no longer work, have relationships, or experience the hardships of life, such as parking tickets and computer crashes. You would be perfectly happy.

We have presented this question to thousands of students in classes we have taught. In our experience, about 95 percent of the students opt for work, social connections, and pain over orgasmic bliss. The other 5 percent prefer the easy route. Perhaps their jobs and families are not that rewarding. Perhaps they don't fully realize what they would be giving up. Although we can't be certain what people would choose if actually faced with an experiencing machine, our results underscore Nozick's basic assertion: people generally want to be happy, *but for the right reasons*. Most people would prefer to live according to a clearly held sense of values. They are willing to accept some anxiety and disappointment en route to the deep satisfaction of an important personal achievement. It may even be that a little hardship and effort makes the payoff more rewarding.

The founder of positive psychology, Martin E. P. Seligman, has pointed to the distinction between pleasurable happiness and happiness based on meaning and purpose in life. For people with a genetic predisposition toward negativity, this will come as welcome news, because engagement and meaning are possible even when pleasant feelings are low. Conversely, it is possible to experience many pleasant feelings without feeling happy in the life-satisfaction sense of the word. Playing computer games, eating ice cream, and singing a catchy song may all be pleasurable activities, but they are often not linked to a deeper sense of life satisfaction. Happiness is a matter of balance. Too much pleasure without purpose can be destructive. Hedonism without pursuing meaning leaves most people feeling empty. However, too much purpose without actually feeling good leaves something to be desired as well. Consummate happiness includes both pleasure and meaning.

Consummate Happiness

A person with high subjective well-being is someone who experiences a preponderance of joy and affection (positive affect) along with only occasional guilt, worry, anger, and sadness (negative affect), feels satisfied with her life (life satisfaction), and with important aspects of it. To put this into a formula, subjective well-being = positive affect − negative affect + life satisfaction + flourishing.

By looking at both pleasant and unpleasant moods, as well as broad and domain-specific satisfaction, we have a definition of happiness that works for most people. We allow for personal variation in definitions of happiness; for example, some people emphasize contentment while others focus on joy. Such variation is relatively small, however, when compared to what people have in common where happiness is concerned. Think about it: whatever definition of happiness you prefer, all humans share a basic biology that determines that certain emotions – joy, contentment, curiosity, affection, and hope – will feel pleasant. We have yet to come across a culture in which people experience crippling depression as pleasant, or think that cultivating lasting hatred is the emotional ideal. In the end, happiness – however the word is used – refers to a set of feelings that are pleasant, and the evaluation the person makes that his or her life is going well.

There are sometimes conflicts and trade-offs between types of happiness. In fact, people sometimes sacrifice one element of happiness for another. People commonly turn down offers to participate in emotionally rewarding activities in the present so that they can continue to work toward goals that will reap larger psychological rewards in the future. You might pass on a dinner date, for example, in favor of working on a campaign to raise money for a local literacy program. There is also a trade-off between aspects of happiness as we get older. As we age, we tend to experience emotions less intensely. The burning passions of our twenties subside into the warm embers of our seventies. But this is not to say that the elderly are unhappy – not by a long shot. In fact, research shows that older people are often higher than younger folks in life satisfaction, even while younger people tend to be higher in the experience of intense pleasant emotions.

Scientifically Measuring Happiness

When Ed began his studies of happiness, he focused his early work on measurement. He developed a new scale for assessing life satisfaction, but his biggest focus was testing whether scales to measure happiness are truly valid. What he discovered is that happiness can be measured in many different ways, not just through surveys.

Some researchers get at the questions of happiness through biological tallies of feelings. Richard Davidson, a neuroscientist at the University of Wisconsin, uses brain imaging to measure the cerebral activity of happy people. He has made strides in identifying brain areas, such as the prefrontal cortex, that are associated with happiness. To oversimplify, Davidson finds that more activity in the very front of the left side of the brain, right behind your left eyebrow, shows more in happy people, whereas depressed people have more activity in their brains right behind their right eyebrow.

One of Davidson's most highly publicized investigations revolves around the emotions of Buddhist monks versus those of university students. Davidson placed his research subjects in a functional magnetic resonance imaging machine and asked them to voluntarily generate emotional compassion at specific intervals. The monks, who had years of experience with meditation, were able to make the machine spike on cue, while the hapless university students could hardly nudge their electronic readings. Apparently, we can generate positive emotional feelings if we are highly practiced at it.

Another biological psychologist, the University of Chicago researcher John Cacioppo, uses electrodes to measure tiny movements in facial muscles associated with various emotions. He shows his participants pleasant, neutral, and unpleasant slides. The images show things like ice cream cones, snakes, chairs, and horrific physical deformities. Cacioppo measures the intensity of the reactions to these photographs, and has found interesting differences between happy individuals and their more distressed counterparts. For instance, dispositionally happy people react to neutral stimuli, such as a chair, as if it were positive. That tells us something very interesting about happy people, and how they approach the world. More specifically, it tells us that in the absence of any perceived threats, happy people are more likely to see the normal environment in a positive way, a tendency that Cacioppo links to evolutionary survival.

Yet another biological approach to measuring happiness is through measuring hormones circulating in the blood and in the brain. For instance, levels of dopamine and serotonin circulating in certain regions of the brain are connected to feelings related to happiness. As you probably know, recent antidepressant drugs work by influencing the levels of natural hormones, such as serotonin, that remain active in the brain. It is easier to assess hormones circulating in the bloodstream, of course, because only a pinprick is required, rather than a needle probe through the skull. Megan Gunnar is one of the world's foremost experts on cortisol, a hormone circulating in the bloodstream that readies our bodies for action, but which can also signify stress. By tracking the rise and fall of cortisol through the day, she tracks our stress reactions in everyday life through biological means.

But biological measures are not the only methods to gauge happiness. Despite the sophistication of the biological measures of happiness, simply asking people how happy they are is still the most frequent way we measure well-being. People tend to be skilled at monitoring their own emotions, and generally know how intensely they are experiencing happiness. Just consider yourself for a moment: if we asked you how happy you are right now, you would probably know whether you are flying high or are down in the dumps. Not only can you distinguish between these two extremes, but you likely also know if you are moderately happy or very happy. If we asked you whether you were generally satisfied with your job, you could likely tell us the specific aspects you are pleased with and those about which you have some complaints. In fact, self-reports of happiness correlate with the biological measures, suggesting that asking folks about their happiness is a valid route to measuring this experience.

But what about people who might be shy about saying they are happy, or are motivated to conceal their discontent? What of people who are currently in a happy mood, and so summarize their entire life as very happy? We recognize these and other problems when measuring happiness, and overcome them by employing other measures in addition to self-report. For instance, we try to obtain the reports of friends and family members, people who know the research participant well and are willing to report on his or her moods. If you think about those folks you are close to – your spouse or your best friend – it is almost certain that you know when they are feeling upbeat and when they are a bit sour. They just can't hide the truth behind their moods day in and day out. We use these "informant reports" to look for agreement or discrepancies in the happiness scores of our research participants.

In addition to informant reports, we use memory measures of good and bad events that have occurred in the recent past. Happy people tend to be able to quickly recall lots of positive events, such as their child's school play, walking the dog, a productive brainstorming session at work, or the clever thing they said at a party. Depressed people, because they have a habit of focusing on the negatives of life, can easily recall recent problems, upsets, failures, and setbacks. Therefore, when we ask research participants to list as many positive or negative events as they can remember in a short period of time, such as sixty seconds, we can see whether or not they lean toward happiness. The renowned Princeton psychologist Daniel Kahneman and his colleague Talya Miron-Schatz have used the listing of daily thoughts, coded into positive and negative categories, as yet another way to assess happiness.

But we don't stop with measures of biology, self-report, informant report, thought listing, and memory. We also commonly use the experience sampling method (ESM), in which we provide research participants with a palmtop computer that periodically rings a random alarm, and ask them to fill out mood reports throughout the day while they are engaged in a wide range of natural situations. The participants report their mood on the palmtop at random moments in the mornings and the afternoons, when they are alone and with friends, and when they are at work and at weekends. In this way, we are able to sample people's moods from moment to moment as they go about their lives in the real world. Although people's momentary moods tend to fluctuate a bit, owing to momentary situational factors, a person's average moods are usually consistent when calculated over time. A happy person goes up and down in moods, but over time she tends to have a higher average mood level than an unhappy person. Thus, the ESM measure is one of the best ways of assessing happiness.

However, ESM has a few costs as well, especially to us researchers. We have lost several expensive palmtops over the years. They occasionally get left in trains, dropped in toilets (we asked that volunteer not to return that computer), and crushed by cars. But the information ESM provides is invaluable. Finally, we can explore measures of how much people smile or frown, for example, in a videotaped interview, as a measure of happiness. Taken together, all these measures can paint a reasonably accurate picture of a person's overall happiness. As it turns out, psychologists can measure happiness about as well as economists can measure income – pretty well, but not perfectly. When several measures of happiness are used together, we can obtain a reasonably accurate measure of happiness.

Further Reading

Argyle, M. 2001. *The psychology of happiness*. 2nd edn. New York: Routledge.

Bryant, F. B., and J. Veroff. 2007. *Savoring: A new model of positive experience*. Mahwah, NJ: Lawrence Erlbaum.

Buckingham, M., and C. Coffman. 1999. *First, break all the rules: What the world's greatest managers do differently*. London: Simon and Schuster.

Csikszentmihalyi, M. 1990. *Flow: The psychology of optimal experience*. New York: Harper Perennial.

Csikszentmihalyi, M., et al. 1975. *Beyond boredom and anxiety*. The Jossey-Bass Behavioral Science Series. San Francisco: Jossey-Bass.

Csikszentmihalyi, M., and I. S. Csikszentmihalyi, eds. 2006. *A life worth living: Contributions to positive psychology*. New York: Oxford University Press.

DePaulo, B. 2006. *Singled out: How singles are stereotyped, stigmatized, and ignored, and still live happily ever after*. New York: St. Martin's Press.

Dutton, J. E. 2003. *Energize your workplace: How to create and sustain high-quality connections at work*. San Francisco: Jossey-Bass.

Emmons, R. A., and M. E. McCullough, eds. 2004. *The psychology of gratitude*. New York: Oxford University Press.

Fromm, E. 1956. *The art of loving*. New York: Harper and Row.

Furnam, A., and M. Argyle. 1998. *The psychology of money*. New York: Routledge.

Gilbert, D. T. 2006. *Stumbling on happiness*. New York: Knopf.

Kahneman, D. 2008. *Thinking about thinking*. New York: Doubleday.

Lama, D., and H. C. Cutler. 1998. *The art of happiness: A handbook for living*. New York: Riverhead Books.

Layard, R. 2005. *Happiness: Lessons from a new science*. New York: Penguin.

Lykken, D. T. 1999. *Happiness: What studies on twins show us about nature, nurture, and the happiness set point*. New York: Golden Books.

Lyubomirsky, S. 2008. *The how of happiness: A scientific approach to getting the life you want*. New York: Penguin.

Lyubomirsky, S., L. King, and E. Diener. 2005. The benefits of frequent positive affect: Does happiness lead to success? *Psychological Bulletin* 131:803–5.

McMahon, D. 2006. *Happiness: A history.* New York: Atlantic Monthly Press.

Myers, D. 1993. The *pursuit of happiness: Discovering the pathway to fulfillment, well-being, and enduring personal joy.* New York: Harper Collins.

Nettle, D. 2005. *Happiness: The science behind your smile.* New York: Oxford University Press.

Nozick, R. 1989. *The examined life: Philosophical meditations.* New York: Simon and Schuster.

Putnam, R. 1995. *Bowling alone: The collapse and revival of American community.* New York: Simon and Schuster.

Sapolsky, R. 1998. *Why zebras don't get ulcers: An updated guide to stress, stress-related disease and coping.* 2nd edn. New York: Henry Holt.

Schwartz, B. 2004. *The paradox of choice: Why more is less.* New York: Ecco.

Seligman, M. E. P. 2002. *Authentic happiness: Using the new positive psychology to realize your potential for lasting fulfillment.* New York: Free Press.

Vaillant, G. E. 2003. *Aging well: Surprising guideposts to a happier life from the landmark Harvard study of adult development.* New York: Little, Brown.

Wagner, R., and J. K. Harter. 2006. *12: The elements of great managing.* New York: Gallup Press.

References

Abbe, A., C. Tkach, and S. Lyubomirsky. 2003. The art of living by dispositionally happy people. *Journal of Happiness Studies* 4:385–404.

Adler, N. E., T. Boyce, M. A. Chesney, S. Cohen, S. Folkman, R. L. Kahn, and S. L. Syme. 1994. Socioeconomic status and health: The challenge of the gradient. *American Psychologist* 49:15–24.

Ai, A. L., C. Peterson, T. N. Tice, S. F. Bolling, and H. G. Koenig. 2004. Faith-based and secular pathways to hope and optimism subconstructs in middle-aged and older cardiac patients. *Journal of Health Psychology* 9:435–50.

Amabile, T. M., S. G. Barsade, J. S. Mueller, and B. M. Staw. 2005. Affect and creativity at work. *Administrative Science Quarterly* 50:367–403.

Anderson, C. J., and L. C. Vogel. 2003. Domain-specific satisfaction in adults with pediatric-onset spinal cord injuries. *Spinal Cord* 41:684–91.

Ardelt, M. 2003. Effects of religion and purpose in life on elders' subjective well-being and attitudes toward death. *Journal of Religious Gerontology* 14:55–77.

Baron, J. 2000. *Thinking and deciding.* 3rd edn. New York: Cambridge University Press.

Bartolini, S., E. Bilancini, and M. Pugno. 2007. *Did the decline in social capital decrease American happiness? A relational explanation of the Happiness Paradox.* University of Siena Department of Economics Series, no. 513. Retrieved September 7, 2007, from.

Bazerman, M. H., D. A. Moore, A. E. Tenbrunsel, K. A. Wade-Benzoni, and S. Blount. 1999. Explaining how preferences change across joint versus separate evaluation. *Journal of Economic Behavior and Organization* 39:41–58.

Bergman, L. R., and D. Daukantaite. 2006. The importance of social circumstances for Swedish women's subjective well-being. *International Journal of Social Welfare* 15:27–36.

Berscheid, E. 2003. The human's greatest strength: Other humans. In *A psychology of human strengths: Fundamental questions and future directions for a positive psychology*, edited by L. G. Aspinwall and U. M. Staudinger. Washington, DC: American Psychological Association.

Biswas-Diener, R. 2008. Material wealth and subjective well-being. In *The science of subjective well-being*, edited by M. Eid and R. J. Larsen. New York: Guilford Press.

Biswas-Diener, R., and E. Diener. 2001. Making the best of a bad situation: Satisfaction in the slums of Calcutta. *Social Indicators Research* 55:329–52.

Biswas-Diener, R., and E. Diener. 2006. The subjective well-being of the homeless, and lessons for happiness. *Social Indicators Research* 76:185–205.

Biswas-Diener, R., J. Vittersø, and E. Diener. 2005. Most people are pretty happy, but there is cultural variation: The Inughuit, the Amish, and the Maasai. *Journal of Happiness Studies* 6:205–26.

Blanchflower, D. G., and A. J. Oswald. 2006. Hypertension and happiness across nations. Unpublished manuscript.

Bonanno, G. A., C. B. Wortman, D. R. Lehman, R. G. Tweed, M. Haring, J. Sonnega, et al. 2002. Resilience to loss and chronic grief: A prospective study from pre-loss to 18 months post-loss. *Journal of Personality and Social Psychology* 83:1150–64.

Bonanno, G. A., C. B. Wortman, and R. M. Nesse. 2004. Prospective patterns of resilience and maladjustment during widowhood. *Psychology and Aging* 19:260–71.

Brickman, P., and D. T. Campbell. 1971. Hedonic relativism and planning the good society. In *Adaptation level theory: A symposium*, edited by M. H. Appley. New York: Academic Press.

Brickman, P., D. Coates, and R. Janoff-Bulman. 1978. Lottery winners and accident victims: Is happiness relative? *Journal of Personality and Social Psychology* 36:917–27.

Brown, S. L., R. M. Nesse, A. D. Vinokur, and D. M. Smith. 2003. Providing social support may be more beneficial than receiving it: Results from a prospective study of mortality. *Psychological Science* 14:320–7.

Bryant, F. B., and J. Veroff. 2007. *Savoring: A new model of positive experience*. Mahwah, NJ: Lawrence Erlbaum.

Cacioppo, J. T., L. C. Hawkley, A. Kalil, M. E. Hughes, L. Waite, and R. A. Thisted. 2008. Happiness and the invisible threads of social connection: The Chicago health, aging, and social relations study. In *The science of subjective well-being*, edited by M. Eid and R. J. Larsen. New York: Guilford Press.

Campbell, W. K., E. A. Krusemark, K. A. Dyckman, A. B. Brunell, J. E. McDowell, J. M. Twenge, and B. A. Clementz. 2006. A magneto-encephalographic investigation of neural correlates for social exclusion and self-control. *Social Neuroscience* 1:124–34.

Canli, T., M. Qiu, K. Omura, E. Congdon, B. W. Hass, Z. Amin, M. J. Herrmann, T. Constable, and K. P. Lesch. 2006. Neural correlates of epigenesist. *Proceedings of the National Academy of Sciences* (US) 103:16033–8.

References

Carson, T. P., and H. E. Adams. 1980. Activity valence as a function of mood change. *Journal of Abnormal Psychology* 89:368–77.

Caspi, A., K. Sugden, T. E. Moffitt, A. Taylor, I. W. Craig, H. Harrington, J. McClay, J. Mill, J. Martin, A. Braithwaite, and R. Poulton. 2003. Influence of life stress on depression: Moderation by a polymorphism in the 5-HTT gene. *Science* 301:386–9.

Cheney, G. E., T. E. Zorn, S. Planalp, and D. J. Lair. In press. Meaningful work and personal/social well-being: Organizational communication engages the meanings of work. In *Communication Yearbook* 32, edited by C. S. Beck. Mahwah, NJ: Lawrence Erlbaum.

Cherkas, L. F., A. Aviv, A. M. Valdes, J. L. Hunkin, J. P. Gardner, G. L. Surdulescu, M. Kimura, and T. D. Spector. 2006. The effects of social status on biological aging as measured by white-blood-cell telomere length. *Aging Cell* 5:361–5.

Cohen, S. 2004. Social relationships and health. *American Psychologist* 59:676–84.

Cohen, S., W. J. Doyle, and A. Baum. 2006. Socioeconomic status is associated with stress hormones. *Psychosomatic Medicine* 68:414–20.

Cohen, S., W. J. Doyle, R. B. Turner, C. M. Alper, and D. P. Skoner. 2003. Emotional style and susceptibility to the common cold. *Psychosomatic Medicine* 65:652–7.

Cox, W. M. 1999. *Myths of rich and poor: Why we're better off than we think.* New York: Basic Books/Perseus Books Group.

Cropanzano, R., K. James, and M. A. Konovsky. 1993. Dispositional affectivity as a predictor of work attitudes and job performance. *Journal of Organizational Behavior* 14:595–606.

Cropanzano, R., and T. A. Wright. 1999. A five-year study of change in the relationship between well-being and job performance. *Consulting Psychology Journal: Research and Practice* 51:252–65.

Csikszentmihalyi, M., and I. S. Csikszentmihalyi, eds. 2006. *A life worth living: Contributions to positive psychology.* New York: Oxford University Press.

Cunningham, M. R. 1988. Does happiness mean friendliness? Induced mood and heterosexual self-disclosure. *Personality and Social Psychology Bulletin* 14:283–97.

Cunningham, M. R. 1988. What do you do when you're happy or blue? Mood, expectancies, and behavioral interest. *Motivation and Emotion* 12:309–31.

Cunningham, M. R. 1997. Social allergens and the reactions that they produce: Escalation of annoyance and disgust in love and work. In *Aversive interpersonal behaviors*, edited by R. M. Kowalski. New York: Plenum Press.

Danner, D. D., D. A. Snowden, and W. Friesen. 2001. Positive emotions in early life and longevity: Findings from the Nun Study. *Journal of Personality and Social Psychology* 80:804–13.

Davenport, R. J. 2005. Optimistic for longevity. *The Science of Aging Knowledge Environment* 17:33.

Davidson, R. J. 2005. Emotion regulation, happiness, and the neuroplasticity of the brain. *Advances in Mind-Body Medicine* 21:25–58.

Dawkins, R. 2006. *The God delusion.* Boston: Houghton Mifflin.

Deci, E. L., and R. M. Ryan, eds. 2002. *Handbook of self-determination research.* Rochester, NY: University of Rochester Press.

Diener, E. 1984. Subjective well-being. *Psychological Bulletin* 95:542–75.

Diener, E. 2000. Subjective well-being: The science of happiness, and a proposal for a national index. *American Psychologist* 55:34–43.

Diener, E. 2008. Myths in the science of happiness, and directions for future research. In *The science of subjective well-being,* edited by M. Eid and R. J. Larsen. New York: Guilford Press.

Diener, E., and R. Biswas-Diener. 2002. Will money increase subjective well-being? A literature review and guide to needed research. *Social Indicators Research* 57:119–69.

Diener, E., and D. Clifton. 2002. Life satisfaction and religiosity in broad probability samples. *Psychological Inquiry* 13:206–9.

Diener, E., C. R. Colvin, W. G. Pavot, and A. Allman. 1991. The psychic costs of intense positive affect. *Journal of Personality and Social Psychology* 61:492–503.

Diener, E., and C. Diener. 1996. Most people are happy. *Psychological Science* 7:181–5.

Diener, E., and M. Diener. 1995. Cross-cultural correlates of life satisfaction and self-esteem. *Journal of Personality and Social Psychology* 68:653–63.

Diener, E., M. Diener, and C. Diener. 1995. Factors predicting the subjective well-being of nations. *Journal of Personality and Social Psychology* 69:851–64.

Diener, E., and R. A. Emmons. 1985. The independence of positive and negative affect. *Journal of Personality and Social Psychology* 47:1105–17.

Diener, E., R. A. Emmons, R. J. Larsen, and S. Griffin. 1985. The satisfaction with life scale. *Journal of Personality Assessment* 49:71–5.

Diener, E., and F. Fujita. 1995. Resources, personal strivings, and subjective well-being: A nomothetic and idiographic approach. *Journal of Personality and Social Psychology* 68:926–35.

Diener, E., and F. Fujita. 2005. Hedonism revisited: Happy days versus a satisfying life. Unpublished manuscript, University of Illinois at Urbana-Champaign.

Diener, E., C. L. Gohm, E. Suh, and S. Oishi. 2000. Similarity of the relations between marital status and subjective well-being across cultures. *Journal of Cross-Cultural Psychology* 31:419–36.

Diener, E., J. Horwitz, and R. A. Emmons. 1985. Happiness of the very wealthy. *Social Indicators Research* 16:263–74.

References

Diener, E., R. J. Larsen, S. Levine, and R. A. Emmons. 1985. Intensity and frequency: Dimensions underlying positive and negative affect. *Journal of Personality and Social Psychology* 48:1253–65.

Diener, E., and R. Lucas. 1999. Personality, and subjective well-being. In *Well-being: The foundations of hedonic psychology*, edited by D. Kahneman, E. Diener, and N. Schwarz. New York: Sage.

Diener, E., R. Lucas, and C. N. Scollon. 2006. Beyond the hedonic treadmill: Revising the adaptation theory of well-being. *American Psychologist* 61:305–14.

Diener, E., C. Nickerson, R. E. Lucas, and E. Sandvik. 2002. Dispositional affect and job outcomes. *Social Indicators Research* 59:229–59.

Diener, E., and S. Oishi. 2000. Money and happiness: Income and subjective well-being across nations. In *Culture and subjective wellbeing*, edited by E. Diener and E. M. Suh. Cambridge, MA: MIT Press.

Diener, E., and S. Oishi. 2004. Are Scandinavians happier than Asians? Issues in comparing nations on subjective well-being. In *Asian economic and political issues*, vol. 10, edited by F. Columbus. Hauppauge, NY: Nova Science.

Diener, E., and S. Oishi. 2005. Target article: The nonobvious social psychology of happiness. *Psychological Inquiry* 16:162–7.

Diener, E., S. Oishi, and R. E. Lucas. 2003. Personality, culture, and subjective well-being: Emotional and cognitive evaluations of life. *Annual Review of Psychology* 54:403–25.

Diener, E., E. Sandvik, and W. Pavot. 1991. Happiness is the frequency, not the intensity, of positive versus negative affect. In *Subjective well-being: An interdisciplinary perspective*, edited by F. Strack, M. Argyle, and N. Schwarz. New York: Pergamon.

Diener, E., E. Sandvik, W. Pavot, and F. Fujita. 1992. Extraversion and subjective well-being in a US national probability sample. *Journal of Research in Personality* 26:205–15.

Diener, E., J. Sapyta, and E. Suh. 1998. Subjective well-being is essential to well-being. *Psychological Inquiry* 9:33–7.

Diener, E., and M. E. P. Seligman. 2002. Very happy people. *Psychological Science* 13:81–4.

Diener, E., and M. E. P. Seligman. 2004. Beyond money: Toward an economy of well-being. *Psychological Science in the Public Interest* 5:1–31.

Diener, E., and E. Suh. 1999. National differences in subjective well-being. In *Well-being: The foundations of hedonic psychology*, edited by D. Kahneman, E. Diener, and N. Schwarz. New York: Sage.

Diener, E., E. Suh, and S. Oishi. 1997. Recent findings on subjective well-being. *Indian Journal of Clinical Psychology* 24:25–41.

Diener, E., and E. M. Suh, eds. 2000. *Culture and subjective well-being*. Cambridge, MA: MIT Press.

Diener, E., E. M. Suh, R. E. Lucas, and H. L. Smith. 1999. Subjective well-being: Three decades of progress. *Psychological Bulletin* 125:276–302.

Diener, E., and W. Tov. In press. Culture and subjective well-being. In *Handbook of cultural psychology*, edited by S. Kitayama and D. Cohen. New York: Guilford Press.

Diener, E., and W. Tov. In press. Happiness and peace. *Journal of Social Issues*.

Diener, M. L., and M. B. D. McGavran. 2008. What makes people happy? A developmental approach to the literature on family relationships and well being (by the daughters of a man who thought to ask). In *The science of subjective well-being*, edited by M. Eid and R. J. Larsen. New York: Guilford Press.

Dijkers, M. P. 1999. Correlates of life satisfaction among persons with spinal cord injury. *Archives of Physical Medicine and Rehabilitation* 80:867–76.

Dunn, E. W., M. A. Brackett, C. Ashton-James, E. Schneiderman, and P. Salovey. 2007. On emotionally intelligent time travel: Individual differences in affective forecasting ability. *Personality and Social Psychology Bulletin* 33:85–93.

Easterbrook, G. 2003. *The progress paradox: How life gets better while people feel worse*. New York: Random House.

Easterlin, R. A. 1996. *Growth triumphant: The twenty-first century in historical perspective*. Ann Arbor: University of Michigan Press.

Elliot, A. J., and T. M. Thrash. 2002. Approach-avoidance motivation in personality: Approach and avoidance temperaments and goals. *Journal of Personality and Social Psychology* 82:804–18.

Emmons, R. A. 2008. Gratitude, subjective well-being, and the brain. In *The science of subjective well-being*, edited by M. Eid and R. J. Larsen. New York: Guilford Press.

Emmons, R. A., and E. Diener. 1985. Personality correlates of subjective well-being. *Personality and Social Psychology Bulletin* 11:89–97.

Emmons, R. A., and M. E. McCullough. 2003. Counting blessings versus burdens: An experimental investigation of gratitude and subjective well-being in daily life. *Journal of Personality and Social Psychology* 84:377–89.

Epel, E. S. 2004. Accelerated telomere shortening in response to life stress. *Proceedings of the National Academy of Sciences* (US) 101:17312–15.

Exline, J. J. 2002. Stumbling blocks on the religious road: Fractured relationships, nagging vices, and the inner struggle to believe. *Psychological Inquiry* 13:182–9.

Ferriss, A. L. 2004. Religion and the quality of life. *Journal of Happiness Studies* 3:199–215.

Folkman, S., and J. T. Moskowitz. 2000. Stress, positive emotion, and coping. *Current Directions in Psychological Science* 9:115–18.

Frank, R. H. 1999. *Luxury fever: Why money fails to satisfy in an era of excess*. New York: Free Press.

References

Frank, R. H. 2005. Does money buy happiness? In *The science of well-being*, edited by F. A. Huppert, N. Baylis, and B. Keverne. New York: Oxford University Press.

Frasure-Smith, N., and F. Lesperance. 2005. Depression and coronary heart disease: Complex synergism of mind, body, and environment. *Current Directions in Psychological Science* 14:39–43.

Frederick, S., and G. Loewenstein. 1999. Hedonic adaptation. In *Well-being: The foundations of hedonic psychology*, edited by D. Kahneman, E. Diener, and N. Schwarz. New York: Sage.

Fredrickson, B. L. 1998. What good are positive emotions? *Review of General Psychology* 2:300–19.

Fredrickson, B. L. 2004. Gratitude, like other positive emotions, broadens and builds. In *The psychology of gratitude*, edited by R. A. Emmons and M. E. McCullough. New York: Oxford University Press.

Fredrickson, B. L. 2008. Promoting positive affect. In *The science of subjective well-being*, edited by M. Eid and R. J. Larsen. New York: Guilford Press.

Fredrickson, B. L., and C. Branigan. 2005. Positive emotions broaden the scope of attention and thought-action repertoires. *Cognition & Emotion* 19:313–32.

Fredrickson, B. L., and T. Joiner. 2002. Positive emotions trigger upward spirals toward emotional well-being. *Psychological Science* 13:172–5.

Fredrickson, B. L., and M. F. Losada. 2005. Positive affect and the complex dynamics of human flourishing. *American Psychologist* 60:678–86.

Fredrickson, B. L., R. A. Mancuso, C. Branigan, and M. M. Tugade. 2000. The undoing effect of positive emotions. *Motivation and Emotion* 24:237–58.

Fredrickson, B. L., M. M. Tugade, C. E. Waugh, and G. R. Larkin. 2003. What good are positive emotions in crisis? A prospective study of resilience and emotions following the terrorist attacks on the United States on September 11th, 2001. *Journal of Personality and Social Psychology* 84:365–76.

Friedman, E. T., R. M. Schwartz, and D. A. F. Haaga. 2002. Are the very happy too happy? *Journal of Happiness Studies* 3:355–72.

Friedman, P. H. In press. *The forgiveness solution: 10 steps to releasing depression, anxiety, guilt, and anger, and increasing peace, love, joy, and well-being in your life.* Oakland, CA: New Harbinger Publishers.

Frisch, M. B. 2006. *Quality of life therapy: Applying a life satisfaction approach to positive psychology and cognitive therapy.* Hoboken, NJ: John Wiley and Sons.

Frisch, M. B. 2008. Quality of life coaching and therapy and (QOLC/T): A new system of positive psychology and subjective well-being interventions. In *The science of subjective well-being*, edited by M. Eid and R. J. Larsen. New York: Guilford Press.

Fujita, F. 2008. The frequency of social comparison and its relation to subjective well-being: The frequency of social comparison scale. In *The science of subjective well-being*, edited by M. Eid and R. J. Larsen. New York: Guilford Press.

Fujita, F., and E. Diener. 2005. Life satisfaction set-point: Stability and change. *Journal of Personality and Social Psychology* 88:158–64.

Gable, S. L., H. T. Reis, and A. J. Elliot. 2000. Behavioral activation and inhibition in everyday life. *Journal of Personality and Social Psychology* 78:1135–49.

Gardner, J., and A. J. Oswald. 2007. Money and mental wellbeing: A longitudinal study of medium-sized lottery wins. *Journal of Health Economics* 26:49–60.

George, J. M., and J. Zhou. 2007. Dual tuning in a supportive context: Joint contributions of positive mood, negative mood, and supervisory behaviors to employee creativity. *Academy of Management Journal* 50:605–22.

Germans, M. K., and A. M. Kring. 2000. Hedonic deficit in anhedonia: Support for the role of approach motivation. *Personality and Individual Differences* 28:659–72.

Gerstorf, D., J. Smith, and P. B. Baltes. 2006. A systematic-wholistic approach to differential aging: Longitudinal findings from the Berlin aging study. *Psychology and Aging* 21:645–63.

Gilbert, D. T. 2006. *Stumbling on happiness.* New York: Knopf.

Gilbert, D. T., E. C. Pinel, T. D. Wilson, S. J. Blumberg, and T. P. Wheatley. 1998. Immune neglect: A source of durability bias in affective forecasting. *Journal of Personality and Social Psychology* 75:617–38.

Gottman, J. M. 1994. *What predicts divorce? The relationship between marital processes and marital outcomes.* Hillsdale, NJ: Lawrence Erlbaum.

Grant, N., J. Wardle, and A. Steptoe. 2007. The relationship between life satisfaction and health behavior: A cross-cultural analysis of young adults. Keynote address presented at the Second World Congress of Stress, Budapest.

Grant, N., J. Wardle, and A. Steptoe. In press. The relationship between life satisfaction and health behavior: A cross-cultural analysis of young adults. *International Journal of Behavioral Medicine.*

Gunnar, M. R., and B. Donzella. 2002. Social regulation of the cortisol levels in early human development. *Psychoneuroendocrinology* 27:199–220.

Harker, L. A., and D. Keltner. 2001. Expressions of positive emotion in women's college yearbook pictures and their relationship to personality and life outcomes across adulthood. *Journal of Personality and Social Psychology* 80:112–24.

Harris, S. 2006. *Letter to a Christian nation.* New York: Knopf.

Harter, J. K., Schmidt, F. L., and Hayes, T. L. 2002. Business-unit level relationship between employee satisfaction, employee engagement, and business outcomes: A meta-analysis. *Journal of Applied Psychology* 87:268–79.

Hastorf, A. H., and H. Cantril. 1954. They saw a game: A case study. *Journal of Abnormal and Social Psychology* 49:129–34.

Haybron, D. M. 2008. Philosophy and the science of subjective well-being. In *The science of subjective well-being*, edited by M. Eid and R. J. Larsen. New York: Guilford Press.

Headey, B., J. Kelley, and A. Wearing. 1993. Dimensions of mental health: Life satisfaction, positive affect, anxiety, and depression. *Social Indicators Research* 29:63–82.

Helgeson, V. S., and S. E. Taylor. 1993. Social comparisons and adjustment among cardiac patients. *Journal of Applied Social Psychology* 23:1171–95.

Helliwell, J. F. 2006. Well-being, social capital and public policy: What's new? *Economic Journal* 116:C34–C45.

Herbert, T. B., and S. Cohen. 1993. Depression and immunity: A meta-analytic review. *Psychological Bulletin* 113:472–86.

Hewitt, P. L., and G. L. Flett. 1991. Perfectionism in the self and social contexts: Conceptualization, assessment, and association with psychopathology. *Journal of Personality and Social Psychology* 60:456–70.

Hill, S. E., and D. M. Buss. 2008. Evolution and subjective well-being. In *The science of subjective well-being*, edited by M. Eid and R. J. Larsen. New York: Guilford Press.

Hope, optimism, and other business assets: Why "psychological capital" is so valuable to your company. 2007. *Gallup Management Journal* (January 11, 2007). Retrieved January 11, 2007, from www.gmj.gallup.com/content/print/25708/Hope-Optimism-and-Other-Business-Assets.aspx.

Hsee, C. K., S. Blount, G. F. Loewenstein, and M. H. Bazerman. 1999. Preference reversals between joint and separate evaluations of options: A review and theoretical analysis. *Psychological Bulletin* 125:576–90.

Huebner, E. S., and C. Diener. 2008. Research on life satisfaction of children and youth: Implications for the delivery of school-related services. In *The science of subjective well-being*, edited by M. Eid and R. J. Larsen. New York: Guilford Press.

Isen, A. M. 1999. On the relationship between affect and creative problem solving. In *Affect, creative experience, and psychological adjustment*, edited by S. Russ. Philadelphia: Taylor and Francis.

Isen, A. M. 1999. Positive affect. In *The handbook of cognition and emotion*, edited by T. Dalgleish and M. Power. Chichester: Wiley.

Iyengar, S. S., and M. R. Lepper. 1999. Rethinking the value of choice: A cultural perspective on intrinsic motivation. *Journal of Personality and Social Psychology* 76:349–66.

Iyengar, S. S., and M. R. Lepper. 2000. When choice is demotivating. *Journal of Personality and Social Psychology* 79:995–1006.

Iyengar, S. S., R. E. Wells, and B. Schwartz. 2006. Doing better but feeling worse: Looking for the "best" job undermines satisfaction. *Psychological Science* 17:143–50.

Jacobs, N., I. Myin-Germeys, C. Derom, P. Delespaul, J. van Os, and N. A. Nicolson. 2007. A momentary assessment study of the relationship between affective and adrenocortical stress responses in daily life. *Biological Psychology* 74:60–6.

James, W. 1902. *The varieties of religious experience: A study in human nature.* New York: Longmans, Green.

Johnson, W., and R. F. Krueger. 2006. How money buys happiness: Genetic and environmental processes linking finances and life satisfaction. *Journal of Personality and Social Psychology* 90:680–91.

Jonas, E., J. Schimel, J. Greenberg, and T. Pyszcynski. 2002. The Scrooge effect: Evidence that mortality salience increases prosocial attitudes and behavior. *Personality and Social Psychology Bulletin* 28:1342–53.

Judge, T. A., and R. Klinger. 2008. Job satisfaction: Subjective well-being at work. In *The science of subjective well-being,* edited by M. Eid and R. J. Larsen. New York: Guilford Press.

Judge, T. A., and R. Larsen. 2001. Dispositional affect and job satisfaction: A review and theoretical extension. *Organizational Behavior and Human Decision Processes* 86:67–98.

Judge, T. A., C. J. Thoresen, J. E. Bono, and G. K. Patton. 2001. The job satisfaction-job performance relationship: A qualitative and quantitative review. *Psychological Bulletin* 127:367–407.

Kahneman, D. 1999. Objective happiness. In *Well-being: The foundations of hedonic psychology,* edited by D. Kahneman, E. Diener, and N. Schwarz. New York: Sage.

Kahneman, D., E. Diener, and N. Schwarz. 1999. Does living in California make people happy? A focusing illusion in judgments of life satisfaction. *Psychological Science* 9:340–6.

Kahneman, D., E. Diener, and N. Schwarz. 1999. Well-being: The foundations of hedonic psychology. In *Well-being: The foundations of hedonic psychology,* edited by D. Kahneman, E. Diener, and N. Schwarz. New York: Sage.

Kahneman, D., B. L. Fredrickson, C. A. Schreiber, and D. A. Redelmeier. 1993. When more pain is preferred to less: Adding a better end. *Psychological Science* 4:401–5.

Kahneman, D., and A. Tversky. 1979. Prospect theory: An analysis of decisions under risk. *Econometrika* 47:263–91.

Kahneman, D., and A. Tversky. 1984. Choices, values, and frames. *American Psychologist* 39:341–50.

Kahneman, D., P. P. Wakker, and R. Sarin. 1997. Back to Bentham? Explorations of experienced utility (In memory of Amos Tversky, 1937–1996). *Quarterly Journal of Economics* 112:375–405.

Kasser, T. 2002. *The high price of materialism.* Cambridge, MA: MIT Press.

Kasser, T. 2006. Materialism and its alternatives. In *A life worth living: Contributions to positive psychology,* edited by M. Csikszentmihalyi and I. S. Csikszentmihalyi. New York: Oxford University Press.

Keyes, C. L. M. 2006. Mental health in adolescence: Is America's youth flourishing? *American Journal of Orthopsychiatry* 76:395–402.

References

Keyes, C. L. M. 2007. Promoting and protecting mental health as flourishing: A complementary strategy for improving national mental health. *American Psychologist* 62:95–108.

Kiecolt-Glaser, J. K., L. McGuire, T. F. Robles, and R. Glaser. 2002. Emotions, morbidity, and mortality: New perspectives from psychoneuroimmunology. *Annual Review of Psychology* 53:83–107.

Kim, J., and E. Hatfield. 2004. Love types and subjective well-being: A cross-cultural study. *Social Behavior and Personality* 32:173–82.

King, L. A. 2008. Interventions for enhancing SWB: Can we make people happier and should we? In *The science of subjective well-being*, edited by M. Eid and R. J. Larsen. New York: Guilford Press.

King, L. A., and C. M. Burton. 2003. The hazards of goal pursuit. In *Virtue, vice, and personality: The complexity of behavior*, edited by E. C. Chang and L. J. Sanna. Washington, DC: American Psychological Association.

King, L. A., J. E. Eells, and C. M. Burton. 2004. The good life, broadly and narrowly considered. In *Positive psychology in practice*, edited by P. A. Linley and S. Joseph. Hoboken, NJ: John Wiley and Sons.

King, L. A., and J. A. Hicks. 2007. Whatever happened to "what might have been"?: Regrets, happiness, and maturity. *American Psychologist* October.

King, L. A., J. A. Hicks, J. L. Krull, and A. K. Del Gaiso. 2006. Positive affect and the experience of meaning in life. *Journal of Personality and Social Psychology* 90:179–96.

Kitayama, S., B. Mesquita, and M. Karasawa. 2006. Cultural affordances and emotional experience: Socially engaging and disengaging emotions in Japan and the United States. *Journal of Personality and Social Psychology* 91:890–903.

Kohler, H. P., J. R. Behrman, and A. Skytthe. 2005. Partner + Children = Happiness? The effects of partnerships and fertility on well-being. *Population and Development Review* 31:407–45.

Krause, N. 2004. Common facets of religion, unique facets of religion, and life satisfaction among older African Americans. *Journals of Gerontology*, ser. b: Psychological Sciences and Social Sciences, 59B(2):S109–S117.

Krause, N. 2006. Church-based social support and mortality, *Journals of Gerontology*, ser. b: Psychological Sciences and Social Sciences, 61B:S140–S146.

Kuppens, P., A. Realo, and E. Diener. In press. The role of emotions in life satisfaction judgments across cultures. *Journal of Personality and Social Psychology*.

Larsen, R. J., and E. Diener. 1985. A multitrait-multimethod examination of affect structure: Hedonic level and emotional intensity. *Personality and Individual Differences* 6:631–6.

Larsen, R. J., and Z. Prizmic. 2004. Affect regulation. In *Handbook of self-regulation: Research, theory, and applications*, edited by R. F. Baumeister and K. D. Vohs. New York: Guilford Press.

Larsen, R. J., and Z. Prizmic. 2008. Regulation of emotional well-being: Overcoming the hedonic treadmill. In *The science of subjective well-being*, edited by M. Eid and R. J. Larsen. New York: Guilford Press.

Layard, R. 2005. *Happiness: Lessons from a new science*. New York: Penguin.

Lepper, H. S. 1998. Use of other-reports to validate subjective well-being measures. *Social Indicators Research*, 44:367–79.

Levin, J. S. 1996. How religion influences morbidity and health: Reflections on natural history, salutogenesis and host resistance. *Social Science and Medicine* 43:849–64.

Loewenstein, G., and D. Schkade. 1999. Wouldn't it be nice? Predicting future feelings. In *Well-being: The foundations of hedonic psychology*, edited by D. Kahneman, E. Diener, and N. Schwarz. New York: Sage.

Lucas, R. E. 2005. Time does not heal all wounds: A longitudinal study of reaction and adaptation to divorce. *Psychological Science* 16:945–50.

Lucas, R. E. 2008. Personality and subjective well-being. In *The science of subjective well-being*, edited by M. Eid and R. J. Larsen. New York: Guilford Press.

Lucas, R. E. In press. Adaptation and the set-point model of subjective well-being: Does happiness change after major life events? *Current Directions in Psychological Science*.

Lucas, R. E. In press. Long-term disability is associated with lasting changes in subjective well being: Evidence from two nationally representative longitudinal studies. *Journal of Personality and Social Psychology*.

Lucas, R. E., and B. M. Baird. 2004. Extraversion and emotional reactivity. *Journal of Personality and Social Psychology* 86:473–85.

Lucas, R. E., and A. E. Clark. 2006. Do people really adapt to marriage? *Journal of Happiness Studies* 7:405–26.

Lucas, R. E., A. E. Clark, Y. Georgellis, and E. Diener. 2003. Reexamining adaptation and the set point model of happiness: Reactions to changes in marital status. *Journal of Personality and Social Psychology* 84:527–39.

Lucas, R. E., A. E. Clark, Y. Georgellis, and E. Diener. 2004. Unemployment alters the set-point for life satisfaction. *Psychological Science* 15:8–13.

Lucas, R. E., and E. Diener. 2001. Understanding extraverts' enjoyment of social situations: The importance of pleasantness. *Journal of Personality and Social Psychology* 81:343–56.

Lucas, R. E., and E. Diener. 2003. The happy worker: Hypotheses about the role of positive affect in worker productivity. In *Personality and work: Reconsidering the role of personality in organizations*, edited by M. R. Barrick and A. M. Ryan. The Organizations Frontiers Series. San Francisco: Jossey-Bass.

Lucas, R. E., E. Diener, A. Grob, E. M. Suh, and L. Shao. 2000. Cross-cultural evidence for the fundamental features of extraversion. *Journal of Personality and Social Psychology* 79:452–68.

References

Lucas, R. E., E. Diener, and E. Suh. 1996. Discriminant validity of well-being measures. *Journal of Personality and Social Psychology* 71:616–28.

Lucas, R. E., and P. S. Dyrenforth. 2006. Does the existence of social relationships matter for subjective well-being? In *Self and relationships: Connecting intrapersonal and interpersonal processes*, edited by K. D. Vohs and E. J. Finkel. New York: Guilford Press.

Lucas, R. E., and F. Fujita. 2000. Factors influencing the relation between extraversion and pleasant affect. *Journal of Personality and Social Psychology* 79:1039–56.

Lucas, R. E., and U. Schimmack. Forthcoming. Income and life satisfaction in the GSOEP. Manuscript in preparation.

Luthans, F. 2002. The need for and meaning of positive organizational behavior. *Journal of Organizational Behavior* 23:695–706.

Lykken, D. 1999. *Happiness: What studies on twins show us about nature, nurture, and the happiness set point.* New York: Golden Books.

Lykken, D., and A. Tellegen. 1996. Happiness is a stochastic phenomenon. *Psychological Science* 7:186–9.

Lyubomirsky, S. 1997. Hedonic consequences of social comparison: A contrast of happy and unhappy people. *Journal of Personality and Social Psychology* 73:1141–57.

Lyubomirsky, S. 2001. Why are some people happier than others? The role of cognitive and motivational processes in well-being. *American Psychologist* 56:239–49.

Lyubomirsky, S. 2008. *The how of happiness: A scientific approach to getting the life you want.* New York: Penguin.

Lyubomirsky, S., L. King, and E. Diener. 2005. The benefits of frequent positive affect: Does happiness lead to success? *Psychological Bulletin* 131:803–55.

Lyubomirsky, S., and L. Ross. 1999. Changes in attractiveness of elected, rejected, and precluded alternatives: A comparison of happy and unhappy individuals. *Journal of Personality and Social Psychology* 76:988–1007.

Lyubomirsky, S., and K. L. Tucker. 1998. Implications of individual differences in subjective happiness for perceiving, interpreting, and thinking about life events. *Motivation and Emotion* 22:155–86.

Lyubomirsky, S., K. L. Tucker, and F. Kasri. 2001. Responses to hedonically conflicting social comparisons: Comparing happy and unhappy people. *European Journal of Social Psychology* 31:511–35.

McIntosh, D. N., R. C. Silver, and C. B. Wortman. 1993. Religion's role in adjustment to a negative life event: Coping with the loss of a child. *Journal of Personality and Social Psychology* 65:812–21.

McMahon, D. M. 2008. The pursuit of happiness in history. In *The science of subjective well-being*, edited by M. Eid and R. J. Larsen. New York: Guilford Press.

Magnus, K., E. Diener, F. Fujita, and W. Pavot. 1993. Extraversion and neuroticism as predictors of objective life events: A longitudinal analysis. *Journal of Personality and Social Psychology* 65:1046–53.

Maltby, J. and L. Day. 2003. Religious orientation, religious coping and appraisals of stress: Assessing primary appraisal factors in the relationship between religiosity and psychological well-being. *Personality and Individual Differences* 34:1209–24.

Maselko, J., L. Kubansky, I. Kawachi, J. Staudenmayer, and L. Berkman. 2006. Religious service attendance and decline in pulmonary function in a high-functioning elderly cohort. *Annals of Behavioral Medicine* 32: 245–53.

Matthews, K. A. 2005. Psychological perspectives on the development of coronary heart disease. *American Psychologist* 60:783–96.

Matthews, K. A., K. Raikkonen, K. Sutton-Tyrrell, and L. H. Kuller. 2004. Optimistic attitudes protect against progression of carotid atherosclerosis in healthy middle-aged women. *Psychosomatic Medicine* 65:640–4.

Michalos, A. C. 1985. Multiple discrepancies theory (MDT). *Social Indicators Research* 16:347–413.

Michalos, A. C. Forthcoming. The good life: Eighth century to fourth century BCE.

Michalos, A. C. Forthcoming. In *Handbook of Social Indicators and Quality of Life Research*, edited by K. Land.

Michalos, A. C., and B. D. Zumbo. 2002. Healthy days, health satisfaction and satisfaction with the overall quality of life. *Social Indicators Research* 59:321–38.

Middleton, R. A., and E. K. Byrd. 1996. Psychosocial factors and hospital readmission status of older persons with cardiovascular disease. *Journal of Applied Rehabilitation Counseling* 27:3–10.

Moreira-Almeida, A., F. L. Neto, and H. G. Koenig. 2006. Religiousness and mental health: A review. *Revista Brasileira de Psiquitra* 28:242–50.

Myers, D. G. 2008. Religion and human flourishing. In *The science of subjective well-being*, edited by M. Eid and R. J. Larsen. New York: Guilford Press.

Myers, D. G., and E. Diener. 1995. Who is happy? *Psychological Science* 6:10–19.

Nicholson, V., and S. Smith. 1977. *Spend, spend, spend*. London: Jonathan Cape.

Nickerson, C., N. Schwarz, E. Diener, and D. Kahneman. 2003. Zeroing in on the dark side of the American Dream: A closer look at the negative consequences of the goal for financial success. *Psychological Science* 14:531–6.

Nozick, R. 1974. *Anarchy, state, and utopia*. New York: Basic Books.

Nozick, R. 1989. *The examined life: Philosophical meditations*. New York: Simon and Schuster.

Oishi, S., E. Diener, and R. E. Lucas. In press. Optimal level of well-being: Can people be too happy? *Perspectives on Psychological Science*.

References

Oishi, S., E. Diener, R. E. Lucas, and E. Suh. 1999. Cross-cultural variations in predictors of life satisfaction: Perspectives from needs and values. *Personality and Social Psychology Bulletin* 25:980–90.

Oishi, S., and M. Koo. In press. Two new questions about happiness: "Is happiness good?" and "Is happier better?" In *Handbook of subjective well-being*, edited by R. J. Larsen and M. Eid. New York: Oxford University Press.

Oishi, S., and K. O. Seol. Forthcoming. Was he happy? Cultural differences in images of Jesus.

Oishi, S., U. Schimmack, and S. J. Colcombe. 2003. The contextual and systematic nature of life satisfaction judgments. *Journal of Experimental Social Psychology* 39:232–47.

Oishi, S., U. Schimmack, and E. Diener. 2001. Pleasures and subjective well-being. *European Journal of Personality* 15:153–67.

Oishi, S., and H. W. Sullivan. 2006. The predictive value of daily vs. retrospective well-being judgments in relationship stability. *Journal of Experimental Social Psychology* 42:460–70.

Ostir, G. V., I. M. Berges, K. S. Markides, and K. J. Ottenbacher. 2006. Hypertension in older adults and the role of positive emotions. *Psychosomatic Medicine* 68:727–33.

Ostir, G. V., K. S. Markides, S. A. Black, and J. S. Goodwin. 2000. Emotional well-being predicts subsequent functional independence and survival. *Journal of the American Geriatrics Society* 48:473–8.

Paloutzian, R. F. 2006. Psychology, the human sciences, and religion. In *The Oxford handbook of religion and science*, edited by P. Clayton and Z. Simpson. Oxford: Oxford University Press.

Pargament, K. I. 2002. The bitter and the sweet: An evaluation of the costs and benefits of religiousness. *Psychological Inquiry* 13:168–81.

Pargament, K. I., and C. L. Park. 1997. In times of stress: The religion-coping connection. In *The psychology of religion: Theoretical approaches*, edited by B. Spilka and D. N. McIntosh. Boulder, CO: Westview Press.

Pavot, W. 2008. The assessment of subjective well-being: Successes and shortfalls. In *The science of subjective well-being*, edited by M. Eid and R. J. Larsen. New York: Guilford Press.

Pavot, W., and E. Diener. 1993. The affective and cognitive context of self-reported measures of subjective well-being. *Social Indicators Research* 28:1–20.

Pavot, W., and E. Diener. 1993. Review of the satisfaction with life scale. *Psychological Assessment* 5:164–72.

Pavot, W., and E. Diener. In press. New review of SWLS. *Journal of Positive Psychology*.

Pavot, W., E. Diener, C. R. Colvin, and E. Sandvik. 1991. Further validation of the satisfaction with life scale: Evidence for the cross-method convergence of well-being measures. *Journal of Personality Assessment* 57:149–61.

Pavot, W., E. Diener, and F. Fujita. 1990. Extraversion and happiness. *Personality and Individual Differences* 11:1299–306.

Peterson, C., and M. E. P. Seligman. 2004. Hope: Optimism, future-mindedness, future orientation. In *Character strengths and virtues: A handbook and classification*, edited by C. Peterson and M. E. P. Seligman. Washington, DC: American Psychological Association and Oxford University Press.

Peterson, C., and R. S. Vaidya. 2003. Optimism as virtue and vice. In *Virtue, vice, and personality: The complexity of behavior*, edited by E. C. Chang and L. J. Sanna. Washington, DC: American Psychological Association.

Pomerantz, E. M., J. L. Saxon, and S. Oishi. 2000. The psychological trade-offs of goal investment. *Journal of Personality and Social Psychology* 79:617–30.

Pressman, S. D., and S. Cohen. 2005. Does positive affect influence health? *Psychological Bulletin* 131:925–71.

Proffitt, D. 2006. Embodied perception and the economy of action. *Perspectives on Psychological Science* 1:110–22.

Putnam, R. D. 2000. *Bowling alone: The collapse and revival of American community*. New York: Simon and Schuster.

Rath, T. 2006. *Vital friends: The people you can't afford to live without*. New York: Gallup Press.

Redelmeier, D. A., and D. Kahneman. 1996. Patients' memories of painful medical treatments: Real-time and retrospective evaluations of two minimally invasive procedures. *Pain* 66:3–8.

Redelmeier, D. A., J. Katz, and D. Kahneman. 2003. Memories of colonoscopy: A randomized trial. *Pain* 104:187–94.

Riener, C., J. K. Stefanucci, D. R. Proffitt, and G. Clore. 2003. Mood and the perception of spatial layout. Poster presented at the 44th Annual Meeting of the Psychonomic Society, Vancouver, Canada.

Robinson, M. D. 2007. Gassing, braking, and self-regulating: Error self-regulation, well-being, and goal-related processes. *Journal of Experimental Social Psychology* 43:1–16.

Robinson, M. D., and R. J. Compton. 2008. The happy mind in action: The cognitive basis of subjective well-being. In *The science of subjective well-being*, edited by M. Eid and R. J. Larsen. New York: Guilford Press.

Roese, N. J. 1997. Counterfactual thinking. *Psychological Bulletin* 121:133–48.

Roese, N. J. 2005. *If only*. New York: Random House.

Rusting, C., and R. J. Larsen. 1995. Moods as sources of stimulation: Relationships between personality and desired mood states. *Personality and Individual Differences* 18:321–9.

Ryff, C. D. 1989. Happiness is everything, or is it? Explorations on the meaning of psychological well-being. *Journal of Personality and Social Psychology* 57:1069–81.

Ryff, C. D., G. D. Love, H. L. Urry, D. Muller, M. A. Rosenkranz, E. M. Friedman, R. J. Davidson, and B. Singer. 2006. Psychological well-being and ill-being: Do they have distinct or mirrored biological correlates? *Psychotherapy and Psychosomatics* 75:85–95.

Ryff, C. D., and B. H. Singer. 2006. Best news yet on the six-factor model of well-being. *Social Science Research* 35:1103–19.

Samuelson, R. J. 1995. *The good life and its discontents: The American dream in the age of entitlement, 1945–1995.* New York: Times Books/Random House.

Sandvik, E., E. Diener, and L. Seidlitz. 1993. Subjective well-being: The convergence and stability of self-report and non-self-report measures. *Journal of Personality* 61:317–42.

Schimmack, U. 2008. The structure of subjective well-being. In *The science of subjective well-being,* edited by M. Eid and R. J. Larsen. New York: Guilford Press.

Schimmack, U., E. Diener, and S. Oishi. 2002. Life-satisfaction is a momentary judgment and a stable personality characteristic: The use of chronically accessible and stable sources. *Journal of Personality* 70:345–84.

Schimmack, U., and R. Lucas. 2007. Marriage matters: Spousal similarity in life satisfaction. *Schmollers Jahrbuch* 127:1–7.

Schimmack, U., and S. Oishi. 2005. The influence of chronically and temporarily accessible information on life satisfaction judgments. *Journal of Personality and Social Psychology* 89:395–406.

Schimmack, U., P. Radhakrishnan, S. Oishi, V. Dzokoto, and S. Ahadi. 2002. Culture, personality, and subjective well-being: Integrating process models of life-satisfaction. *Journal of Personality and Social Psychology* 82:582–93.

Schkade, D. A., and D. Kahneman. 1998. Does living in California make people happy? A focusing illusion in judgments of life satisfaction. *Psychological Science* 9:340–6.

Schwartz, B. 1994. *The costs of living: How market freedom erodes the best things in life.* New York: Norton.

Schwartz, B. 2000. Self-determination: The tyranny of freedom. *American Psychologist* 55:79–88.

Schwartz, B. 2004. *The paradox of choice: Why more is less.* New York: Harper Collins.

Schwartz, B., and A. Ward. 2004. Doing better but feeling worse: The paradox of choice. In *Positive psychology in practice,* edited by P. A. Linley and S. Joseph. Hoboken, NJ: John Wiley and Sons.

Schwartz, B., A. Ward, S. Lyubomirsky, J. Monterosso, K. White, and D. R. Lehman. 2002. Maximizing versus satisficing: Happiness is a matter of choice. *Journal of Personality and Social Psychology* 83:1178–97.

Schwartz, R. M., and G. L. Garamoni. 1989. Cognitive balance and psychopathology: Evaluation of an information processing model of positive and negative states of mind. *Clinical Psychology Review* 9:271–94.

Schwarz, N., and F. Strack. 1999. Reports of subjective well-being: Judgmental processes and their methodological implications. In *Well-being: The foundations of hedonic psychology*, edited by D. Kahneman, E. Diener, and N. Schwarz. New York: Sage.

Scollon, C. N., and L. A. King. 2004. Is the good life the easy life? *Social Indicators Research* 68:127–62.

Scollon, C. N., Diener, E., Oishi, S., and Biswas-Diener, R. 2004. Emotions across cultures and methods. *Journal of Cross-Cultural Psychology* 35:304–26.

Seligman, M. E. P., K. Reivich, L. Jaycox, and J. Gillham. 1995. *The optimistic child*. Boston: Houghton Mifflin.

Semmer, N. K., F. Tschan, A. Elfering, W. Kälin, and S. Grebner. 2005. Young adults entering the workforce in Switzerland: Working conditions and well-being. In *Contemporary Switzerland: Revisiting the special case*, edited by H. Kriesi, P. Farago, M. Kohli, and M. Zarin-Nejadan. New York: Palgrave Macmillan.

Sheldon, K. M., and S. Lyubomirsky. 2006. How to increase and sustain positive emotion: The effects of expressing gratitude and visualizing best possible selves. *Journal of Positive Psychology* 1:73–82.

Shmotkin, D., and J. Lomranz. 1998. Subjective well-being among Holocaust survivors: An examination of overlooked differentiations. *Journal of Personality and Social Psychology* 75:141–55.

Sieff, E. M., R. M. Dawes, and G. Loewenstein. 1999. Anticipated versus actual responses to HIV test results. *American Journal of Psychology* 112:297–311.

Silver, J. M. 2005. Happiness is healthy. *Journal Watch Psychiatry* 706:3.

Simons, D. J., and C. F. Chabris. 1999. Gorillas in our midst: Sustained inattentional blindness for dynamic events. *Perception* 28:1059–74.

Simons, D. J., and D. T. Levin. 1997. Change blindness. *Trends in Cognitive Sciences* 1:261–7.

Simons, D. J., and D. T. Levin. 1998. Failure to detect changes to people during a real-world interaction. *Psychonomic Bulletin and Review* 5:644–9.

Sirgy, M. J. 1998. Materialism and quality of life. *Social Indicators Research* 43:227–60.

Smith, S., and P. Razzell. 1975. *The pools winners*. London: Calibon Books.

Smith, T. W. 2007. Job satisfaction in the United States. Unpublished manuscript. National Opinion Research Center (NORC), University of Chicago. Retrieved September 7, 2007, from www.norc.org.

Snyder, C. R., D. R. Sigmon, and D. B. Feldman. 2002. Hope for the sacred and vice versa: Positive goal-directed thinking and religion. *Psychological Inquiry* 13:234–8.

Solberg, E. G. 2007. Examining the role of affect on worker productivity: A task based analysis. PhD dissertation, University of Illinois at Urbana-Champaign.

Solberg, E. G., E. Diener, and M. Robinson. 2004. Why are materialists less satisfied? In *Psychology and consumer culture: The struggle for a good life in a materialistic world*, edited by T. Kasser and A. D. Kanner. Washington, DC: American Psychological Association.

Staw, B. M., and S. G. Barsade. 1993. Affect and managerial performance: A test of the sadder-but-wiser vs. happier-and-smarter hypotheses. *Administrative Science Quarterly* 38:304–31.

Staw, B. M., R. I. Sutton, and L. H. Pelled. 1994. Employee positive emotion and favorable outcomes at the workplace. *Organization Science* 5: 51–71.

Steger, M. F., P. Frazier, S. Oishi, and M. Kaler. 2006. The meaning in life questionnaire: Assessing the presence of and search for meaning in life. *Journal of Counseling Psychology* 53:80–93.

Steptoe, A., and J. Wardle. 2005. Positive affect and biological function in everyday life. *Neurobiology of Aging* 26:S108–S112.

Sternberg, R. J. 1986. A triangular theory of love. *Psychological Review* 93: 119–35.

Sternberg, R. J., and M. L. Barnes, eds. 1988. *The psychology of love*. New Haven, CT: Yale University Press.

Stone, A. A., J. E. Schwartz, D. Schkade, N. Schwarz, A. Krueger, and D. Kahneman. 2006. A population approach to the study of emotion: Diurnal rhythms of a working day examined with the day reconstruction method. *Emotion* 6:139–49.

Storbeck, J., and G. L. Clore. 2005. With sadness comes accuracy; with happiness, false memory: Mood and the false memory effect. *Psychological Science* 16:785–91.

Strine, T. W., Chapman, D. P., Balluz, L. S., Moriarty, D. G., and A. H. Mokdad. 2008. The associations between life satisfaction and health-related quality of life, chronic illness and health behaviors among US community-dwelling adults. *Journal of Community Health* February.

Stroebe, W., and M. Stroebe. 1996. The role of loneliness and social support in adjustment to loss: A test of attachment versus stress theory. *Journal of Personality and Social Psychology* 70:1241–9.

Suh, E. M., E. Diener, and F. Fujita. 1996. Events and subjective well-being: Only recent events matter. *Journal of Personality and Social Psychology* 70:1091–102.

Suh, E. M., E. Diener, and J. A. Updegraff. In press. From culture to priming conditions: Self-construal influences life satisfaction judgments. *Personality and Social Psychology Bulletin*.

Svanum, S., and Z. B. Zody. 2001. Psychopathology and college grades. *Journal of Counseling Psychology* 48:72–6.

Tamir, M., and E. Diener. In press. Approach-avoidance goals and well-being: One size does not fit all. In *Handbook of approach and avoidance motivation*, edited by A. J. Elliot. Mahwah, NJ: Lawrence Erlbaum.

Tassinary, L. G., and J. T. Cacioppo. 1992. Unobservable facial actions and emotion. *Psychological Science* 3:28–33.

Tatarkiewicz, W. 1976. *Analysis of happiness*. Warsaw: Polish Scientific Publishers; The Hague: Martinus Nijhoff.

Taylor, S. E., L. C. Klein, B. P. Lewis, T. L. Gruenewald, R. A. R. Gurung, and J. A. Updegraff. 2000. Biobehavioral responses to stress in females: Tend-and-befriend, not fight-or-flight. *Psychological Review* 107:411–29.

Tellegen, A., D. T. Lykken, T. J. Bouchard, K. J. Wilcox, N. L. Segal, and S. Rich. 1988. Personality similarity in twins reared apart and together. *Journal of Personality and Social Psychology* 54:1031–9.

Tkach, C., and S. Lyubomirsky. 2006. How do people pursue happiness? Relating personality, happiness-increasing strategies, and well-being. *Journal of Happiness Studies* 7:183–225.

Tomarken, A. J., R. J. Davidson, R. E. Wheeler, and R. C. Doss. 1992. Individual differences in anterior brain asymmetry and fundamental dimensions of emotion. *Journal of Personality and Social Psychology* 62:676–87.

Tov, W., and E. Diener. 2007. The well-being of nations: Linking together trust, cooperation, and democracy. In *Cooperation: The political psychology of effective human interaction*, edited by B. A. Sullivan, M. Snyder, and J. L. Sullivan. Oxford: Blackwell.

Tsai, J. L., B. Knutson, and H. H. Fung. 2006. Cultural variation in affect valuation. *Journal of Personality and Social Psychology* 90:288–307.

Tsai, J. L., F. F. Miao, and E. Seppala. 2007. Good feelings in Christianity and Buddhism: Religious differences in ideal affect. *Personality and Social Psychology Bulletin* 33:409–21.

Tugade, M. M., B. L. Fredrickson, and L. F. Barrett. 2004. Psychological resilience and positive emotional granularity: Examining the benefits of positive emotions on coping and health. *Journal of Personality* 72:1161–90.

Twenge, J. M., and L. A. King. 2005. A good life is a personal life: Relationship fulfillment and work fulfillment in judgments of life quality. *Journal of Research in Personality* 39:336–53.

Uchida, Y., V. Norasakkunkit, and S. Kitayama. 2004. Cultural constructions of happiness: Theory and empirical evidence. *Journal of Happiness Studies* 5:223–39.

Vaillant, G. E. 2008. *Faith, hope and joy: The neurobiology of the positive emotions*. New York: Morgan Road Books.

Vinokur, D., and D. M. Smith. 2003. Providing social support may be more beneficial than receiving it: Results from a prospective study of mortality. *Psychological Science* 14:320–7.

Vohs, K., N. L. Mead, and M. R. Goode. 2006. The psychological consequences of money. *Science* 314:1154–6.

References

Wagner, R., and J. K. Harter. 2006. *The elements of great managing*. New York: Gallup Press.

Warr, P. 1999. Well-being and the workplace. In *Well-being: The foundations of hedonic psychology*, edited by D. Kahneman, E. Diener, and N. Schwarz. New York: Sage.

Warr, P. 2007. *Work, happiness, and unhappiness*. Mahwah, NJ: Lawrence Erlbaum.

Wheeler, R. E., R. J. Davidson, and A. J. Tomarken. 1993. Frontal brain asymmetry and emotional reactivity: A biological substrate of affective style. *Psychophysiology* 30:82–9.

Wilson, T. D., J. Meyers, and D. T. Gilbert. 2003. "How happy was I, anyway?" A retrospective impact bias. *Social Cognition* 21:421–46.

Wilson, T. D., T. Wheatley, J. M. Meyers, D. T. Gilbert, and D. Axsom. 2000. Focalism: A source of durability bias in affective forecasting. *Journal of Personality and Social Psychology* 78:821–36.

Wirtz, D., J. Kruger, C. N. Scollon, and E. Diener. 2003. What to do on spring break? The role of predicted, on-line, and remembered experience in future choice. *Psychological Science* 14:520–4.

Witter, R. A., W. A. Stock, M. A. Okun, and M. J. Haring. 1985. Religion and subjective well-being in adulthood: A quantitative synthesis. *Review of Religious Research* 26:332–42.

Wolf, S. 1959. The pharmacology of placebos. *Pharmacology Review* 11:689–704.

Wright, T. A., and D. G. Bonett. 2007. Job satisfaction and psychological well-being as non-additive predictors of workplace turnover. *Journal of Management* 33:140–60.

Wright, T. A., and R. Cropanzano. 2000. Psychological well-being and job satisfaction as predictors of job performance. *Journal of Occupational Health Psychology* 5:84–94.

Wright, T. A., and R. Cropanzano. 2004. The role of psychological well-being in job performance: A fresh look at an age-old quest. *Organizational Dynamics* 33:338–51.

Wright, T. A., R. Cropanzano, and D. G. Bonett. 2007. The moderating role of employee positive well being on the relation between job satisfaction and job performance. *Journal of Occupational Health* 12:93–104.

Wright, T. A., R. Cropanzano, P. J. Denny, and G. L. Moline. 2002. When a happy worker is a productive worker: A preliminary examination of three models. *Canadian Journal of Behavioral Science* 34:146–50.

Wright, T. A., and B. M. Staw. 1999. Affect and favorable work outcomes: Two longitudinal tests of the happy-productive worker thesis. *Journal of Organizational Behavior* 20:1–23.

Wrzesniewski, A. 2003. Finding positive meaning in work: In *Positive organizational scholarship: Foundations of a new discipline*, edited by K. S. Cameron, J. E. Dutton, and R. E. Quinn. San Francisco: Barrett-Koehler.

Wrzesniewski, A., C. R. McCauley, P. Rozin, and B. Schwartz. 1997. Jobs, careers, and callings: People's relations to their work. *Journal of Research in Personality* 31:21–33.

Xu, J. 2006. Subjective well-being as predictor of mortality, heart disease, and obesity: Prospective evidence from the Alameda County Study (California). PhD dissertation, University of Texas School of Public Health. *Dissertation Abstracts International* 66:3671.

Yip, W., S. V. Subramanian, A. D. Mitchell, D. T. S. Lee, J. Wang, and I. Kawachi. 2007. Does social capital enhance health and well-being? Evidence from rural China. *Social Science and Medicine* 64:35–49.

Zelenski, J. M., and R. J. Larsen. 2002. Predicting the future: How affect-related personality traits influence likelihood judgments of future events. *Personality and Social Psychology Bulletin* 28:1000–10.

Zinnbauer, B. J., K. I. Pargament, B. Cole, M. S. Rye, E. M. Butter, T. G. Belavich, et al. 1997. Religion and spirituality: Unfuzzying the fuzzy. *Journal for the Scientific Study of Religion* 36:549–64.

Index

Index